Practical Solutions to U.K Immigration & Nationality Matters

Second Edition

Solomon-Soul FARINTO   LLB (Hons.), PGD (Econ. Dev.)

Muyiwa JIBOWU   B.Sc (Hons.), LLB (Hons.) Barrister

Published by: M.J.Solomon & Co.
3a Stroud Green Road
Finsbury Park
London   N4 2DQ

Telephone: 0171 561 0505

FAX: 0171 272 8161

ISBN 0 9520559 1 0

Printed in Great Britain by
Edward Charles 10 Hoxton Street London N1

M.J.Solomon & Co.
(London)

PREFACE

This book has been written with the aim of reducing the problems and anxieties of people with immigration and nationality concerns, by providing a readable, comprehensive and up-to-date guide to resolving these problems.

There is wide consensus that Immigration rules are designed to benefit 'well-to-do' (affluent) countries, hence it is not surprising that the rules and procedures have been constantly frowned upon by generality of people from 'poorer' nations.

One cannot but recognise the constant changes in this area of law, most especially in the Immigration Rules. These rules and the Nationality legislation are subject of interpretation, and are not readily understood by a majority of non-practitioners. Furthermore, it is not easy for such people to keep abreast of these changes, hence, it is not uncommon for visitors to erroneously request an extension of their six month's visitor's visa.

This is, thus, an indispensable piece of work, emanating from ingenious researches of the authors, touching directly on common problems and solutions, such as, How to Obtain a Work permit, What to do as an Overstayer and why one should not overstay, How to bring Family Members and Relatives to the UK, How to Obtain Permanent Residence, What Welfare Benefits are available to immigrants, as well as incorporating application procedures for Entry Clearance, Variation and Extension of Visas.

We have, therefore, adopted a style and format in the book which makes this complex subject readable by people who wish to travel to the UK, those in the UK, and immigration practitioners alike. This work is given additional flavour by some examples, practical advice, case studies and useful suggestions.

The inconveniences and hardships encountered by immigrants due to ignorance of immigration rules and procedures, the loss of liberty that may result from omissions and the cost of restoring one's immigration credibility may be avoided by familiarising yourself with the contents of this book.

ACKNOWLEDGEMENTS

We also thank the Controller of Her Majesty's Stationary Office and the Home Office for granting us permission to reproduce documents, stamps, forms and notices in this work.

We thank God by whose grace and favour we have been able to produce this material and pray that it will be a blessing to all readers: Amen.

Our sincere thanks to our colleague Samson Adelowo, our special friend David Jide Johnson, and all our friends and families for their assistance and encouragement. We dedicate this book to our families for their patience, sacrifice and endurance whilst we spent enormous time on this work.

For ease of expression in this book, we have chosen to adopt the practice of using 'he' for 'he or she', unless the contrary can be inferred. Also, while the word 'visa' is the documentary evidence of permission to enter or remain and 'leave to enter or remain' is the status conferred by the visa, they shall, however, be used interchangeably, and 'permanent residence' may be used instead of 'indefinite leave to enter or remain'; Secretary of State for the Home
Office (Home Secretary) is used for the Home Office.

The abbreviations E.C.O and I.O stand for Entry Clearance and Immigration Officers respectively.

The following countries belong to the European Economic Area (E.E.A): Austria, Belgium, Denmark, Finland, France, Germany, Greece, Iceland, Ireland, Italy, Liechtenstein, Luxembourg, Norway, Portugal, Spain, Sweden and the United Kingdom.

The contents of this book reflect the state of affairs as at the date of print, 8th January, 1997.

Contents

CONTENTS

CONTENTS

CONTENTS

CONTENTS

CONTENTS

CONTENTS

CONTENTS

CONTENTS

CONTENTS

CONTENTS

CONTENTS

CONTENTS

CONTENTS

CONTENTS

CONTENTS

CONTENTS

CONTENTS

CONTENTS

CONTENTS

VISITING

1.1   INTRODUCTION

A visitor (other than one seeking leave to enter or remain for Private Medical Treatment) is a person living and working outside the United Kingdom who comes to the United Kingdom for a holiday, vacation, or to transact business (such as attending meetings and briefings, fact finding, negotiating or making contracts with the United Kingdom, business to buy or sell goods or services).[1]   Visitors are granted 6 months leave to enter which can not be renewed or extended on the same basis except for other reasons which are recognised within or outside the immigration rules.

1.3   CRITERIA FOR ENTRY CLEARANCE
AND ENTRY

A visitor may be admitted for a period not exceeding 6 months, subject to a condition prohibiting employment, provided the immigration officer is satisfied that he:

a)   is genuinely seeking entry as a visitor for a limited period as stated by him, not exceeding 6 months; and

b)   intends to leave the United Kingdom at the end of the period of the visit as stated by him; and

c)   does not intend to take employment in the United Kingdom; and

d)   does not intend to produce goods or provide services within the United Kingdom, including the selling of goods or services direct to members of the public; and

e)   does not intend to study at a maintained school; and

f)   will maintain and accommodate himself and any dependants adequately out of resources available to him without recourse to public funds or taking employment; or will, with any dependants, be maintained and accommodated adequately by relatives or friends; and

g)   can meet the cost of the return or outward journey.[2]

1.4   IMPORTANCE OF ENTRY CLEARANCE

It is necessary for some visitors to obtain entry clearance before departing from their home country. These are:-

●   foreigners (full visa nationals), and

●   some commonwealth nationals (classified as semi visa nationals), the list of which was broadened on 4th April, 1996.

Full and semi visa nationals are those listed in figure 1.34. Semi visa nationals are those few commonwealth countries who now need visas to come to the UK, list of which is below. Non visa-nationals are those countries not included in the list referred to in chapter one and in the list of commonwealth countries mentioned below.

A full or semi visa national who has no entry clearance or appropriate leave to remain (visa) in the UK would not normally be allowed to board a plane or vessel and may be refused entry into the UK.

Semi - visa nationals (i.e. citizens of **Bangladesh, Bahrain, Cameroon, The Dominican Republic, Fiji, Gambia, Ghana, Guyana, India, Kenya, Maldives, Mauritius, Mozambique, Nigeria, Pakistan, Papua New Guinea, Sierra Leone, South Africa, Sri Lanka, Tanzania, Uganda and Zambia**), who need entry clearance to come to the UK are still treated for other purposes as commonwealth citizens, so that other requirements such as registration with the police as discussed in other parts of this book are not imposed on them. The remaining other commonwealth nationals do not need entry clearance to visit the UK.

Furthermore, nationals of the countries that are parties to the EEA (European Economic Area) agreement do not need entry clearance or visa to come the UK as they have freedom of movement.

1.5   ENTRY CLEARANCE: Optional For Non Visa And Mandatory For Full/Semi Visa National

As a general rule, non visa nationals coming to the UK are not required to obtain entry clearance before setting out on their journey. There are some situations, however, where obtaining entry clearance is mandatory and should be obtained. This mandatory requirement will apply to non visa, and semi/full visa nationals alike, [see individual topics to find out if entry clearance is mandatory for your purpose of entry to the UK]. Where entry clearance for a particular purpose is not mandatory, obtaining one may be an indication of the passenger's chances of entry.

Additionally, the possession of an entry clearance will usually afford the passenger a right of appeal exercisable whilst in the UK against refusal of entry.

Full/semi visa nationals coming to the UK must obtain entry clearance before starting their journey.

1.6   ENTRY CLEARANCE PROCESSING

It is not uncommon for the Entry Clearance Officer (ECO) to question applicants about their background in an attempt to check their credibility, as well as to determine whether they do not require to stay longer than the requested duration.

Such questions may include:

● Who is going to look after your children/business while you are away?

- Do you have any relatives in the UK?
- How long would you like to stay in the UK?

The ECO may be concerned where a person's annual income is signific antly less than the cost of his travel fare. Documents such as letters from the employer, confirming the length of his holiday and when he is expected back at work, (or college letter, if a student, confirming when the next term will begin) may help to dispel any doubts.

Non-visa nationals coming to the UK will have to meet the same entry clearance criteria to the satisfaction of the immigration officer at the port of entry. Please note that the grant of an entry clearance certificate/visa does not guarantee entry to the UK.

1.7   REFUSAL OF ENTRY CLEARANCE

An application for entry clearance is to be decided in the light of the circumstances existing at the time of the decision as well as in accordance with the provisions governing the grant or refusal of leave to enter

This means that applicants may be refused for various reasons, such as:

-      inability to fulfil any of the criteria laid down for entry clearance as discussed above;

-      the ECO having reasons to believe that the real purpose of the intended journey is to seek employment, provide services, sell goods to the members of the public or that the applicant intends to remain longer than indicated;

-      previous breaches of immigration law by the applicant;

-      where someone is a subject of deportation order;

-      where the Home Secretary has personally directed that the exclusion of the applicant from the UK is conducive to the public good;

-      medical grounds (for people with communicable diseases); and

- the applicant's criminal record.

There is no Right of Appeal against such a refusal of a visitor's entry clearance.[3]

1.8   HOW TO SPONSOR A VISITOR TO THE UK

Where a visitor is applying for entry clearance or is arriving at the port of entry with or without one, the following may be required:

- current passport (together with the old passport if applicable);

- evidence that adequate funds will be available in the UK to support the visitor and any dependants travelling with him. Any or a combination of the following should suffice;

    - Travellers Cheque;

    - Up-to-date bank statement, or Authority to obtain foreign exchange (where appropriate) in order to maintain and accommodate himself; and

    - an undertaking from the sponsor, confirming that he is willing and able to maintain and accommodate him, together with evidence to back up the undertaking such as a letter from the sponsor's employer showing his current income or recent payslips and an up-to-date bank statement;

    - Letter of sponsorship/invitation from the sponsor in the UK;

    - Proof of purpose of visit, for example, wedding invitation;

    - Proof that the visitor will be in the UK only temporarily, for example:

* a letter from his employer, or

* evidence that he has a family to return to, and

* a return ticket.

1.9   DURATION AND VALIDITY OF ENTRY CLEARANCE

The validity of entry clearance is usually for a period of six months. However, people on frequent visits to the UK may be granted multiple entry clearance for a period between 1 and 5 years. When an entry clearance is granted, it is usually endorsed valid for presentation at the UK port within six months of the date of issue (or longer if multiple entry clearance). The holder must then travel to the UK within that period.

A six month entry clearance is only valid for one visit and may not be used for a second journey to the UK. On the other hand, the holder of a multiple entry clearance may travel to the UK as many times as possible within the validity of this entry clearance.

Multiple entry clearance is commonly granted to business men and women as well as people who frequently travel to the UK.

At the port of entry, an immigration officer will usually grant leave to enter, usually for 6 months. This is not the same as entry clearance, and the duration of stay in the UK begins from the date of entry and not from the date the entry clearance is granted.

Possession of an entry clearance does not guarantee entry to the UK as passengers will still have to be screened at the port of entry. Where a passenger in possession of an entry clearance is refused entry clearance, there will be a right of appeal exercisable while the passenger is in the UK for which a temporary admission may be granted, provided that the passenger is not declared an illegal entrant. A passenger declared an illegal entrant may only appeal after leaving the UK.

Sample copies of entry clearance certificates

Fig 1.10   *Single visit*   Fig 1.11   *Multiple visits*

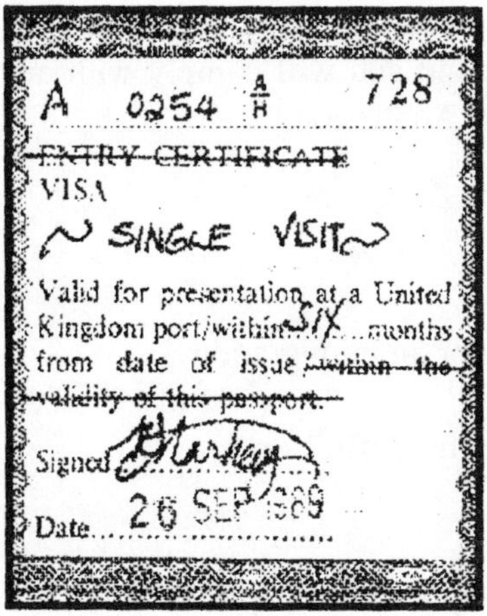

1.12   LEAVE TO ENTER

Immigration officers (I.O) can grant or refuse leave to enter the UK. Leave to enter is a notice in writing, usually in the form of a visa stamp specifying a certain period of time in some cases or for an indefinite period. Anything short of this is, therefore, not leave to enter.

Those granted Temporary Admission can physically enter the UK but this does not mean they have leave to enter, as there would not be a visa stamp on their passport.[4] Infact, their passport would have been retained by the immigration authority. Those who remain beyond the time limit of their temporary admission without authority are, therefore, classified as illegal entrants.

1.13 TEMPORARY ADMISSION

By its nature, temporary admission amounts to formal permission, short of formal Entry (even though there is physical entry) usually granted as a favourable alternative to detention. Temporary admission will usually be granted to a passenger where the immigration authorities are confident that such a passenger is highly unlikely to abscond and will comply with any restrictions and conditions of the Temporary Admission.

Restrictions or conditions may be to:

1) reside at an address given to them,
2) report weekly or monthly to a police or an immigration officer,
3) return to the port of entry or immigration office on a particular date.

Temporary admission may also be granted in the following situations:

1) Where further investigation is necessary due to suspicion or need to clarify certain facts before entry is allowed.
2) Where entry is refused but the passenger is allowed in for a short period.
3) Where the purpose of the passenger's visit is no longer achievable.
4) Where the passenger is a minor or vulnerable person accompanied by an adult or guardian resident in the UK, whose status of immigration category is yet to be determined or confirmed.
5) Where the passenger has applied for Asylum at the Port of Entry.
6) Where the person is declared an illegal entrant but is subsequently allowed to remain pending the consideration of other or outstanding matters.

Where temporary admission is granted, the immigration authorities will usually retain the person's passport (if one is available) and instruct him to report back to them on a particular date. Where this is the case, the passenger should seek legal advice immediately. If the decision on whether to admit or refuse has not been reached, it may be possible to influence the immigration officer in reaching a favourable decision. However, where entry is refused, it is rare to have such a decision reversed unless there are exceptional and compelling circumstances, or the passenger is now able to substantiate his claim thoroughly beyond the initial attempt.

It should also be noted that temporary admission is not a visa and cannot be varied, although it can be renewed in appropriate cases. Furthermore, a passenger granted temporary admission will not have a right of appeal exercisable in the UK where he has arrived without an entry clearance.

Fig 1.14

Port Reference: **GAN/32921**

Home Office Reference:

IS 96

Check-In

HM IMMIGRATION OFFICE
NORTH TERMINAL
GATWICK AIRPORT - LONDON
GATWICK WEST SUSSEX
RH6 0PJ   **Tel:**   **01293 892500**
               Fax: **01293 892560**

IMMIGRATION ACT 1971 -   NOTIFICATION OF TEMPORARY ADMISSION TO A PER SON WHO IS LIABLE TO BE DETAINED

To: ....

LIABILITY TO DETENTION

A   You are a person who is liable to be detained*

TEMPORARY ADMISSION RESTRICTIONS

B   I hereby authorise your (further) temporary admission to the United Kingdom subject to the following restrictions**:-

*   You must reside at:-   ....

                       ....

                       .... Tel ....

*   You may not enter employment, paid or unpaid, or engage in any business or profession.

*   You must report to the **GATWICK NORTH BRITISH AIRWAYS**
ticket/check-in desk for flight no.   **BA265**
to KINGSTON by 10:30 hrs on 23-DEC-96 with your baggage and
obtain a boarding card. Please present the attached form to the airline check-in staff.

*   You must then report to the Immigration Officer at the departures control not later than 11:30 hrs on **23-DEC-96.**

ANY CHANGE OF RESTRICTION

If these restrictions are to be changed an Immigration Officer will write to you.

N.B.   **NORMAL BAGGAGE ALLOWANCES APPLY.**

If you have excess baggage and do not pay the charge demanded, the airline may refuse to carry your baggage.

If the flight departs later than tomorrow please telephone this office between 0800 and 2000 hours on the day before you are due to report to ensure that the arrangements for your departure have not been changed.

*   Although you have been temporarily admitted, you remain liable to be detained.

*   You have NOT been given leave to enter the United Kingdom within the meaning of the Immigration Act 1971.

                     Immigration Officer..

Date **1st DEC-96**   * Paragraph 16 of Schedule 2 to the Act

                     ** Paragraph 21 of Schedule 2 to the Act

1.15   REFUSAL OF LEAVE TO ENTER

There are numerous reasons for which a passenger might be refused entry into the UK, some of which are the following:

1.   Where there has been a material change in circumstances since the issue of entry clearance (e.g. where you want to come to the UK for a wedding ceremony and it took place before your arrival). This change in circumstances will be sufficient to remove the basis of the holder's claim for Admission.

2.   Where the Immigration Officer reasonably believes that the visitor will not be able to maintain and accommodate himself adequately without recourse to public funds.

3.   Where an immigration Officer has reasons to believe that the real purpose of seeking entry is to take up employment, or that the applicant will not return to his country at the end of his requested period.

4.   Where false representations were used to obtain entry clearance whether or not to the holders knowledge.

5.   Where material facts were not disclosed in obtaining entry clearance.

6.   Where restricted returnability is concerned i.e. where passengers do not satisfy immigration officers that they will be admitted back to their country after their short stay in the UK.

7.   Previous breaches of UK immigration law, for example, if one was caught taking up employment in breach of his landing conditions during a previous visit, or overstaying.

8.   Where the passenger had previously obtained leave to enter by deception.

9. Refusal by sponsor of the passenger, if requested to do so, to provide an undertaking in writing to be responsible for the passenger's maintenance and accommodation for the period of leave requested.

10. Whether or not to the holder's knowledge, the making of false representations or the failure to disclose any material fact for the purpose of obtaining a work permit.

11. Failure by a child under the age of 18 years who is travelling alone, and not applying for asylum, if required, to provide written consent from his parent(s) or guardian.

12. Where information is available to immigration officers of the passenger's undesirable character, conduct or association which makes his exclusion conducive to the public good.

13. Medical grounds:- Where people have communicable disease.

14. Where the passenger has a criminal conviction in any country including the UK of an offence which, if committed in the UK, is punishable with imprisonment for a term of 12 months or more (although the other provisions under this sub-topic usually applies to those who have indefinite leave to remain in the UK, this particular provision is commonly involved).

15. People subject to deportation order cannot return to the UK until such order has been revoked.

16. Where it transpires that he intends to produce goods or provide services within the United Kingdom including the selling of goods or services direct to members of the public.

17. Where it transpires that he intends to study at a maintained school.

18. Where, he does not intend to leave the United Kingdom at the end of the period of visit as stated by him.

1.16 REFUSAL OF ENTRY TO A PERSON IN POSSESSION OF AN ENTRY CLEARANCE

A passenger seeking leave to enter the UK who holds an entry clearance duly issued to him which is still current may, nevertheless, be refused entry where the Immigration Officer is satisfied that:

1. whether or not to the holder's knowledge, false representations were employed or material facts were not disclosed, either in writing or orally, for the purpose of obtaining the entry clearance; or

2. where change of circumstances since the entry clearance was issued has removed the basis of the holder's claim to admission; or

3. refusal is justified:-
    a)   on grounds of criminal record(s),
    b)   on medical grounds,
    c)   because exclusion would be conducive to the public good.

Passengers are sometimes questioned by Immigration Officers, who may search their luggage and read any letter or documents from which inference may be drawn.

1.17   Example:

Mr Bello has arrived from The Gambia on the 6th of March 1993 without an entry clearance for the purpose of studying. On being questioned, Mr Bello said his wife was in Gambia. His luggage was subsequently searched and some letters addressed to a certain Miss Promise were found. Mr Bello later admitted that this lady was his wife in the UK and he gave reasons for the prior untrue information.

The fact is that, this false information had affected Mr Bello's credibility.

Mr Bello was refused entry, and because he had no entry clearance, he had to return to Gambia before exercising his right of appeal. Mr Bello had spent about £500 on his fare and £700 on his college fees - all down the drain.

Where entry is refused, the sample stamp in figure 1.18 will be endorsed and coded with two ink lines across it.

Fig 1.18

```
┌─────────────────────────┐
│ IMMIGRAT...ION OFFICER   │
│   *        (69)      *   │
│   27  SEP  1996          │
│   GATWICK   (N)          │
└─────────────────────────┘
```

1.19   Practical Point to Note

Immigration Officers or E.C.O may ask applicants whether they will work if a job is offered to them. The answer to this should emphatically be NO, except where applicants are coming to the UK purposely to work under a recognised category, or where it may be incidental to their stay in the UK, also under a recognised category.

DISPLAY OF ENTRY VISA STAMPS

Note the difference in prohibition and restriction stamps as they affect employment.

Fig 1.20   Prohibition

Fig 1.21 Restriction
(BB 909 804)

```
LEAVE TO ENTER FOR SIX MONTHS
    EMPLOYMENT PROHIBITED
```

Leave to remain in the United Kindom, on Condition that the holder does not enter or change employment paid or unpaid without the consent of the Secretary of State for Employment and does not engage in any business or profession without the consent of the Secretary of State for the Home Department, is hereby given

until . . . .

HOME OFFICE
IND
23 DEC 1992
(953)
IMMG & NAT. DEPARTMENT

Fig 1.22   Prohibition

(BB 909 804)

Leave to enter the United Kingdom, on condition that the holder does not enter employment paid or unpaid and does not engage in any business or profession, is hereby given for/until

. . . .

| 2 7 | 0 6 | 1 9 66 |

1.23   VISAS GIVEN BY MISTAKE

An Immigration Officer may erroneously believe that a passenger has the Right of Abode and thus allow him into the country without placing any stamp at all in the passport, or by merely placing a date stamp.

It is worth bearing in mind that visas can be withdrawn or curtailed even if obtained legitimately and in the absence of any fraud or dishonesty on the part of the visitor/applicant. Withdrawal or curtailment may be possible only if the Home Office is aware of it's mistakes, but there are occasions where such mistakes will not be in favour of the visitor or applicant, for example, where a 'Date Stamp only or 'No Stamp at all is placed in the passport.

1.24   'Date Stamp' only and 'No Stamp at all'

Where the visitor is aware that a mistake has been made, such a person may contact the Home Office so as to rectify this mistake, and he may be granted a proper visa. As earlier stated, such entry into the UK would be without a visa and the visitor may be treated as an illegal entrant.

A visitor who has a 'Date Stamp' on his passport would have proof of the mistake, whilst the one with 'No Stamp' at all may bring a presumption of illegal entry, for example, passing through the back door.

1.25   Unclear Stamps

Presently, a holder of an unclear stamp is deemed to have a six month leave to remain with prohibition (4) on employment, while those who may have been given such a stamp before the 10th July 1988 have a deemed indefinite leave to remain.[5]

For the sake of clarity, a visit to the Home Office for rectification or re-stamping would be a sensible thing to do.

1.26   Too Much Power

As immigration law is an exclusionary law (i.e. designed to exclude unwanted foreigners), it is not strange to realise that this law confers those performing immigration functions, especially Immigration and Entry Clearance Officers, with abundant power to grant or refuse entry or leave to remain.

Experience also suggests that E.C.Os and I.Os, in performing their duties, accord special treatment to affluent passengers, while passengers from less developed countries are more likely to be refused entry.

1.27   Like Cases Alike

Also, it is common knowledge that Immigration and Entry Clearance Officers do not always treat like cases alike; therefore, identical twins may present identical documents and one application may be successful while the other is refused.

A lot of people have generally attributed these inconsistencies to 'the mood' of the interviewing officers and 'luck'. It is also not uncommon to hear that entry to the UK is better through Gatwick Airport than Heathrow, that Seaports' officers are more sympathetic than those at Airports, and that officers are friendlier around festive periods e.g. Xmas period.

One cannot but agree that the wide discretion given to these officers amounts to too much power.

1.28   PRACTICAL ADVICE

1.   A visitor coming to stay with a sponsor whose immigration history is unclear or bad, or who is relying on public funds, may be refused entry clearance or entry.

2.   After an interview with an E.C.O or I.O, it is advisable that questions asked and answers provided should be noted and kept. Such records are kept by the immigration authorities and may be referred to on a request for variation, extension, entry or for appeal purposes. **It is important to make such notes immediately after leaving the interview, or where possible, request for copies from the interviewing officer.**

1.29   A VISITOR IN TRANSIT

A person not being a member of the crew of a ship, aircraft, hovercraft, hydrofoil or train) seeking leave to enter the United Kingdom as a visitor in transit may be granted such leave provided he:-

a)   is in transit to a country outside the common travel area; and

b)   has both the means and the intention of proceeding at once to another country; and

c)   is assured of entry there; and

d)   intends and is able to leave the United Kingdom within 48 hours.

The maximum leave permitted which may be granted to a visitor in transit is 48 hours, and an application for an extension of stay beyond 48 hours from a person admitted in this category is to be refused.[6]

1.30   Common Travel Area

A person is allowed to travel within the common travel area, that is, between the Isle of Man, the Channel Island, the Republic of Ireland and the UK, without the need to obtain visas from these countries provided he has a visa to enter one of them. A person without a visa, that is, an overstayer, is not free to travel as such.

Since there is no immigration barrier between these countries, everyone is theoretically free to travel without any problem. It is also true that you do not need your passport to travel within these countries.

Anything to identify you, for example, Drivers Licence, may suffice. However, an overstayer in the UK who travels to Republic of Ireland, for example, may be treated as an illegal entrant if he returns to the UK. Although his travel to that country will not be known to the authorities except when he is interviewed and this is revealed.

1.31   IRISH IMMIGRATION LAW

We have decided to provide this sub-topic because as you may soon find out, the Republic of Ireland is mentioned in some few pages.

1.32   The Primarily Law

Irish Immigration Law is contained in the Aliens Act 1935 and delegated legislation made thereunder, particularly the Aliens Order 1946 and 1975. There are no published immigration rules and no Appellate Authority as we have here. However, there is a written constitution, and a Supreme Court on the USA which has made very astonishing inroad into immigration law.

1.33   Few Points to Note

There is no Immigration barrier between the UK and the Republic of Ireland.

● Leave to enter in the UK is leave to land in Ireland, while leave to remain in the UK is leave to stay in Ireland.

● Leave to land is usually always for 3 months in Ireland as against 6 months in the UK.

● Ireland requires the nationals of certain countries to have entry clearance and these have usually always been the ones on the UK list, although UK visa is equally good for entry over there and Irish visa is also equally good for entry here.

- Aliens who have permission to work must register at the Aliens Registration office in Dublin (the capital city), or with the Superintendent of one of the main Garda (Police) stations if living outside Dublin. You have a Green Book as proof of this registration.

- Work Permit is renewable annually and it does not lead to indefinite leave to remain like we do in the UK.

- Aliens are rarely deported in Ireland, possibly about 6 a year.

- Aliens can acquire citizenship much more easily than it is in the UK.

- Spouse can apply for citizenship 3 years after marriage. If you meet the requirements, you will get it as it is not based on discretion as we have in the UK. Fee is £500, payable if the application is successful. The fee is much higher than we have in the UK.

- A child born in Ireland is an Irish from birth, although registration of this may be necessary.

- Parents of Irish infants may be allowed to remain in Ireland.

- Republic of Ireland is a member of the EEA.

1.34   COUNTRIES WHOSE CITIZENS NEED VISAS FOR THE UK

a) Nationals or citizens of the following countries:-

Afghanistan	Guyana	Sao Tome Principle
Albania	Haiti	Saudi Arabia
Algeria	India	Senegal
Angola	Indonisia	Sierra Leone
Armenia	Iran	Somalia
Azerbaijan	Iraq	Sri Lakan
Bangladesh	Ivory Coast	Sudan
Belarus	Jordan	Surinam
Benin	Kazakhstan	Syria
Bhutan	Kenya	Taiwan Tajikistan
Bosnia-Herzegovina	Kirgizstan	Tanzania
Bulgaria	Korea (North)	Thailand
Burkina	Kuwait	Togo
Burma	Laos	Tunisia
Burundi	Lebanon	Turkey
Cambodia	Liberia	Turkmenistan .
Cameroon	Libya	Uganda
Cape Verde	Macedonia	Ukraine
Central African Republic	Madagascar	United Arab Emirates
Chad	Mali	Uzbekistan
China	Maldives	Vietnam
Comoros	Mauritania	Zaire
Congo	Mauritius	Zambia
Cuba	Moldova	
Djibouti	Mongolia	
Dominican	Morocco	
Egypt	Mozambique	
Equatorial Guinea	Nepal	
Eritrea	Niger	
Ethiopia	Nigeria	
Fiji	Oman	
Gabon	Pakistan	
Georgea	Phillipines Romania	
Ghana	Russia	
Guinea Bissau	Rwanda	

The territories formerly comprising the Socialist Federal Republic of Yugoslavia excluding Croatia and Slovenia.

b)   Persons who hold passports or travel documents issued by the former Soviet Union or by the former Socialist Federal Republic of Yugoslavia.

c)   Stateless persons.

d)   Persons who hold Non-National documents.

Chapter 1   VISITING

PERSONS WHO DO NOT NEED VISAS FOR THE UK

Persons who do not need visas for the UK are:-

a)   British Citizens;

b)   those who qualify for admission to the United Kingdom as returning residents;

c)   those who seek leave to enter the United Kingdom within the period of their earlier leave unless that leave was for a period of six months or less; or was extended by statutory instrument;

c)   those holding refugee travel documents issued under the 1951 Convention relating to the Status of Refugees by countries which are signatories of the Council of Europe Agreement of 1959 on the Abolition of visas for Refugees if coming on visits of 3
months or less.

FOOTNOTES

1.   HC 395 paragraph 40

2.   HC 395 paragraph 41

3.   S.11 (1) Immigration Act 1971

4.   Immigration Act 1988 Sch.1 paragraph 8

5.   HC 395 paragraph 50

Chapter 2

STUDENTS

2.1 INTRODUCTION

A person seeking leave to enter or remain in the UK as a student may be admitted or allowed to remain for an appropriate period depending on the length of his course of study and his means, with a condition restricting his freedom to take employment, provided the Immigration Officer is satisfied that the conditions of the immigration rules are met.

2.2 COMING TO THE UK FOR STUDIES

A person may come to the UK as a prospective student or in the alternative as a student. In any case, a visa-national will need to obtain entry clearance before setting out on his journey to the UK. A non-visa national may, however, be able to switch from another category to that of student. Conditions for entry clearance as a prospective student and student are, but for a little difference, similar. See figure 13.4 for list of countries whose citizens need visas for the UK.

2.3 PROSPECTIVE STUDENTS

It is possible for a person to come to the UK not as a student but a prospective student, that is, where arrangements have not been concluded with regard to enrolment at a bona-fide college.

2.4 Conditions For Entry or Entry Clearance

A prospective student seeking leave to enter or entry clearance to the UK must:-[1]

a)   be able to demonstrate a genuine and realistic intention of undertaking, within 6 months of his date of entry, a course of study which would meet the requirements for an extension of stay as a student and

b)   must intend to leave the United Kingdom on completion of his studies or on the expiry of his leave to enter if he is not able to meet the condition for an extension of stay as a student.

c)   must be able, without working or recourse to public funds, to meet the costs of his intended course and accommodation and maintenance of himself and any dependents while making arrangements to /study and during the course of his studies.

At the interview for entry clearance or at the port of entry, the prospective student should expect questions which are similar to the following:

● When did you make up your mind to study in the UK?

● Why can't you study in your home country?

● Have you any relatives in the UK?

● Who is going to be responsible for your school fees?

● How are you going to maintain and accommodate yourself in the UK?

● Have you applied for admission in any other country apart from the UK?

● What is the duration of your intended course?

● What do you intend to do at the end of your course?

● What is your sponsor's annual income? etc.

A successful applicant should be admitted into the UK for a period of six months. Once in the UK, he is expected to pursue admission into a bona fide school after which he should forward to the Home Office:

- his College Admission Letter,
- his Passport, and
- evidence of funds,

so that he may be granted leave to remain as a student.

2.5   STUDENTS

A visa national who has made conclusive arrangements for a course of study in the UK from his home country will need an entry clearance while a non-visa national can come to the UK without an entry clearance. An applicant should come with his college admission letter and evidence of funds, and should be granted a student visa at the port of entry.

For a non-visa national, it is also possible to come to the UK for a short visit, have a genuine change of circumstance, and seek to switch to become a student. While semi/full visa-nationals must obtain entry clearance for this purpose.

2.6   Conditions for Entry or Entry Clearance

A person who has made conclusive arrangements for a course of study will have to satisfy the E.C.O and or I.O at the port of entry that he:[2]

a)   has been accepted for a course of study at;

i)   a publicly funded institution of further or higher education; or

ii)   a *bona fide* private education institution which maintains satisfactory records of enrolment and attendance; or

iii)   an independent fee paying school outside the maintained sector; and

b)   is able and intends to follow either:

   i)   a recognised full-time degree course at a publicly funded institution of further or higher education; or

   ii)   a weekday full-time course involving attendance at a single institution for a minimum of 15 hours organised daytime study per week of a single subject or directly related subjects; or

   iii)   a full-time course of study at an independent fee paying school; and

c)   is under the age of 16 years and is enrolled at an independent fee paying school on a full-time course of studies which meets the requirements of the Education Act 1944; and

d)   intends to leave the United Kingdom at the end of his studies; and

e)   does not intend to engage in business or to take employment, except part-time or vacation work undertaken with the consent of the Secretary of State for Employment; and

f)   is able to meet the costs of his course and accommodation and the maintenance of himself and any dependents without taking employment or engaging in business or having recourse to public funds.

On the question of funds, it may be sufficient to show that the funds needed to meet the cost of studies will be available from a reliable source such as private or government sponsorship. In such a situation, a sponsorship letter and evidence of capacity for example, bank statement may suffice.

It is also important to note that whilst the spouse of a student may be permitted to work and his income could be taken into account while being considered for further extension of the student visa, a spouse's anticipated earnings will be of no assistance or benefit to an applicant coming into the UK to study or a person varying his status to that of a student.

A student or prospective student seeking entry clearance, entry, variation or extension of his visa should note that correspondence courses are not acceptable. Additionally, it is important to note that students are no longer allowed to enroll on a variety of part-time courses to make up the required 15 hours. The New Immigration Rules require students to enroll for a single subject or directly related subjects at a single institution.

2.7   REASONS FOR REFUSAL OF ENTRY CLEARANCE OR ENTRY

In addition to the general reasons for refusal of entry clearance or entry, a student or prospective student's application may also be refused for the following reasons:

● where the conditions as stipulated above are not met either in part or in full, or

● Where an entry clearance has been granted and it is still valid, the passenger holding such may be refused leave to enter at the port of entry if:

- the immigration officer is satisfied that the student or prospective student has no genuine intention to study, or

- he is discovered to have used fraud to obtain an entry clearance, or

- he is found not to have fulfiled any of the conditions as mentioned above.

Where such a passenger who has a valid entry clearance is refused entry, his right of appeal is exercisable whilst in the UK except if he is declared an illegal entrant, the consequences of which are discussed on figure 19.9.

Note, however, that as a result of the Asylum and Immigration Appeals Act 1993, prospective students or students accepted on courses for less than 6 months duration, together with their dependents, no longer have a right of appeal against refusal of entry clearance or entry, although there is a right of appeal for those who have entry clearance and are refused entry to the UK at the port of entry, such right is exercisable whilst in the UK. However, there is a right of appeal against refusal of entry clearance where a student is accepted on a course for more than 6 months duration.

2.8   Non Visa Nationals

Prospective students and those who have completed arrangements to study in the UK may be granted entry without an entry clearance. However, they may be required to satisfy all other conditions just like visa nationals before they are granted leave to enter the UK.

Also, visitors to the UK who are here for temporary purpose may have genuine change of mind and can, therefore, apply to become students. *THIS IS NOT POSSIBLE FOR SEMI/FULL VISA NATIONALS WHO MUST OBTAIN STUDENT ENTRY CLEARANCE BEFORE THEY SET OUT ON THEIR JOURNEY TO THE UK.*

2.9   VARYING TO BECOME A STUDENT

An applicant who arrived in the UK for a temporary purpose and is varying his status to that of a student may be asked the following or similar questions:

1.   What was the original purpose of your visit to the UK?

2.   Why did you not apply for your visa at the port of entry?

3.   What was your occupation before you came to the UK?

    a.   If you were employed, what arrangements have you made with   your employer?

    b.   Do you have a job to return to in your home country? Please submit documentary evidence.

4. Do you have a wife and/or children in your home country or elsewhere?

   a. If yes, who will be supporting them financially while you study in the UK?

5. From what source would you receive funds to study in the UK?

6. How long do you intend to study in the UK?

7. How will you benefit from the course for which you have enrolled?

8. What are your intentions at the end of this course of study?

9. When do you intend to return to your home country?

2.10   REMAINING IN THE UK AS A STUDENT

2.11   Visa or Non-Visa Nationals

A student whose leave to remain in the UK has not expired, and has not breached his landing conditions, may be allowed to remain further in this capacity. Also, a non-visa national who is switching can make an application for variation of his visitor's visa, and semi/full visa-national who have prior entry clearance before entry will also have to apply for visa as a student. Applications will have to be made to the Home Office for an extension or variation before the expiration of the existing visa.

2.12   Making the application

You will need to send to the Home Office:

● Your Passport,

● Evidence of funds (e.g. your recent bank balance or itemised statement covering the last 6 months, or sponsor's letter and bank balance), and

● A college letter stating:

- the course of study.
- commencement date and duration of the course.
- how many hours will be spent on the course in a week
- how much of the school fees have been paid, and other relevant details.

A person who is varying his visa for the first time may be questioned at the Home Office (where he appears in person) or may be sent a questionnaire (where the application was by post). The likely questions may be similar to those in figure 2.9

2.13   Extension of Student Visa

A student whose leave to remain is coming to an end must apply to extend such leave if he wants to remain further in that capacity. The extension required may be for the same course, or another, or an advanced course of study. While an application for extension of visa for another stage or level of a course, or advanced level may not encounter so much difficulty, one seeking an extension to pursue another course without completing the earlier one (i.e. moving from one course to another) may encounter some difficulties, and have to provide proof or justification that he is not moving from one course to another as a 'time buying' exercise.

To obtain an extension, a student is expected to meet the following conditions. He must prove that he:-

1. has been accepted for a course of study at:

   a) a publicly funded institution of further or higher education; or

   b) a bona fide private education institution which maintains satisfactory records of enrolment and attendance; or

    c)   an independent fee paying school outside the maintained sector; and

2.   is able and intends to follow either:

    a)   a recognised full-time degree course at a publicly funded institution of further or higher education; or

    b)   a weekday full-time course involving attendance at a single institution for a minimum of 15 hours organised daytime study per week of a single subject or directly related subjects; or

    c)   a full-time course of study at an independent fee paying school; and

3.   if under the age of 16 years is enrolled at an independent fee paying school on a full-time course of studies; and

4.   intends to leave the United Kingdom at the end of his studies; and

5.   does not intend to engage in business or to take up employment, except part-time or vacation work undertaken with the consent of the Secretary of State for Employment; and

6.   is able to meet the costs of his course and accommodation and the maintenance of himself and any dependents without taking up employment or engaging in business or having recourse to public funds; and

7.   has produced evidence of his enrolment on a course; and

8.   can produce, if requested, *satisfactory evidence of regular attendance* during any course which he has already begun; or any other course for which he has been enrolled in the past; and

9.   can show evidence of *satisfactory progress in his course of study* including the taking and passing of any relevant examinations; and

10.   would not, as a result of an extension of stay, spend more than 4 years on short courses (i.e. courses of less than 2 years duration, or longer courses broken off before completion); and

11.   has not come to the end of a period of government or international scholarship agency sponsorship, or has the written consent of his original sponsor for a further period of study in the United Kingdom and satisfactory evidence that sufficient sponsorship funding is available.

This is a specimen of a student visa usually with restriction on employment

Fig 2.14

Leave to remain in the United Kindom, on Condition that the holder does not enter or change employment, paid or unpaid without the consent of the Secretary of State for Employment and does not engage in any business or profession without the consent of the Secretary of State for the Home Department, is hereby given for/until.

. . . .

| 0 5 | 1 1 | 1990 |

2.15   Refusal of Extension of Student Visa

Where a student fails to fulfil any of the conditions for extension stated above, his application may be refused. The most commonly encountered reasons for refusing applications are:-

i)   where there is reason to believe that the student does not intend to leave the UK at the end of his studies. This may be inferred, for example, where the student had shown a previous intention, expressly or by implication, of remaining permanently in the UK.

ii)   where the Home Office is not satisfied that the applicant intends to and is able to follow a full-time course of study. Such an inference is not uncommon where there has been persistent or continuous lack of success (though this is a question of degree) Where there are a genuine reasons or explanations for the student's lack of success proof of such should be provided to the Home Office (e.g. Medical Letter).

iii)   where the student appears to be moving from one course to another without any intention of bringing his education to an end.

2.16   ADVICE

It is the practice of the immigration department to employ a double edged sword while providing reason for refusal. It is not therefore uncommon to find reasons for refusal combining, for example, 'lack of success' and 'no intention to return home'. Perhaps proof of prospective employment back home and or evidence that the applicant has acquired ownership of property back home will thwart this second limb.

Additionally, a person who has shown a previous intention to remain permanently in the UK will most likely be refused further extension to remain as a student. This is because the Home Office can infer that he has 'no intention of returning home'.

2.17   VARIATION OF STUDENT VISA

A student may be allowed to vary his existing student visa to any status which does not have mandatory entry clearance requirement, provided he satisfies the necessary conditions for the grant of such visa (status).

For example, a student may be allowed to switch to train or gain experience in the field of his studies.

2.18   Important Points to Note

Students from full and semi visa countries must be careful in switching status. For example, a student from India who varies his student status to another category, if he travels out of the UK and on his return makes another application as a student may encounter some problems. This student application may be refused by the Home office, unless he has obtained an entry clearance for the purpose of study from outside the UK before this application. The refusal will be for the simple reason that his continuous residence as a student had been broken when he changed his status. Such a person will now need a new entry clearance to revert to student status.

Although students can at times switch to another status, they should be careful in doing this because an application to revert to student status at the expiration of the new leave may be refused, perhaps on the premise that the applicant has no intention of going back to his country.

2.19   EMPLOYMENT AND JOB PROSPECTS FOR STUDENTS

Student visas would normally restrict employment paid or unpaid, as well as establishment of business. Students may, nevertheless, be allowed to do some part-time job, but a work permit for the job with a specific employer is necessary. Taking up, or carrying on in, an employment without such a permit will amount to a breach of landing condition.

While such a breach may seem trivial, it may, in some cases, lead to a rejection of subsequent visa application to extend or vary, or curtailment of a current visa, followed by a notice of intention to deport. This breach of landing condition is also a criminal offence which may lead to prosecution in a Magistrates' court in some cases.

2.20   HOW TO OBTAIN A STUDENT'S WORK PERMIT

Such a permit can be obtained at the local job centre nearest to the job location.

To apply, the following documents are required:

● a letter of employment,

● a college letter consenting to the proposed employment, and

● the applicants passport

A student's work permit will usually be issued for a *particular job* with *a particular employer,* and will usually stipulate the maximum number of hours the student is allowed to work which may be up to 24 hours a week during the school session and much longer during vacation.

Students should also note that once they leave the employment for which the work permit is issued, a new work permit is needed for a new employment as the earlier work permit lapses on leaving that employment.

2.21   Common Problems

It is not uncommon for students to encounter difficulties in obtaining job offers as most employers would not normally want to employ a student without a work permit, whereas, an employment offer is a precondition for getting a work permit.

Therefore, while the first work permit may be difficult to obtain due to employers' lack of co-operation, a previous permit if shown to a prospective employer, may suggest that should the student be offered a particular job, it would not be too difficult or time consuming to obtain another work permit.

2.22   SPOUSES OF FOREIGN STUDENTS

A student's spouse may be allowed to enter or remain for the same period of the student's authorised stay provided:-

● he can be maintained; and

● accommodated without having to recourse to public funds; and

● each of the parties intends to live with the other as his or her spouse during the applicant's stay and the marriage is subsisting; and

● the applicant (and his spouse) does not intend to take up employment except as permitted by the immigration rules. *Immigration rules now prohibit employment for student's spouses where the period of leave being granted is 12 months or less.*

● The applicant (and his spouse) intends to leave the United Kingdom at the end of any period of leave granted to him. *Also a person with limited leave or who has completed his own studies but subsequently marries a student, may be granted leave corresponding to his spouse's leave.*

2.23   CHILDREN OF FOREIGN STUDENTS

Unmarried children of students under the age of 18 who are not leading independent lives of their own who can be adequately accommodated and maintained without recourse to public funds may be admitted or allowed to remain for a period of leave not in excess of that granted to the student.

Such children are required not to stay in the United Kingdom beyond the period of leave granted to their parents.

Just as in the case of the spouse, employment is to be prohibited where the period of leave being granted is 12 months or less.

Children who are visa nationals will need entry clearance for this purpose although if already in the UK for some other purpose, they may be allowed to remain.

Where the child of a student is over the age of 18, he may also be allowed in but must obtain entry clearance for this purpose, regardless of whether he is a visa or non-visa national.

2.24   Criteria to be Met

- This child must be unmarried and must not have formed an independent family unit and not leading an independent life.

- There must be adequate maintenance and accommodation without recourse to public funds.

- Children under the age of 12 are more likely to be admitted as their exclusion may be undesirable.

2.25   Important Points to Note

1. Occasionally, the Home Office will request an itemised statement of account for the past 6 months. This may, perhaps help to detect those who may have been working, as the bank entries will show the movement of funds from and into the account. *Those who have two separate bank accounts may not face this problem.*

2. Students are no longer allowed to enroll on a variety of part-time courses at a number of educational establishments in order to make up their 15 hours. Students are generally expected, therefore, to enroll for a single course at a single institution of learning.

3. A child under the age of 16, who seeks leave to enter or remain for studies must be in full-time education which meets the requirements of the Education Act 1944 at an independent fee paying school. This

is to ensure that children who should be receiving full-time education for their O'Level tuition are not being enrolled on courses which do not meet that requirement, such as secretarial courses.

4.   The Home Office may request from students or their institutions to provide satisfactory records of enrolment and attendance. Institutions or colleges are therefore advised to maintain such records.

5.   Foreign/Overseas students are not eligible for rebate on Council Tax.

6.   Entry clearance, variation or extention of visa will not be granted for **correspondence courses.**

For special reasons, Student Nurses, Mid-wives, Medical Doctors and Dentists are accorded special treatment and will now be discussed. A person who wishes to study for a P.hD programme should consult his institution with regard to employment and variation/extension of leave to remain.

2.26   NURSES AND MID-WIVES

An applicant accepted for training as a student nurse or mid-wife leading to a Registered Nursing qualification, or an overseas nurse or midwife on an adaptation course leading to registration as a nurse with the United Kingdom Central Council for Nursing,[3] may be granted an entry clearance (if a visa national), or allowed to vary or remain (if non-visa national) as a student, unless there is evidence that he had obtained such an acceptance:

●   by misrepresentation, or

●   that he does not intend, or he is unable to follow the course.

A person seeking leave to vary or enter as a student nurse must:-

●   intend to leave the UK,

- not intend to engage in business or take employment except in connection with his training course, and

- have sufficient funds available for his accommodation and maintenance for himself and any dependents. (The department of employment bursary may be taken into account in assessing whether the student meets the maintenance requirement. Also, training hospitals usually provide hostel accommodation.)

Qualified Nurses and Mid-wives from other countries who are required to do an adaptation course are considered as students, and the above stated requirements for entry clearance or entry will have to be met. For registration purposes, it will be necessary to contact:-

> UK Central Council
>   for Nursing Midwifery and Health Visiting
> 23 Portland Place
> London   W1N 4JT

> Telephone - 0171 637 7181

Full and Semi-Visa nationals should also note that for the purpose of training as a Nurse, they are treated as students and will, therefore, require entry clearance to enter the UK.

2.27   Important Points to Note

1. Student nurses are treated as students, not trainees for which a work permit would be required. Although it is clear that they are working as a trainee-nurse and are being paid, these student nurses will not be regarded as breaching their landing conditions.

2. Student nurses are now required to satisfy the entry clearance officer or immigration officer, like other students, that they intend to leave the UK at the end of their studies.

3. In view of the fact that at the moment the Department of

Employment no longer regard nursing as shortage occupation, student nurses may find it difficult to switch to work permit employment after they have qualified. If provided with employment, they are now required to return to their home countries and seek entry to the UK with their Work Permits, although there are few exceptions. Further information can be obtained from the Overseas Labour Office.

4.   Qualified nurses wishing to undertake postgraduate courses will now have to qualify under the Training and Work experience scheme.

2.28   DOCTORS AND DENTISTS

A Doctor or Dentist seeking postgraduate training in hospital may be admitted, or allowed to remain for an initial period not exceeding 12 months, if he:-

1.   a)   is a graduate from a United Kingdom medical school intending to undertake Pre-Registration House Officer employment for up to 12 months, as required for full registration with the General Medical Council; and

        b)   has not spent more than 12 months in aggregate in Pre-Registration House Officer employment; or

2.   a)   is a doctor or dentist eligible for full or limited registration with the General Medical Council or with the General Dental Council who intends to undertake postgraduate training in a hospital; and

        b)   has not spent more than 4 years in aggregate in the United Kingdom as a postgraduate doctor or dentist, excluding any period spent in Pre-Registration House Officer employment; and

3.   intends to leave the United Kingdom on completion of his training period.[4]

40

Where the applicant has previously spent time in the UK for the purpose of post graduate training, he may be admitted for a further period, but the total aggregate period in the UK for this purpose should not exceed 4 years.

It is interesting to note that Doctors from visa/semi - visa countries do not need to obtain entry clearance for the above purpose. In other words, they may be allowed to switch or remain to pursue a post graduate training without having to fulfil entry clearance requirement, although some doctors are required to pass what is called 'PLAB TEST', that is, Professional & Linguistic Assessments Board test.

2.29 Plab Test

Foreign doctors of some countries are required to pass the Professional and Linguistic Assessments Board Examination [PLAB] before they can be granted limited registration by the Medical Council. Limited registration is usually for a period of 4 years, and exceptionally, for five years. During this limited registration period, the candidate should be working in a hospital for his port graduate training. Trainees are expected to pass Parts 1 & 11 of his medical examinations within this period.

The Home Office will generally allow a total period of 12 months period during which the candidate is expected to pass his PLAB exams. He is, during this period, regarded as a visitor, his leave to remain for this examination having been granted as a concession outside the immigration rules. There is no right of appeal, therefore, against a refusal to vary or extend leave beyond the usual 12 months.

2.30 CLINICAL ATTACHMENT

A foreign doctor may also be allowed by the Home Office to take up an appointment for clinical attachment and will generally be allow a period of 12 months for this purpose. He is also, during this period regarded as a visitor, his leave to remain for this purpose having been granted as a concession outside the immigration rules. There is no right of appeal, therefore, against a refusal to vary or extend leave beyond the usual 12 months.

Our enquiries with the General Medical Council suggest that it is up to the hospital concerned to decide whether or not the candidate should ˙ have passed his PLAB test before he could be offered a position; although limited registration is a prerequisite where the applicant is going to be in contact with patients, otherwise, registration is not necessary.

REGISTRATION WITH THE GMC

For registration with the medical council, it will be necessary to contact:

> Professional Linguistic Assessments Board
> Examination[PLAB]
> General Medical Council
> 44 Hallam Street
> London W1N 6AE
>
> Phone: 0171-580-7642

At the completion of a doctor's training, and after passing his Part Two examination of the General Medical Council, it is commonplace and natural for such a doctor to seek permanent employment. However, the new immigration rules now require him to return to his home country and seek entry to the UK with a Work Permit before he can take up any employment. Further information can be obtained from the Overseas Labour Office. (See figure 12.11 for their address.)

2.31   SEASONAL WORKERS AT AGRICULTURAL CAMPS

An agricultural student may be allowed to come to the UK as a seasonal worker at an agricultural camp for a period not more than 3 months or not until the 30th November of year in question, which ever is the shorter period. An extension may be allowed for a total period of 6 months, which will not make the applicant's stay to be beyond the 30th November of the year in question. Although Entry Clearance is not required for this purpose, Home Office Work Card must be obtained by all applicants who intend to enter the UK for this purpose.

2.32   Criteria for Entry and Extension

A visa national will of course need to obtain an entry clearance in addition to obtaining the mentioned Work Card, while non-visa national does not need to obtain an entry clearance for this purpose. At the port of entry, an applicant will have to fulfil the following criteria:-[5]

a)   must be in full-time education,
b)   must be between 18-25 years inclusive,
c)   holds a valid Home Office Work Card issued by the
        operator/employer of this scheme as approved by the Home Office,
d)   intends to leave the UK at the end of this period,
e)   does not intend to take employment other than as a seasonal worker.

While seeking an extension of the initial 3 months, an applicant will, in addition, have to fulfil the following criteria:

a)   that there is further farm work available under the approved scheme, and
b)   would not as a result of an extension of stay, remain in the UK as a seasonal worker for longer than 6 months in aggregate or beyond 30 November of the year in question, whichever is the shorter period.

2.33   Work Card

It is the responsibility of the operator of the scheme or the employer in the UK to issue this card to anyone he is inviting to come to the UK to work as a seasonal agricultural worker. Prior arrangements between employee and employer is therefore needed to complete the issue of such a card. In order to be allowed to remain for up to 6 months in the UK, it is advisable for applicants to enter the UK in or about the month of June of the year in question.

2.34   USA STUDENTS

As part of a reciprocal programme of student exchanges between the UK and USA, American citizens who are full-time students in the USA can apply to come and work in the UK for a total period of 6 months under this programme, although they need to obtain a Work Permit from their employer's local job centre for each and every job they take. This work permit will normally be granted automatically.

2.35   CASE STUDY

Dear Sir/Madam,

I am 28 years old from the Bahamas. I arrived in the UK on the 16th of January 1996 as a visitor. I was granted a six month visa which is expiring soon.

Whilst here in the UK, I visited some colleges and libraries and my interest was captured when I went to Holborn Law Tutors. I have heard a lot about this private college, and as I have always wanted to study law, the course structure did nothing but fascinate me.

The problem is that I have only obtained the application forms and would have to write home so that my past results can be sent. However by the time I have done this, my visa would have expired, and I understand that I would not be able to extend my visa if I allow it to expire. Though the college has given me some advice, I thought it fit to consult an expert on this issue to avoid 'had I known'.   The college is resuming in November. It will be money down the drain if I have to go back to the Bahamas and come back in September. Also, I am yet to remit funds to the UK for my school fees as well as my maintenance.

Please advise me on what to do.

Yours faithfully,

Anthony

2.36   Suggested solution

Interestingly, you are from a commonwealth country from which an entry clearance is not needed, either to come in as a visitor, or for purpose of studies. Provided you have a genuine change of mind you may be able to vary your current status (visiting) to that of a student.

Your visa is going to expire in a few weeks, and the college is not resuming until November 1996, that is, in about five months time.

Immigration rules provide for prospective students to be admitted into the UK if they satisfy the Immigration Officer at the port of entry of certain criteria. Unfortunately, a person cannot be a prospective student after entry. Notwithstanding this, the Home Office has abundant discretion to allow such persons to remain until the school starts, and experience shows that if the interval between expiration of the person's visitors visa and the college date of resumption is not too far apart, the Home Office will generally allow this. Although a period of five months seems a fairly long time, a word of advice from your lawyer or your college welfare officer should assist.

FOOTNOTES

1.   *HC 395 paragraph 82*

2.   *HC 395 paragraph 57*

3.   *HC 395 paragraph 63*

4.   *HC 395 paragraph 70*

5.   *HC 395 paragraph 104*

Specimen of letter form the Home Office which may accompany a passport on a grant of Student visa

Fig 2.37

**Immigration and
Nationality Department**

Lunar House 40 Wellesley Road
Croydon CR9 2BY
Telephone: 071-760

HOME OFFICE

ind

M. J. Solomon & Co.
3a Stroud Green Road
Finsbury Park
London
N4 2DQ

Your Reference

Our Reference

Date   30th Sept 1991

Dear Miss Hanah,

I am returning the enclosed passport(s) endorsed with an extension of stay in the United Kingdom to enable you to continue or complete your studies.

Any application for a further extension of stay as a student must be accompanied by verifiable evidence of adequate funds for the duration of your studies without recourse to public funds, and evidence of regualr attendance on a full-time couse of day-time study. In additon you should forward evidence of the results of all examinations taken since your arrival in the United Kingdom. A further extension of stay as a student is unlikely to be granted unless the Secretary of State is satisfied that you are able to meet fully all the requirements of the Immigration Rules.

Please read the endorsement carefully.

*The enclosed police registration certificate(s) has/have also been endorsed.

                              Yours sincerely

ENCS Bank Statements

Chapter 3

WORKING HOLIDAY

3.1 WHAT IS A WORKING HOLIDAY

This is a visa granted to young Commonwealth Citizens aged 17-27 inclusive who on application are able to meet the requirements for leave to enter. *Entry clearance is now a must as no one would be allowed to switch to this category after entry.*

3.2 REQUIREMENTS FOR LEAVE TO ENTER

The requirements to be met by a person seeking leave to enter the UK as a working holiday maker are that he:[1]

i)   is a Commonwealth Citizen; and

ii)   is aged 17-27 inclusive or was so aged when first given leave to enter in this capacity; and

iii) is unmarried or is married to a person who meets the requirements of this paragraph and the parties to the marriage intend to take a working holiday together; and

iv)   has the means to pay for his return or onward journey; and

v)   is able and intends to maintain and accommodate himself without recourse to public funds; and

vi)   is intending to take employment incidental to a holiday but not to engage in business, provide services as a professional sportsman or entertainer or pursue a career in the United Kingdom; and

vii)   does not have dependent children any of whom are 5 years of age or over or who will reach 5 years of age before the applicant completes his working holiday; or commitments which would require him to earn a regular income; and

viii) intends to leave the United Kingdom at the end of his working holiday; and

ix)   if he has previously spent time in the United Kingdom as a working holidaymaker, is not seeking leave to enter to a date beyond 2 years from the date he was first given leave to enter in this capacity; and

x)   holds a valid United Kingdom entry clearance for entry in this capacity.

3.3   ENTRY CLEARANCE REQUIREMENT

A person seeking leave to enter as a working holidaymaker may be admitted for a period not exceeding 2 years with a condition restricting his freedom to take employment, provided he is able to produce to the immigration officer, on arrival, a valid UK entry clearance for entry in this capacity.[2]

By virtue of the immigration rules which came to force in October 1994 (HC 395), it is no longer possible to switch from another category to Working Holiday, neither is it possible to apply for Working Holiday in the UK where one has not entered without a Working Holiday entry clearance.   This applies to both visa and non-visa nationals alike.

Where an application for Working Holiday is made without such an entry clearance this application will be refused without a right of appeal.

3.4   NEW REQUIREMENTS INTRODUCED

New requirements have been introduced from October 1994. Therefore, in addition to the entry clearance requirements already mentioned above, the new requirements will affect applicants:-

- with spouse (who are married),
- with dependent children,
- with commitments,
- those intending to engage in business or provide services as professional sportsmen or entertainers or pursue a career.

The new rules also limit the duration to 2 years without aggregation. These changes are explained below.

3.5   Working Holiday Maker and his Spouse

The rules allow applicants who are unmarried as well as those married . Where the applicant is married, both parties to the marriage must intend to take working holiday together and they must both meet all the requirements of working holiday visa. For example, where an applicant for Working Holiday named H is married and the spouse named W does not qualify under the age or nationality requirement, H is disqualified.

It is also important to note that even where W qualifies in her own right but does not submit an application or does not intend to take a Working Holiday together with H, H is disqualified.

3.6   Children of Working Holiday Makers

There were no specific rules for children of Working Holiday Makers before the new rule which came into force in October 1994. The new rules now make entry clearance requirement mandatory for children under this category.

- The child must be under the age of 5 years.
- The child will still be under the age of 5 years when his parent(s)'s two years as a working holidaymaker are over.
- Both parents are here or coming as working holiday makers.

Where the child's parents are divorced, separated or unmarried, he can only accompany or join the parent who has sole responsibility for his upbringing, and where one parent is dead , he can accompany or join the surviving parent.

3.7   Example 1

Where the child of the applicant is 3 years old or more at the time of making application for an entry clearance intending to come for Working Holiday, then such an application will be refused. This is because such a child would be 5 years or more before the applicant completes his Working Holiday.

3.8   Example 2

Where the child of the applicant is 3 years at the time of making an application for entry clearance, intending to come for between 1 year and 18 months, such application should not be refused. This is because such a child would not be 5 years or more before the applicant completes his Working Holiday.

3.9   Example 3

Where the child of the applicant is 2 years or less at the time of making an application for entry clearance, intending to come for 2 years Working Holiday, such application should not be refused. This is because such a child would not be 5 years or more before the applicant completes his Working Holiday.

The requirement concerning children would have to be satisfied both at the time of application for entry clearance as stated above and at the port of entry in the UK when applying for leave to enter.

3.10   COMMITMENTS REQUIRING APPLICANTS TO EARN REGULAR INCOME

This requirement seems to cover a broad area and although the rule does not make clear what would amount to such commitments, it is likely that the immigration authority would be using this provision as a minefield to exclude applicants who have:-

● dependent children,

● dependent relatives e.g. grandparents, nephews etc.,

● outstanding mortgage repayments,

● outstanding loans or repayments, or

● other financial commitments.

Applicants would therefore have to watch out so as not to give a wrong impression of having any of such commitments which would require them to earn a regular income (whilst in the UK for Working Holiday).

3.11   BUSINESS, SPORTS PERSON, ENTERTAINER OR CAREER PURSUIT

The rule requires employment to be incidental to applicant's holiday (incidental to holiday explained below) and does not allow a working holiday maker to :-

● engage in business,

● provide services as a professional sportsman,

● provide services as an entertainer, or

● pursue a career.

This provision will also affect those intending to pursue academic career, train or undergo work experience.

3.12   EMPLOYMENT INCIDENTAL TO HOLIDAY

This phrase may be understood to mean that an employment or intended employment must not be the main objective of the applicant. The applicant's intention must be to take up employment which he may likely come across during his holiday. Such employment should not occupy the whole period of the Holiday.

While a working holiday maker may engage in full-time employment, he is not expected to spend the entire working holiday period in such employment. In proportion, about half of the working holiday period may be spent in full-time employment, while part-time employment for the whole period may be perfectly alright.

Also, a working holiday maker returning after spending some time outside the UK is likely to be questioned about his previous work pattern and future intentions.

One must also be careful when answering some difficult questions, for example, a person who admits that he could not find a job in his home country may be refused a working holiday visa on the basis that his primary objective was to work in the UK rather than to enjoy a holiday.

3.13   2 YEAR LIMIT (NO AGGREGATION)

In the past where part of the Working Holiday has been spent outside the UK, extension may be granted to make up for such time. This is no longer the case. The effect of the new rule is that if an applicant has previously spent time in the UK as a working holidaymaker, he would not be granted leave to enter to a date beyond 2 years from the date he was first given leave to enter in this capacity.

3.14   Example

Mr Hassani was granted Entry Clearance for Working Holiday in January 1995 and entered the UK in April 1995. He will not be able to remain or return to the UK as a Working Holidaymaker beyond April 1997. Please note that time starts to run from the date of first entry.

Other requirements, which need to be fulfiled are now explained.

3.15   17-27 YEARS OLD INCLUSIVE

No application should be made except the applicant is at least 17 years old and not more than 27 years old on the day of application.[3]

A person is 27 years old up until A DAY before his 28th birthday.

3.16   MEANS OF RETURNING, MAINTENANCE AND ACCOMMODATION

Two important requirements must be borne in mind:

- the applicant must have means to pay for his return journey (possibly through a sponsor), and

- the applicant must not recourse to public funds.

A working holiday maker is expected to be able to maintain and accommodate himself without having to recourse to public funds. Therefore, cheques in favour of applicant, bank drafts, travellers cheques, bank balance/statement, or sponsorship letter from relative or friend in the UK, together with payslips or bank statement/balance of such relative or friend may be forwarded with an application.

The sponsor may also be required to provide proof of adequate accommo-dation such as his rent book, tenancy agreement or proof of ownership.

3.17 HOW TO APPLY FOR ENTRY CLEARANCE FOR WORKING HOLIDAY

Application should be made to a British Embassy or High Commission by filling the appropriate form and paying the required fees. Such applicants would normally be invited to attend an interview where their home circumstances, commitments, reasons for working holiday and intentions can be ascertained.

The following are some of the necessary documents which may be required:-

1)   Applicant's Passport and Birth Certificate.
2)   Children's Birth Certificate (where applicable).
3)   Marriage Certificate (where applicable).
4)   Letter of Sponsorship/Invitation Letter from Sponsor in the UK.
5)   Sponsor's Bank Statement/Pay slips.
6)   Evidence of Accommodation in the UK e.g. Tenancy Agreement.
7)   Educational Certificates/College Admission Letter or Employment Letter.
8)   Up-to-date Bank Statement of Applicant.
9)   Any documentary Evidence from which it may be inferred that applicant will likely return home after his working holiday in the UK.

Applicant should note that they are not expected to have secured employment in the UK in order to satisfy the working holiday requirement. Also, applicant's interest should be more of a holiday, as employment is just going to be incidental to this holiday.

3.18 WHAT NEXT AFTER WORKING HOLIDAY?

A person who has been in the UK as a Working Holiday maker may be allowed to vary this status to another category which requires no mandatory entry clearance. Such applicant seeking variation to another status will have to show that there has been a change of circumstance, for example, marriage to a person settled in the UK during the existence of the working holiday.

It is necessary to reiterate that no one may be able to vary to a category where entry clearance is mandatory, for example, as a minister of religion; and while a non-visa national may be able to vary his working holiday status to that of student, the Immigration Rules categorically state that applications by full and semi - visa nationals (who are in the UK for any other temporary purpose), to remain in the UK as students, should be refused.

3.19   Illustration

Nyaki, a Ugandan (semi-visa national) who is in the UK on a working holiday visa wishes to remain in order to complete a 3 year degree course she had started just 6 months before the end of this working holiday visa. Nyaki would have to travel back home so as to be able to obtain an entry clearance for this purpose.

This can be contrasted with the case of Mr Alex from Australia (non visa national) who, provided he satisfies the conditions for being a student, may be able to obtain a variation of status, without needing to travel home for an entry clearance (although he is not expected to have embarked on the studies during the course of his working holiday).

3.20   Important Points to Note

1.   A working holiday maker does not need a work permit as there will not be any restrictions or prohibitions on his visa once a working holiday visa is granted. This working holiday visa will also make one eligible for a National Insurance number which is normally required by would-be-employers.

2.   You may also wish to note that Cameroon, Mozambique and South Africa are now Commonwealth countries. Cameroon and Mozambique have semi visa status while South Africa has non visa status.

3.21   COMMONWEALTH COUNTRIES

Antigua and Barmuda	Mauritius
Australia	Namibia
The Bahamas	Naura
Bangladesh	New Zealand
Barbados	Nigeria
Belize	Pakistan
Botswana	Papua New Guinea
Brunei	Republic of Cyprus
Canada	Saint Christopher and Nevis
Cameroon	Saint Lucia
Dominica	St.Vincent and the Grenadines
Fiji	Seychelles
The Gambia	Sierra Leone
Ghana	Solomon Islands
Grenada	South Africa
Guyana	Sri Lanka
India	Singapore
Jamaica	Swaziland
Kenya	Tanzania
Kiribati	Tonga
Lesotho	Trinidad and Tobago
Malawi	Tuvulu
Malaysia	Uganda
Maldives	Vanuatu
Malta	Western Samoa
	Zambia
	Zimbabwe

FOOTNOTES

1. ·   HC 395 paragraph 95
2.   HC 395 1 paragraph 96
3.   HC 395 paragraph 95(ii)

Chapter 4

MARRIAGE

4.1 INTRODUCTION

In order to preserve the integrity of family units, immigration law has been carefully drawn in this area, with provisions for entry and settlement of spouses, as well as fiancé(e)s.

These provisions do not allow polygamous marriages or those of the under age (i.e. where a spouse is under the age of 16). [1]

Although immigration law provisions have been unique in this area, they are nonetheless viewed as unfair because of the 'primary purpose test', and its stringent requirements.

We have endeavoured to provide a comprehensive analysis on the entry of fiancé(e)s and spouses of settlers and non-settlers, their leave to remain and some other practical hints which should assist people with concerns in this area. Also discussed are subjects relating to Leave to Remain for EEA spouses and applications outside the immigration rules.

4.2 BRINGING IN FIANCÉS/FIANCEES BY THOSE WHO ARE SETTLED IN THE UK

It is possible for someone who is settled in the UK or who is being admitted for settlement, to bring his/her fiancee/fiancé in anticipation of marriage, but an entry clearance is needed for this purpose. The in-coming fiancé(e)s will initially be admitted for a period of six months, within which he is expected to marry. An extension of leave to remain in this capacity may be granted where there are good grounds for the delay in marriage, and where there is satisfactory evidence that the marriage will take place soon afterwards.

4.3   CONDITIONS FOR ENTRY CLEARANCE FOR FIANCÉ(E)S

An Entry Clearance Officer will have to be satisfied:[2]

- that the applicant is seeking leave to enter the UK for marriage to a person present and settled in the UK or who is on the same occasion being admitted for settlement;

- that it is not the primary purpose of the intended marriage to obtain admission to the UK;

- that the parties to the marriage intend to live together permanently in the UK as husband and wife;

- that both parties to the marriage have met and there will be adequate maintenance and accommodation for the applicant until the date of marriage without having to recourse to public funds;

- that after the marriage there will be *adequate accommodation* for the parties and their dependants without having to recourse to public funds; and

- that after the marriage, the parties will be able to *maintain* themselves and their dependants without having to recourse to public funds.

4.4   What Happens After Your Marriage?

Once the marriage has taken place, variation of stay for a period of one year will normally be granted, after which an application for indefinite leave to remain should be made, provided the couple can meet the Home Office's requirements. For further discussion, see figure 4.12

4.5   ADMISSION OF SPOUSES OF SETTLED PERSONS

A passenger seeking admission to the UK as the spouse of a person who is present and settled in the UK or who is on the same occasion being admitted for settlement must hold an entry clearance granted for that purpose.

4.6   Who is Settled in the UK?

One is settled for this purpose if he is ordinarily resident in the UK without being subject to any restriction on his stay under the Immigration Laws. Such a person may be a British Citizen, a person with a Right of Abode, a person with Indefinite Leave to Enter or Remain, or a member of HM Forces in the UK serving overseas

4.7   CONDITIONS FOR ENTRY CLEARANCE FOR SPOUSES

Before the grant of entry clearance, an entry clearance officer must be satisfied:

- that the applicant is married to a person present and settled in the UK or who is on the same occasion being admitted for settlement;

- that the marriage was not entered into primarily to obtain admission to the UK;

- that both parties to the marriage have the intention of living permanently with each other as his or her spouse and the marriage is subsisting;

- that parties to the marriage have met, and that there will be *adequate accommodation* for the parties and their dependants (if any) without having to recourse to public funds;

- that the parties will be able to *maintain* themselves and their dependants adequately without having to recourse to public funds.

On arrival, such a passenger holding an entry clearance would normally be admitted for an initial period of 12 months.

Towards the end of this period of 12 months, such a spouse will then have to make an application for indefinite leave to remain. See below for necessary documents in support of this application.

4.8   HOW TO APPLY FOR ENTRY CLEARANCE FOR SPOUSE/FIANCÉ(E)S

Spouses and fiancé(e)s have to apply by themselves. The sponsoring partners cannot apply for them, but must support their applications. The applying partners should apply to the British High Commission or Embassy (usually in their Home country).

An interview may be granted in order to establish among other things:

● the primary purpose of the marriage,

● that the couple have met,

● that they intended to live permanently together as husband and wife and that the marriage is subsisting (where already married),

● that there will be adequate accommodation for the couple and their dependants without having to recourse to public funds.

4.9   WHAT IS NEEDED FOR THE INTERVIEW

For the interview, applicants will have to provide a number of documents in their original form or certified copies from themselves and their sponsors. Such documents will usually include:-

● Certified copies of the sponsor's current and old passport to show his or her immigration status in the UK; if he or she is a British Citizen, the first five pages with personal details. If a settled person, the first five pages and all pages with Immigration stamps on them.

- Where marriage has been contracted, proof of marriage in form of original marriage certificate will be needed. If the original marriage certificate is in the UK, it should be sent to the spouse abroad while a certified copy should be retained by the partner in the UK. Where there is no such certificate in existence, the applicant should explain the reason for this.

- Proof that the couple are free to marry: if either party has been married before, proof that the previous marriage has ended by death, divorce or annulment. The proof should be in it's original form.

- Proof of financial support available in the UK; recent payslips and/or bank statements from the sponsor or letter from his employer confirming his salary. Where the sponsor is not in gainful employment, the applicant would have to provide proof that he (the applicant) has sufficient funds or prospects of securing employment without being a burden on the state resources in the UK.

- Evidence of accommodation available in the UK; If the accommodation is rented, a rent book or tenancy agreement and where possible, a letter from the Landlord/Council to confirm the size of the accommodation and the number of rooms available. If owned or mortgaged, the mortgage documents or letter from the building society showing the essential details. Such accommodation should be owned or exclusively occupied by the parties.

- Letter of sponsorship from the sponsoring spouse or fiancé(e)s in the UK supporting the application including any other information which may assist the entry clearance officer to arrive at a satisfactory decision.

- Where available, letters exchanged between the couple to show an existing relationship between them.

●   Proof that the couple have met. This may include photographs together, old family photographs etc. Letter of sponsorship from the sponsoring spouse/fiancé(e)s may also state when and where the couple have met.

The spouse or fiancé(e)s in the UK may also be interviewed where the couple have only recently engaged or married, and such interview will be to establish the purpose of the marriage.

An applicant may be asked why he wants to come to the UK and questions to the sponsor may include why he or she does not prefer going abroad to live with the spouse, whether the applicant has attempted to come to the UK before and for what purpose, whether he had previously planned to travel abroad to work or for any other purpose and many more detailed and personal questions.

Applicants from poor countries may be asked a lot of questions, many of these being repeated over and again in slightly different forms, to see if any negative inference can be drawn as to the primary purpose of the marriage.

Also while the interviewing procedure and methods may be similar for intending settlers and those coming for temporary purpose, it is normally expected that those coming to settle receive greater scrutiny.

4.10   What next after the interview?

After the interview, an entry clearance office may make enquiries as to the authenticity of facts and documents provided. This may include finding out whether a former spouse is truly dead or that the divorce papers or any other papers are genuine. Sometimes, the Entry Clearance Officer may visit the applicant's home to obtain further information, and may ask the Home Office in London to make enquiries about the sponsor.

The Home Office may also ask the sponsor to sign an undertaking in support of the application, that the applicant will not have to recourse to public funds. If the authorities are satisfied, an entry clearance will be granted and this is valid for six months.

At the port of entry, the spouse of a settler may be granted a year visa after which an indefinite leave to remain should be sought.   Fiancé(e)s are normally granted a six months visa at the port of entry. (Spouses of those who are in the UK for a temporary purpose may be granted either six months visa or for the same period as those of their sponsors).

4.11   PROVING THE MARRIAGE

It is logical to expect the E.C.O or I.O to ask for proof of the marriage before allowing the spouse-applicants to *join or settle* with their partners. Usually, the best proof of marriage is a Marriage Certificate, but problems may occur where the marriage has taken place under a local custom and there is no such certificate. Proving the existence of such marriage may be a big task.

Experience has shown that the spouse of a settler who is coming to or who is already in the UK and seeking settlement, will always have to do more than other spouses in proving this marriage.

Proving a customary marriage is largely one of evidence of credibility, and the onus is on the couple to do this. Sworn affidavit(s) stating the custom or law under which the marriage was contracted, date of marriage and the way and manner such custom or law allows the marriage to be conducted, should normally be sufficient in most cases.

4.12   APPLICATION AFTER ENTRY

Fiancé(e)s should apply for leave to remain immediately after their marriage. A spouse who entered the UK for a short visit may have a genuine change of circumstances and request to remain as a spouse. Also, a person in the UK for temporary purpose who is now married to a person settled here will also have to make an application for leave to remain as a foreign spouse.

An extension will not be granted unless the Home Office is satisfied with the following conditions:-

- that the applicant has leave to remain in the UK,

- that the marriage was not entered into primarily to obtain settlement in the UK;

- that the parties to the marriage have met and the applicant has not remained in breach of the immigration law (e.g. being in employment without authority);

- that the marriage has not taken place after a decision has been made to deport the applicant or after having been given notice to leave the country;

- that the marriage has not been terminated and each of the parties has the intention of living permanently with the other as husband and wife;

- that there will be adequate accommodation for the parties and their dependants without having to recourse to public funds in accommodation which they own or occupy exclusively and

- that the parties will be able to maintain themselves and their dependants adequately without having to recourse to public funds.

As you can see from the above conditions, leave to remain would be considered within the rules provided that the applicant has leave to remain and he is not in breach of immigration rules (e.g. as an overstayer). Where you have no visa or you are in breach of immigration rules, or where your immigration status is unclear, your application would most probably be considered outside the immigration rules.

The application process leading to the final grant of permanent residence is in two stages.

4.13   THE FIRST STAGE

4.14   The Probationary Period: 12 Months Visa

On satisfying these conditions, the Home Office should grant the applicant an extension of stay for a period of 12 months. While a Questionnaire may be given to the couple for completion, they may also be interviewed. A visit by an immigration officer to the couple's residence is equally possible.

Although the rules allow the Home Office to extend this probationary period of 12 months, they rarely do so.

4.15   Necessary Documents for this Application

Where an applicant is making an application either by post or in person, the following documents should be forwarded:

● the applicant's Passport;

● the spouse's passport (not a British Visitor's Passport) showing that he is settled in the UK, or if he is a British Citizen, he has full birth certificate may be acceptable although, it must be supported with other evidence of identity e.g. Driving Licence, National Insurance/Health Service Registration cards;

● the couple's civil or religious marriage certificate;

● evidence that the applicant and spouse are free to marry where either had been married before;
● wedding photographs;

● consent letter from the 'settled' spouse;

● Spouse's Home Office reference number (if he is not a British citizen by birth or descent);

● birth certificates of children of the marriage (if any), and or medical certificate as proof of pregnancy (where appropriate);

- evidence of accommodation; rent book, tenancy agreement etc.; bank statements of the couple (joint or separate);

- last three or four wage slips for the couple (where appropriate); and

- any official correspondence addressed to the couple, possibly, at the matrimonial address.

Where an application is made by post, a questionnaire form may be sent to the applicant for completion, and this must be signed by both the applicant and his spouse. The following questions are commonly asked:

1. How and where did you meet your spouse and when did you first meet?

2. When did the relationship become serious, and when did you start living together?

3. When and why did you decide to marry?

4. How long has your spouse lived in the UK, and what relatives do you and your spouse have in the UK?

5. What relatives do you and your spouse have in other countries?

6. Do you or your spouse have children of an earlier relationship who are living with you or whose maintenance you are responsible for? If yes, provide details.

7. At what address are you and your spouse living? Please state if it is rented, mortgaged or owned by the council, together with the number of rooms, names of people living there, and the full weekly rent or mortgage repayment of this property.

8. If the applicant and /or spouse are in current employment please

forward their last three wage slips. Please supply NI (National Insurance) numbers.

9.   If neither of them is in current employment please advise us of the source(s) of their funds and provide documentary evidence.

10.   What savings do they both have? Please provide evidence.

It is not unusual for the Home Office to ask applicants to provide names, addresses, phone numbers and immigration status of third parties who will be willing to confirm information that have been provided in support of the marriage application. Such a third party will also be expected to indicate his willingness to attend the Home Office or an interview, if called upon.

This is a 12 month visa without any restriction or prohibition on employment.

Fig 4.16

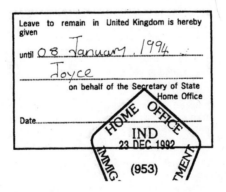

The applicant's passport will be returned, together with a letter informing him that he is allowed to work and do business, but should not have recourse to public funds.

This is the sample letter from the Home Office for stage one application

Fig 4.17

Immigration and Nationality Department	HOME OFFICE
Lunar House 40 Wellesley Road Croydon CR9 2BY Telephone: 071-760	**ind**

Your Reference

Our Reference M 170272

Date 15 April, 1993

Dear Michael,

I am writing about your application to remain in the United Kingdom following your marriage.

A person who marries someone settled in this country may be allowed to stay here for an initial period of up to 12 months, provided that the requirements of the Immigration Rules are met. You may now stay in the United Kingdom until 16 April 1994 . . . . .and may set up a business or take employment without a work permit.

During this period you will be expected not to rely on public funds to support yourself, although there is no objection to your spouse receiving any assistance to which he or she is entitled in his or her own right. Public funds means housing under Part III of the Housing Act 1985 and income support, family credit and housing benefit under Part II of the Social Security Act 1986.

You may apply for the time limit attached to your stay in this country to be removed shortly before your leave expires. It is important that this application is made before then and you should enclose your passport and the birth certificate or passport of your spouse for identification purposes with it.

For the application to be granted, we will need to be satisfied that your marriage has not ended and that you and your spouse both still intend living permanently with each other as husband and wife. If you provide a statement to this effect, signed by you both, this will assist us in considering your application.

We shall also need to ask if you have received any of the public funds described above since the date of this letter, and any information you can provide about this could again save further enquiry on our part. Short term assistance from public funds, and in particular it is clear that you are unable to maintain and accommodate yourself without further help, your application may be refused under the general considerations in paragraph 100 of the Immigration Rules.

4.18   SECOND STAGE

4.19   Indefinite Leave to Remain

Before the expiry of the initial 12 months, another application should be forwarded to the Home Office so that the time limit on stay could be removed.

The requirements for Indefinite Leave to Remain for the spouse of a person present and settled in the United Kingdom are that:-

a)   the applicant was admitted to the United Kingdom or given an extension of stay for a period of 12 months and has completed a period of 12 months as the spouse of a person present and settled here; and

b)   the applicant is still the spouse of the person he or she was admitted or granted an extension of stay to join and the marriage is subsisting; and

c)   each of the parties intends to live permanently with the other as his or her spouse.

Necessary documents will include those stated under stage one above as well as correspondence proving that the couple are still living together as husband and wife from the grant of the one year probationary period up till the time of this new application for Indefinite Leave. These correspondence should include intermingling of official letters sent to both parties of the marriage addressed to them at their residence and will be preferred to have come from of the following sources:-

-   Notice of Poll or Council Tax Registration
-   British Telecom
-   Mercury/Cable Telephone Services
-   Local Housing Authority
-   Credit Card Company
-   Department of Employment

- Bank/Building Society
- British Gas
- Electricity Authority
- Social Services Department
- Health Authority
- Inland Revenue, etc.
- Custom and Excise
- Tenancy Agreement

This is a Permanent Residence visa

Fig 4.20

4.21   Important Points to Note

1. Where someone is not sure that he has met or can fulfil the above listed conditions, (for example, where he is an overstayer) the Home Office should be approached with care and caution. Please see sub-topic: Marriage Application Outside the Rules.

2. Where an application is made in person, it is the practice of the Home Office to interview both spouses separately and individually asking

identical questions. These questions may cover the background of each spouse, and will be verified with the other spouse.

3.   The Home Office usually make enquiries with other government departments such as the benefits office. As such it not uncommon for some people to run into some difficulties where records with the benefit office are different from that with the Home Office. For example, Mr Fostin is married to Freda who has been on income support for many years. Mr Fostin's pay advice shows a salary of £2,000 per month and Freda is unwilling to stop her income support. Benefit office records will not show that Freda is now married. This of course can be a source of suspicion for the immigration office which may lead to further enquiries from which it may be inferred that the couple are not living together, or that they do not intent to live permanently together as husband and wife.

4.22   ESSENTIAL POINTS IN MARRIAGE APPLICATIONS

4.23   Interview Questions

Where an application is made in person, or where the couple are interviewed, questions asked may be similar to the following:-

-    why did you decide to marry?
-    who proposed the marriage?
-    are your parents in agreement to this marriage?
-    how many brothers and sisters has your spouse?
-    what food does your spouse like best?
-    who cooked last night?
-    what is your spouse's favourite colour?
-    how did you travel to the interview? etc.

You may find a mock interview helpful prior to the real interview.

Few and minor discrepancies in answers provided at the interview are unlikely to jeopardise one's application but very serious and crucial gaps, errors or omissions which go to the root of the marriage or relationship by way of giving contradictory answers between the spouses may result in a refusal.

We strongly advise that all questions asked and answers provided should be noted down during or as soon as the parties leave the interview. Such interview notes may be needed in the future, e.g. for an appeal against refusal, or to substantiate future claims where seeking further extension..

Problems commonly encountered with marriage applications are usually in the following arrears:

- Primary purpose,
- intention to live permanently together as husband and wife,
- the requirement that the couple have met,
- accommodation, and
- maintenance without having to recourse to public funds.

4.24   Primary Purpose Rule

This rule is to check thoroughly that the marriage was not entered into primarily to obtain admission or settlement in the UK.

The burden is on the applicant (and his spouse) to satisfy immigration/ entry clearance officers, that it is not the primary purpose of the marriage to obtain admission or settlement in the UK. The intention of the couple, therefore, becomes paramount. Where the marriage has been arranged, the intention of those who arranged it will also be considered. Evidence of intervening devotion such as the birth of a child of the marriage should greatly assist in satisfying the primary purpose test.

The primary purpose rule has generated a lot of anger and created inconvenience. It has also been easy tool for entry clearance officers to deny entry clearance. However, there is a concession that an application should not be refused where the couple have been married for over 5 years. Another concession is that refusal should not be based on primary purpose where the couple have a child who has a right of abode in the UK.[3]

4.25   Intention to Live Permanently Together

Fiancé(e)s and newly married couples will have to show that they intend to live together permanently.

In practice, such intention will be demonstrated by joint residence and absence of any contrary evidence which may suggest otherwise.   Such contrary evidence may be separation, divorce proceedings or an admission or statement by one of the parties to a governmental body or agency (e.g. Department of Social Security) that he resides elsewhere.

4.26   That the Parties Have Met

There must be a meeting by the parties to the extent that the parties recognise and know each other.   This criterion is in the rules so as to weed out marriages where parties have never met at all up till the day of marriage or arrival in the UK.   Old photographs of the couple taken together before marriage may be very useful in this area.

4.27   Adequate and Exclusive Possession of Accommodation

Quite apart from availability, the accommodation must also be adequate for the occupiers as well as the in-coming partners or spouses.   Where a bedroom should be adequate for a couple, this may not be so where there are children in the household. This accommodation must be owned or occupied exclusively by the couple. [4]

4.28   Maintenance

This is the sponsor's ability to maintain himself and his fiancee or spouse. Therefore, his income or savings must be such that will be considered reasonable to support them without having to recourse to public funds. Where the sponsor's income or savings are inadequate or he or she is unemployed the application will usually encounter some difficulties. However, proof of employment or prospect of one for the applicant, in the UK, or evidence of the applicant's own funds upon which he may rely will be very helpful.

Please note that by virtue of rule order CM 3365, August 1996, it is a requirement that when applying for indefinite leave to remain, the parties to the marriage must have been maintaining themselves and any dependants without recourse to public funds in their accommodation and maintenance. This is to say that the 'settled spouse' must also not have recourse to public funds.

4.29   MARRIAGE APPLICATION OUTSIDE THE RULES

The immigration rules provide that application to remain in the United Kingdom for any purpose, including application to remain with spouse should be made before current leave expires.

From the view point of the Home Office, all applications considered to fall for consideration outside the immigration rules should best be made outside the UK, and as such, not all applications which fall for consideration outside the rules will be favourably considered by the Home Office.

An application may still, however, be made by someone who is:

1.   on appeal due to refusal of variation or extension , or

2.   an overstayer/illegal entrant, or

3.   appealing against an intention to deport, or

4.   subject of a deportation order, or

5.   cohabiting with a settled partner.

The Home Office's current internal policy in relation to such application, commonly referred to as DP3/96, gives guidelines for consideration of applications which may fall under the above-named categories. These internal instructions are supposed to reflect recent European cases with respect to Right for the family and private life, and any interference with this must be in accordance with the law. Before DP3/96 was DP2/93 which we intend to reproduce for the benefit of few cases which are still to be considered under it, and also for comparison between the two documents. DP3/96 came into operation and will be the basis for considering applications received by the Home Office from the 14th March 1996.

4.30   DP2/93

4.31   Home Office Internal Policy on Marriage Applications, Outside the Rules.

1.   All deportation and illegal entry cases must be considered on their individual merits. Where enforcement action is under consideration or has been initiated and the offender is married, a judgement will need to be reached on the weight to be attached to the marriage as a compassionate factor.

2.   As a general rule deportation action under section 3(5)(a) or section 3(5)(b) (in criminal cases), or illegal entry action should not be initiated or pursued where the subject has a genuine and subsisting marriage to a person settled in the United Kingdom if:-

   a)   the marriage pre-dates enforcement action; **and**

   b)   (i) the marriage has lasted 2 years or more or, in the case of a common-law relationship, the couple have cohabited for 2 years or more. It does not automatically follow, however, that deportation/removal is the right course where this test is not met. Full account should be taken of any evidence that a strong relationship has existed for more than 2 years (this will include any reasons why the couple did not marry earlier, e.g. waiting for a divorce to be finalised, saving to buy their own home); **or**

c)   (ii) the settled spouse has lived here from an early age or it is otherwise unreasonable to expect him/her to accompany on removal; **or**

d)   (iii) one or more children of the marriage has the right of abode in the United Kingdom, most commonly as a result of having been born in the United Kingdom to a parent settled here. It should be noted that an illegitimate child born in the United Kingdom only obtains British Citizenship under the British Nationality Act 1981 if the mother is a British Citizen or settled here.   Under the 1981 Act, the status of the father of an illegitimate child has no bearing on the nationality of the child unless he subsequently marries the mother and legitimises the child.

NOTE:

i)   The subject's immigration history is of little relevance once it has been concluded that the marriage is genuine and subsisting.

ii)   Enforcement action may be inappropriate where the spouse or the foreign national is pregnant with a child who would have the right of abode here even if born outside the United Kingdom.

iii)   The presence of the settled spouse's children by a former relationship will also be an availing factor provided that the children have the right of abode in the United Kingdom, are still dependent and that we can be satisfied that they either live with or have frequent contact with the settled spouse.

3)   In considering whether it is reasonable for a spouse to accompany on removal under paragraph 2(c) above, whilst the onus is on the United Kingdom settled spouse to make out a case why it is unreasonable for him/her to join the family outside the United Kingdom, in general terms, cases should be conceded if the United Kingdom settled spouse:-

a)   has strong family ties in the United Kingdom; or
b)   has lengthy residence in the United Kingdom; or
c)   suffers from ill health such that his/her quality of life would be significantly impaired if he/she were to accompany his/her removal.

4)   There will be a presumption to proceed with section 3(5)(a), 3(5)(b) (in non-criminal cases) or illegal entry action (subject to consideration of other relevant factors) in marriage cases where there are no children with the right of abode in the United Kingdom if:-

a)   neither parent is settled in the United Kingdom; or
b)   the marriage is one of convenience, that is, the couple do not intend to live together permanently as husband and wife; or
c)   the couple are separated.

Divorced or Separated Parents

5)   The fact that the European Court is strongly disposed to find a breach of Article 8 of the European Convention where the effect of an immigration decision is to separate a parent from his/her child is also relevant in cases involving divorced or separated parents. Where one parent is settled in the UK and the removal of the other would result in deprivation of frequent and regular access currently enjoyed by either parent, section 3(5)(a), 3(5)(b) (in non-criminal cases) or illegal entry action should be abandoned. Reliance cannot be placed on the argument that the UK settled parent can travel abroad to continue access.

6)   Cases will arise where a person to be deported/removed has custody of a child with the right of abode in the UK by a previous partner who is no longer in contact with the child. Here the crucial question is whether it is reasonable for the child to accompany the parent to live abroad. The factors to be considered are:

a)   the age of the child (in most cases a pre-school age child could reasonably be expected to adapt to life abroad);

b)   the strength of the child's ties with the UK, including other UK resident family members;

c)   any medical conditions which would be better treated here;

d)   the standard of living (including educational facilities) in the country to which the parent is being removed.

Common-Law Relationships

7)   Where there is conclusive evidence that a genuine and subsisting common-law relationship akin to marriage exists, it should be considered under this instruction as if it were a marriage. The onus rests firmly on the individual who seeks to benefit to provide conclusive evidence of the nature of the relationship.
Criminal Convictions

8)   The test is, where someone liable to immigration control has family ties here which would normally benefit him/her under paragraphs 1-6 above yet has criminal convictions, whether removal can be justified as 'necessary in the interests of a democratic society'. This is usually interpreted by the European Court as serious crime punished with imprisonment (for example, crimes of violence, drug offences [other than possession], murder, terrorism) but minor offences (even though an individual has a long criminal record) or a poor immigration history do not carry much weight. What is reasonable in any particular case will depend not only on the nature of the offence but also on the settled spouse's strength of ties with the United Kingdom. Where action is deemed to be in the interests of a democratic society it would normally be capable of being taken under section 3(5)(b) or 3(6) deportation powers.

Marriages of Convenience to EC Nationals

9)   Foreign nationals who contract a valid marriage to an EC national exercising Treaty rights in the UK (for example by working) have

hitherto been allowed to benefit from the provisions of Community law in line with his/her spouse, effectively preventing enforcement action (barring serious criminal convictions) at least whilst the spouse continues to exercise Treaty rights. It has become clear, however, that immigration offenders can exploit this approach by entering into marriage of convenience with EC nationals.

10) Current legal advice is that the removal of a person who has married an EC national exercising Treaty rights may be justified where there are exceptionally strong grounds for suspicion that the marriage is one of convenience, i.e. that the couple do not intend to live together permanently as man and wife and the marriage was contracted for immigration purposes.

4.32   DP3/96

Introduction

This notice provides guidance, in general terms, on the consideration of cases of those liable to be removed as illegal entrants or deported who have married a person settled in the United Kingdom. This notice supersedes DP2/93 which is hereby cancelled, subject to the transitional provisions set out in paragraph 10 of this instruction. Deportation cases fall to be considered within the framework of the Immigration Rules and the attached guidance should be read in conjunction with those Rules. Although illegal entry cases are considered outside the Rules, any relevant compassionate circumstances, including those referred to below, should be considered before a decision to remove is taken.

Policy

2. Paragraph 364 of the Immigration Rules explains that deportation will normally be the proper course where a person has failed to comply with or

has contravened a condition or has remained here without authority but that all the known relevant factors must be taken into account before a decision is reached. These include:

i)   age;
    ii)   length of residence in the UK;
    iii)   strength of connections with the UK;
    iv)   personal history, including character, conduct and employment record;
    v)   domestic circumstances;
    vi)   previous criminal record and the nature of any offence;
    vii)   compassionate circumstances;
    viii)   any representations.

3.   Where persons do not qualify for leave to remain under the Immigration Rules and are to be considered for deportation, or where they are illegal entrants liable to removal, but seek nevertheless to remain on the basis of marriage in the UK, the following paragraphs of this guidance apply.

4.   Where enforcement action is under consideration and the offender is married to someone settled here a judgement will need to be reached on the weight to be attached to the marriage as a compassionate factor. Caseworkers should bear in mind that paragraph 284 of the Immigration Rules, which sets out the requirements to be met for an extension of stay as the spouse of a person present and settled in the UK, specifically requires, amongst other things, a person to have a limited leave to remain here and to have not remained here in breach of the immigration laws, in order to obtain leave to remain on that basis. Therefore, the fact that an offender is married to a person settled here does not give him/her any right to remain under the Rules.

Marriages that Pre-date Enforcement Action

5.   As a general rule, deportation action under 3(5)(a) or (3)(5)(b) (in non-criminal cases) or illegal entry action should not normally be

initiated in the following circumstances (but see notes below):

a)   where the subject has genuine and subsisting marriage with someone settled here and the couple have lived together in this country continuously since their marriage for at least 2 years before the commencement of enforcement action

and

b)   it is unreasonable to expect the settled spouse to accompany his/her spouse on removal.

Notes

i)   In this instruction, "settled" refers to British citizens who live in the UK or to other nationals who have Indefinite Leave to Enter or Remain in the UK.

ii)   In considering whether or not, under paragraph 5(b) above, it would be unreasonable for a settled spouse to accompany the subject of enforcement action on removal the onus rests with the settled spouse to make out a case with supporting evidence as to why it is unreasonable for him/her to live outside the UK. Factors which caseworkers should take into account, if they are made known to them, will include whether the UK settled spouse:

a.   has very strong and close family ties in the UK such as older children from a previous relationship that form part of the family unit; or

b.   has been settled and living in the UK for at least the preceding 10 years; or

c.   suffers from ill-health and medical evidence conclusively shows that his/her life would significantly be impaired or endangered if he/she were to accompany his/her spouse on removal.

iii)   In this instruction commencement of enforcement action is to be taken as either:-

a.   a specific instruction to leave with a warning of liability to deportation if the subject fails to do so; or

b.   service of a notice of intention to deport or service of illegal entry papers (including the service of papers during a previous stay in the UK where the subject has returned illegally:; or

c.   a recommendation by a court that a person should be deported following a conviction.

iv)   The commencement of enforcement action ''stops the clock'' in terms of the 2 years qualifying period referred to in paragraph 5a above in which a marriage must have subsisted. No further time can then be accrued to meet this criterion, for example, whilst making representations, appealing against the decision or applying for judicial review.

v)   This notice contains guidance as to the approach to be adopted in the generality of cases but it must be remembered that each case is to be decided on its individual merits and, for instance, a particularly poor immigration history may warrant the offender's enforced departure from the UK notwithstanding the factors referred to above.

Criminal Convictions

6.   In cases where someone liable to immigration control has family ties here which would normally benefit him/her under paragraph 4 above but has criminal convictions, the severity of the offence should be balanced against the strength of the family ties. Serious crimes which are punishable with imprisonment or a series of lesser crimes which show a propensity to re-offend, would normally outweigh the family ties. A very poor immigration history may also be taken into account. Caseworkers must use their judgement to decide what is reasonable in any individual case.

Children

7.   The presence of children with a right of abode in the UK (see note below) is a factor to be taken into account. In cases involving children

who have the right of abode, the crucial question is whether it is reasonable for the child to accompany his/her parents abroad. Factor to be considered includes:

a)   the age of the child (in most cases a child of 10 or younger could reasonably be expected to adapt to life abroad);

b)   serious ill-health for which treatment is not available in the country to which the family is going.

Note

1)   Children will have the right of abode most commonly as a result of having been born in the UK to a parent settled here. It should be noted that under the British Nationality Act 1981 an illegitimate child born in the UK obtains British citizenship only if the mother is a British citizen or is settled in the UK. Under the 1981 Act the status of the father of a child born illegitimate has no bearing on the nationality of the child unless he subsequently marries the mother and thus legitimises the child.

Marriages that Post-date enforcement action

8.   Where a person marries after the commencement of enforcement action removal should normally be enforced. The criteria set out in paragraph 5 does not apply in such cases. Paragraph 284 of the Immigration Rules makes it clear that one of the requirements for an extension of stay as the spouse of a person present and settled in the UK is that '' the marriage has not taken place after a decision has been made to deport the applicant or he has been recommended for deportation or has been given notice under Section 6(2) of the Immigration Act 1971''. Marriage cannot therefore in itself be considered a sufficient compassionate factor to militate against removal. Detailed enquiries in order to ascertain whether the marriage is genuine and subsisting should not normally be undertaken. The onus is on the subject to put forward any compelling compassionate factors that he/she wishes to be considered which must be supported by documentary evidence. Only in the most exceptional

circumstances should removal action be stopped and the person allowed to stay.

Marriage to European Economic Area (EEA) national

9.   Any foreign national who contracts a marriage to an EEA national should have his/her case considered in the first instance by EC group, B6 Division to whom the case must be referred, irrespective of whether the marriage took place before or after the initiation of enforcement action.

Transitional Arrangements

10   This instructions will not apply retrospectively. It has immediate effect in cases where marriage came to the notice of the Immigration and Nationality Department after 13 March 1996 irrespective of the date on which the marriage took place. Cases where the marriage came to notice on or prior to 13 March 1996 should be considered under the terms of DP2/93.

DP3/96, as it can be seen, is fairly straight forward but very strict, compared with the previous document, that is, DP2/93.

On the next page is a diagram which may assist you to understand how DP3/96 works.

It should also be noted that leave to enter or remain will no longer be granted as from the 23rd February 1996 on the basis of Common Law Relationship, unless there are particularly compassionate reasons. Those who are granted a year visa on this basis may, however, still apply to remain indefinitely on the same basis.

This flow chart should be used as a *guide* only. There will occasionally be cases which fall outside the guidelines.

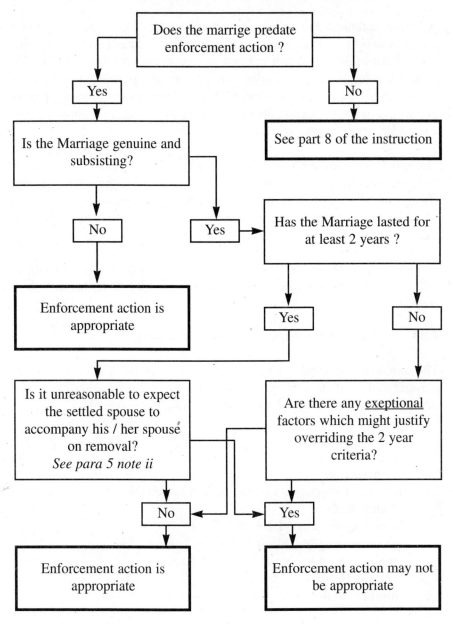

4.33   SPOUSES OF PERSONS IN THE UK ON TEMPORARY PURPOSE

A person seeking leave to enter or remain in the UK as the spouse of a person who is here on temporary purpose may be granted leave for a period of time not in excess of that granted to the person on whose platform he wishes to enter or remain. In relation to an application for leave to enter, he is able on arrival to produce a valid UK entry clearance in that capacity, or in the case of an application for limited leave to remain he is admitted with a valid UK entry clearance for entry in this capacity.

The spouse of a student may not necessarily obtain an entry clearance for this purpose, (that is, he can come to the UK as a visitor and have a genuine change of mind and, therefore, remain with his spouse), though it is advisable to obtain this entry clearance where he has anticipated remaining as such.

The position of the spouse of *students* and *working holiday makers* are quite different and particular examination of those topics will be helpful. Read chapters 2 and 3.

4.34   Persons here on Temporary Purpose

The following categories of people will be here in the UK for temporary purpose as their status is short of that of a settler. These are the categories of people who have come or are remaining for the purpose of:

- Student;
- Au pair;
- EC members;
- Refugee, Exceptional leave to remain as stateless or Asylum seekers;
- Work Experience or Training Scheme;
- A Commonwealth citizen with proof that one of his grandparents was born in the UK and Islands;
- Working Holiday;
- Ministers of Religion;

- Representatives of News agencies on long term
  assignment to the UK;
- Representatives of Overseas Newspapers on long
  term assignment to the UK;
- Representatives of Broadcasting organisations on
  long term assignment to the UK;
- Representatives of Overseas firms which have no
  branch, subsidiary or other representatives in the UK;
- Persons coming for employment by an overseas government or in
  the employment of the U.N.O. or other International Organisation of
  which the UK is a member;
- Teachers and Language assistants coming to schools in the UK
  under exchange schemes approved by the Educational Departments;
- Seamen under contract to join a ship in British waters;
- A person who is in the UK to establish himself in the business or in
  self-employment, including taking-over or joining as a partner of an
  existing business;
- Persons of Independent means,
- Writers, Composers and Artists;
- Private Servants in Diplomatic Households;
- Investors and few more categories allowed to remain temporarily in
  or outside the rules.

*As there is no provision in the immigration rules for fiancé(e)s of persons in
these categories to come to the UK in anticipation of marriage, a lot of
people have been coming as visitors visiting their boyfriend/girlfriend or
even relatives.*

4.35   SPOUSES' ABILITY TO WORK

The freedom of the spouse (and children under the age of 18) to take up
employment should not be restricted unless the sponsor on whose platform
they remain is prohibited from taking employment, in which case, the
prohibition should extend to them.

4.36   MARRIAGE TO EEA NATIONALS

Spouses of EEA Nationals (who are not themselves EEA Nationals), whose partners are working, doing business, self-employed, providing or receiving services in the UK, will be allowed to remain for the same length of time as such partners and should be issued with what is called Residence Permit.

Application for leave to remain for such foreign spouses are not usually subject to the same amount of scrutiny as those of applicants who are spouses of people settled in the UK.

Since EEA nationals do not require leave to remain, most of them, although exercising their rights of residence provisions under the EC Law, do never bother to formalise their presence in the UK by applying for residence permit. Therefore, when they become married to foreigners in the UK and the foreign spouse makes application for leave to remain in the UK with the EEA spouse, the EEA spouse's application for residence permit is considered simultaneously with his foreign spouse's application for leave to remain in the UK.

4.37   Residence Permit

Residence Permit is normally issued for a period of 5 years which is renewable if issued for a period less than 5 years. Residence permit will be issued for less than 5 years in the following instances;

a)   if the employment is between 3 and 12 months, or where the employment is seasonal, 12 months permit may be allowed;
b)   in the case of provision of services, for the period of such services;
c)   in the case of students, the permit may be limited to the duration of the studies, and in the case of studies exceeding 12 months, to 12 in the first instance;
d)   in the case of a retired or self-sufficient person, the permit may be limited to two years in the first instance. Application for a residence permit should be accompanied with the following documents:

1)   Passport or National Identity Card
2)   Two Passport sized Photographs.
3)   Proof that he is in employment, business or self-employed
      occupation.
4)   Evidence of Funds.

4.38   An Application on the Basis of Marriage to EEA Spouse

It is important that the EEA spouse should be exercising his rights of residence under the EC Law. This means that he should, at the time of making this application, be working, doing business, be self-employed or providing or receiving services in the UK, otherwise, such an application for leave to remain in the UK by the foreign spouse may be refused.

Documents required for such application are:-

1)   The above mentioned documents regarding the EEA spouse for her
      own application for residence permit (where he has not formalised
      his presence in the UK or obtained such a residence permit).

2)   Evidence of Cohabitation, for example, Utility Bills and any other
      official correspondence addressed to both parties.

3)   Evidence of accommodation e.g. Tenancy Agreement or
      Rent Book.

4)   Applicant's passport.

At the end of the 4 year period of the EEA national residence permit, both the EEA national and his spouse can apply to the Home Office for Indefinite Leave to Remain. The foreign spouse will be granted Indefinite Leave to Remain provided the marriage is subsisting and the couple intend to live together permanently in the UK as husband and wife. Also, the EEA spouse must still at the time of making this application be exercising his EEA rights.

4.39   DEPORTEE SPOUSE OF EEA NATIONAL

The Home Office Marriage Policy referred to as DP3/96 deals with deportee spouse of British citizens, while rules and policies regarding deportee spouse of an EEA National can be found in case laws within the European countries.

As determined in common law cases, the following interesting points should be noted:

(1)   A deportee married to EEA spouse stands a better chance to remain in the UK than a person married to a British citizen.[5]

(2)   A deportee married to a British citizen may emigrate to another EEA country for a short while, possibly for a year and return to the UK legally, thereby circumvent the UK Immigration Law

The following examples may be of great assistance in understanding the above:

4.40   Example 1

Mr Saheed had been deported to Syria for working in breach of conditions in the UK. His British wife, Hawa, then went to the Republic of Ireland and got a job there. Mr Saheed's application to join her in Ireland was refused but his application for judicial review of this was allowed.

Where spouse of a deportee married to a British citizen can go to Ireland to exercise her EC Rights there, her deportee spouse should be allowed to remain with her in Ireland.

4.41   Example 2

Mr McKerrell, an Irish living in the UK marries Maria, a Thai woman in Thailand. She applied for entry clearance under the British Immigration Law but the British Embassy in Bangkok refuses her on primary purpose ground. Maria then applies for a family permit as the wife of an EEA National under the EC law and this was issued to her. On arrival in the UK, Maria was admitted for 5 years in line with her husband's residence permit. Because Mr McKerrell is also a British citizen (Dual National), Maria applied for indefinite leave to remain just a year after entry under the British Immigration Law. Maria can also go to the Irish Embassy here 3 years after the date of their marriage for an application to become an Irish under the Irish law.

4.42   MARRIAGE & SPOUSE'S AGE

The immigration rules do not permit a person to be granted entry clearance, leave to enter or remain, or any variation as a spouse, where either party to the marriage will be under the age of 16 years on the date on which the leave to remain or variation of leave is being sought.[6]

4.43   POLYGAMOUS MARRIAGES

The immigration rules do not permit a woman to be granted entry clearance, leave to enter or remain or variation of leave as the wife of a man (the husband) if:

● 	her marriage to the husband is polygamous, and there is another woman living with the husband in the UK as his wife, or

● 	there is another woman who has been granted Right of Abode or Entry Clearance as the wife of the husband.[7]

4.44   BREAKDOWN OF MARRIAGE AND YOUR PERMANENT RESIDENCE

The effect of a breakdown of marriage depends on when this breakdown occurs. If there is a breakdown of the marriage before the grant of permanent residence, this will pose a big problem as the application for an indefinite leave to remain is likely to be refused; the marriage must not have been terminated when applying. The practical approach at this juncture may bethat, where the marriage has broken down irretrievably and the applicant had lived in the UK for a substantial period, for example, of up to 7 years, (and possibly where the marriage produced a child), an application outside the rules for indefinite leave to remain may still be made, for example, on the basis of ties and/or long residence. The Home Office may allow this application exceptionally outside the immigration rules.

This approach may equally be best for a spouse whose partner died before an application for indefinite leave could be considered or granted.

Where the termination occurs after the grant of a permanent residence, this visa cannot be withdrawn unless it has been obtained by fraudulent means.

4.45   FREEDOM TO MARRY AND RECOGNITION OF FOREIGN DIVORCES

Where an application to remain in the UK on the basis of marriage is lodged, the applicant may be required to present proof that he is free from his previous marriage. The most acceptable document in such circumstances is a Divorce Certificate.

A divorce which took place in a UK court will generally be accepted as conclusive, while a divorce outside the UK may have to be verified or confirmed from where it was obtained. We have, therefore, discussed a few divorce proceedings, evidence of which may be accepted as conclusive, and for which independent extensive verification may not be necessary.

4.46   A Divorce in the UK

A divorce can be obtained in a UK court where one or both parties (respondent and petitioner) have been ordinarily resident in the UK for a period of one year; a petition will not be entertained until at least a year and a day (366 days) after the marriage.

Also, the only ground for granting a divorce is:

- That the marriage has **broken down irretrievably**, which may be as a result of one of the following:-

    - adultery,
    - unreasonable behaviour,
    - 2 year desertion,
    - 2 year separation with the other spouse's consent, or
    - 5 year separation.

To commence divorce proceedings the couple's marriage certificate will be needed. However, where the marriage was customary one for which there is no marriage certificate, sworn affidavit(s) to prove the subsistence of the marriage should include:

- how the marriage took place
- how the custom works, and
- date and place of the marriage.

4.47   Customary Divorces (West African Countries)

Where the previous marriage was contracted through customary law and the other party to this marriage is not in the UK nor resident here, affidavits from Heads of the Families of both divorcees, confirming the fact of the marriage and subsequent dissolution should suffice. This divorce can only be recognised by the UK marriage registry where the partner in the UK has lived here for less than 365 days immediately before the divorce.

4.48   Recognition of Talaq Divorces

Under the Islamic Law, a husband is able to divorce his wife just by declaring unequivocally that he repudiates the marriage in the presence of two witnesses and without any form of proceedings. This divorce can be registered in that country under the Muslim Family Law Ordinance, and this should make it recognisable in the UK.

4.49   CASE STUDY (1)

Dear Sir/Madam,

My name is Ometha and I am a British Citizen.   My fiancé is a Jamaican and resides in Kingston, Jamaica.   I was in Jamaica for holiday last year and on my return I discovered I was pregnant .   My fiancé is the father of my baby boy born in August 1995 I now want my fiancé to come and live with me in the UK.   I am unemployed at the moment.

I have been to the Home Office to find out the possibility of my fiancé joining me but was told that he must apply for visa from Jamaica.   I reckon that this process may take months to materialise.

I have been told that I can bring my fiancé here as a visitor and later marry him but the Home Office may refuse his application to remain here.   It has also been suggested to me by friends that I can go to Jamaica and marry him and both of us can come back into the UK together, but we have not enough funds to do this.

Could you advise me on the cheapest and fastest way of bringing my Michael here to settle with me and our baby.

Your earnest reply will be appreciated.

Yours faithfully,

Ms Ometha

4.50   Suggested solution

Immigration rules provide that fiancé(e)s of a settled person may come into the UK for purposes of performing the marriage ceremony. A six month visa is normally granted and the marriage is expected to take place within this period. Where the marriage does not take place within this period, an extension of the passenger's visa may be possible provided there are plausible reasons for the delay.

Bringing in your fiancé may truly be a long process but this will depend on the queue at the British High Commission, Jamaica, as well as the availability of adequate documents to satisfy the criteria laid down for entry clearance.

If you bring him as a visitor and marry him soon after entry, the Home Office may suspect this marriage as his main intention of coming into the UK in the first place, and holds that he deliberately avoided applying for a fiancé entry clearance. The Home Office may, therefore, treat your fiancé as an illegal entrant who entered by deception. Notwithstanding, where a person comes to the UK as a visitor and thereafter genuinely decides to get married, he should not be penalised or treated as an illegal entrant, and should therefore be allowed to remain.

Although you can go over to Kingston, Jamaica to marry him, he will have to obtain an entry clearance to come to the UK as your spouse. Coming back with him depends, of course, on the queue at the High Commission in Jamaica, together with your ability to satisfy the criteria laid down for this purpose.

Taking your special circumstances into consideration, it is advisable to see a professional adviser for further confidential advice so that the best of the raised options may be identified.

FOOTNOTES

1.   *HC 395 paragraph 277*

2.   *HC 395 Paragraph 290*

3   *HC 30 June 1992(Answer of Charles Wardle; Immigration Minister*

4   *HC 395 paragraph 281 (v) & 284 (vii)*

5   *R v IAT and Surrinder Singh exparte Secretary of State for the Home Department 1992 IMM AR 565*

6   *HC 395 paragraph 277*

7   *HC 395 paragraph 278*

Chapter 5

SETTLEMENT FOR RELATIVES

5.1   INTRODUCTION

A person settled in the UK may be joined by relatives. The rules now make provisions for limited family members. Restrictive rules apply to sons and daughters over the age of 18 years, as discussed in chapter 6. The same restrictive rules apply to aunts, uncles, sisters and brothers over 18 years. While fairly restrictive rules apply to parents and grandparents who are 65 years old or over, very restrictive ones apply to parents and grandparents below this age.

The rules do not make provision for distant relatives although their entry may be allowed outside the immigration rules; they make provisions for children under the age of 18 who may only be allowed to join or remain with a settled relative in the UK only where there are serious and compelling family or other considerations which make their exclusion undesirable, and suitable arrangements have to be made for their care.

Although entry clearance is required where a person in this category is seeking entry, those who entered for some other temporary purposes may be allowed to switch to this category. (We have also discussed below about parents of Irish children wishing to remain with them).

We shall therefore divide discussion under this topic into the following categories of relatives:-

A)   Parents and Grand Parents.
    i.   Over 65 years
    ii.   Under 65 years

B)   Aunts, Uncles, Sisters and Brothers.
    i.   Over 18 years

C)   Children of Relatives under the age of 18.

D)   Other Relatives not in the Rules.

5.2   [A]{i}   PARENTS AND GRANDPARENTS OVER 65 YEARS

Parents or grandparents coming to the UK or applying for leave to remain with their adult children or grandchildren will have to meet the following requirements,[1]

That:-

● they are widows or widowers of 65 years old or over,

● if married, both must be coming together and one of them must be 65 years or over.

● they must be financially wholly or mainly dependent on the child or grandchild in the UK, (and be able to demonstrate this).

● they can be maintained without recourse to public funds,

● they can be accommodated without recourse to public funds,

● they can demonstrate that they do not have any other close relative in their own country to turn to.

Where a parent or grandparent has remarried, the step parent or grandparent can join or remain with his step children or step grandchildren, on the platform of his new spouse or alone where he becomes a widower as a result of the death of the new spouse.

5.3   [A]{ii}   PARENTS AND GRANDPARENTS UNDER 65 YEARS

Parents and grandparents in this category will have to meet the same requirements as for those over 65 years old, and in addition, they must:-[2]

-   be living alone outside the UK in the most exceptional compassionate circumstances.

This additional criteria is a very tough one to satisfy. See below for the meaning of living alone in the most exceptional compassionate circumstances.

5.4   One Parent:

Where one parent is coming,

*   he or she should be widowed. Note, however, that it was held in the case of *Zanib Bibi*[3] that separated parent who has not remarried should be equated with a widow and that further requirement of exceptional compassionate circumstance should not apply to such a person.

A sponsor bringing his parents may be asked by the Home Office to sign an undertaking that the applicant will not have recourse to public funds, breach of which may be enforced by recouping from him. Undertakings normally cease to be operative after 5 years. See example of an undertaking document figure 11.7

5.5   [B] AUNTS, UNCLES, SISTERS AND BROTHERS OVER 18

The rules now specifically state that aunts, uncles, sisters and brothers, over 18, may be allowed to enter or remain if:-[4]

●   they are living alone outside the UK in the most exceptional compassionate circumstances. This is a tough criterion to be met.

The remaining requirements are that the applicant:-

● is financially wholly or mainly dependent on the sponsor who

● is settled in the UK (and must be able to demonstrate this),

● they can be maintained without recourse to public funds,

● they can be accommodated without recourse to public funds,

● can demonstrate that they do not have any other close relatives in their own country to turn to.

For meaning of *living alone in the most exceptional compassionate circumstances and no close relatives in home country to turn to,* See below.

Where the aunt, uncle, sister or brother is under the age of 18, then he or she may be allowed to enter or remain as discussed in the sub-topic children of relatives under the age of 18. See below.

5.6   [C] CHILDREN OF RELATIVES UNDER THE AGE OF 18

Any child of a relative (presumably CLOSE RELATIVES) for example, children of aunts, uncles, sisters and brothers, (including aunt, uncle, sister or brother) under the age of 18, may be allowed to enter or remain where:-[5]

● there are serious and compelling family or other consideration which makes exclusion of such a child undesirable, and

● suitable arrangements are made for the child's care.

Children of distant relatives under 18 years of age, distant relatives and close relatives not covered by the rules are now discussed.

5.7   [D]   OTHER RELATIVES NOT IN THE RULES

The rule is silent on the admission or leave to remain of certain categories of relatives among which are close relatives such as cousins, half brothers and sisters etc.

The rules mention leave to enter or remain for children of relatives but in practice, children of close relatives may stand a better chance as they are likely to be able to prove the relationship and dependence. It advisable that anyone wishing to sponsor or make application for leave to remain for a person not covered in the sub-topics above should seek professional advice before doing so.

Their admission or leave to remain may be allowed outside the immigration rules where common requirements are met and there are strong exceptional compassionate reasons, for example, where a great-aunt had looked after the sponsor as a child and there are no other closer relatives this great-aunt could turn to in her own country.

An applicant above the age of 70 and who is mentally or physically disabled whose sponsor has sufficient means to maintain and accommodate him should also stand a good chance.

5.8   CLARIFICATION OF IMPORTANT PHRASES

5.9   Dependence

The applicant must be able to show that   he has been wholly or mainly dependent on the person he is coming to join. The current immigration rules mention financial dependence only.

Where a settler is planning to sponsor a relative at some point in the future, it is advisable he keeps documentary evidence of the funds he remits home for such a relative's up-keep, for example, postal order counterfoils, bank receipts/transfer, copies of bank draft etc. It is also advisable to keep proof of emotional dependence and / or close and regular contacts, though not required.

Entry clearance officers and the Home Office usually adopt a lenient approach when considering application from old and fragile applicants e.g. one who is 70 years or more.

5.10   Living Alone Without Close Relatives To Turn To

The applicant must be without other close relatives in their own country to turn to and this criterion will not be met if there are other close relatives who are willing and able to meet the financial and other needs of the applicant. Note, however, that it must be reasonable to depend on these other close relatives other than the sponsor in the UK.

As 'close relatives' has not been defined anywhere in the rules, the usual approach seems to be to consider immediate relatives such as parents, siblings and children for this purpose, (a brother-in-law has once been held to be a close relative)

Also, where parent-applicants have other children in their own country, the E.C.O or the Home Office will want to know why these children are not capable of looking after their parents, checking through their wage slips to determine their capability of doing so. A mere statement from the relatives that they are unwilling to provide the relevant support will not suffice. However, 'to turn to' means that it must be reasonable to expect the applicant to turn to those relatives rather than the sponsor in the UK.

5.11   Sponsor's Ability and Willingness to Maintain and Accommodate

The sponsor must also have the means, as well as the ability and willingness to support and accommodate the in-coming parent(s) and any dependant who may be coming with them, without having to recourse to public funds. A sponsor who is unemployed or who is relying on social security may not be able to satisfy this requirement.

5.12   Exceptional Compassionate Circumstance

This particular requirement seems to the hardest to fulfil in that the applicant's situation should be such that one cannot but be moved with compassion. The problem with this requirement is that such a situation may conflict with the needed proof of financial support given by the sponsor, although other emotional factors may assist.

5.13   Financial Dependence

The applicant must be able to show that they have been financially dependent wholly or mainly on the sponsor they are coming to join.

5.14   MAKING THE APPLICATION

The new rules do not require entry clearance for any application under this chapter where leave to remain is after entry, although a person applying to enter under one of these categories requires an entry clearance. Therefore, a person in the UK for other temporary purpose may apply to switch to any category discussed under this topic. The following documents may be required:

Evidence that the sponsor is settled in the UK: Certified copies of the first five pages of the sponsor's passport, together with the page showing indefinite leave to remain and the Home Office's reference number, or just the first 5 pages only, if it is a British Passport.

● The applicant's passport.

● Evidence of financial dependence:

- Proof of remittance e.g. counter foils of Postal Order, receipts of bank payment, etc. Where money has been sent informally, precise information as to date, amount and method should be given. (We strongly advise formal method as this carries more weight.)

● Evidence of the sponsor's financial position:

    - Wage slips

    - Letter of employment

    - Bank statements or pass books as evidence of funds.

● Evidence of suitable accommodation; stating number of rooms and number of people in the household. It may be necessary to state their age and sex. Rent book, tenancy agreement, mortgage documents can also be made available.

● Documents to show that the applicant is or lived in the most compassionate circumstances.

● Details of the applicant's other children (and close relatives) in their own country or elsewhere, explaining why each is unwilling or unable to support the applicant.

● Other relevant and applicable documents should also be provided, for example:

    - Death Certificate,
    - Medical report stating the medical condition of the relevant person, etc.
    - Divorce Certificate,
    - Sworn Affidavits from other relatives abroad,
    - Letter between applicants and sponsors etc.

5.15   Important Points to Note

1)   It should be borne in mind that relatives coming or requesting to remain in the UK for settlement from *pressure-to-migrate* countries should not expect this task to be an easy one.

2)   Also, a relative whose application for entry clearance to come for settlement is turned down will find it hard, if not impossible, to come to the UK for a visit or any temporary purpose as he is likely to be refused for the simple reason that he might not return home.

3)   Parents or relatives who do not satisfy the requirements discussed above in the first place may still be admitted or allowed to remain with their sponsors provided they can show that they:-

-    are living alone outside the UK in the most exceptional compassionate circumstance

4)   For those applying to remain, there is no Entry Clearance requirement and for those applying to enter there is a requirement for entry clearance

5.16   PARENT OF AN IRISH CHILD

Non-Irish parents of an Irish citizen child have the right to live with their child in Ireland. This right was asserted by the Supreme Court of Ireland in the case of *fajujonu* 1989. This case is about a foreign couple living and working in the republic without authorisation, after moving from England. They had 3 children who were born Irish. The Supreme Court held that under the Constitution, Irish Citizens have the right to live in Ireland, and that an infant citizen can choose through his parents to live in Ireland.

Even if the parents do not have a constitutional right to live there (Ireland), provided they do not represent a threat to the State because of criminal propensities, they (the parents) cannot be deported".

Those who are liable to deportation from the UK should to able to stay in the Republic of Ireland if they are able to travel and have a child there. If leaving from the UK, you do not require visa to enter the Ireland because of the Common Travel Area rule.

FOOTNOTES

1   *HC 395 paragraph 317*
2   *HC 395 paragraph 317(e)*
3   *R v IAT, ex parte Zanib Bibi[1987] Imm AR 392.*
4   *HC 395 paragraph 317 (f)*
5   *HC 395 paragraph 297 & 298*

Chapter 6

CHILDREN JOINING PARENTS IN THE UK

6.1 INTRODUCTION

This topic is designed to cover children who are not British Citizens accompanying or joining their parent(s) who may be here temporarily or settled in the UK. This topic is divided into the following sub headings:-

● children of parents who are here for temporary purpose,

● children settling with parents who are themselves settled in the UK.

6.2 CHILDREN WHOSE PARENTS ARE IN THE UK FOR TEMPORARY PURPOSE

Children accompanying or joining parents who are themselves in, or coming to the UK for a temporary purpose (see figure 4.34 for category of those here on temporary purpose) may be admitted and granted visa for the same length of time as their parents.

This sub-topic is primarily concerned with the admission of children of parents who are here on temporary purpose other than students and working holidaymakers which have already been discussed in Chapters 2 and 3 respectively.

It should also be noted that while some categories of people in the UK for temporary purpose will eventually lead to permanent residence, (for example, the category of workers discussed in chapters 12 and 13), conditions for the admission of their children and criteria to be met whilst these parents are still on temporary visa is the same as with any others on temporary visa.

For those applying to remain under this category, there is no Entry Clearance requirement, those applying to enter must have entry clearance.

6.3   Conditions for Entry Clearance

In addition to other relevant criteria, Entry Clearance Officers would have to be satisfied:-

- that the child is under the age of 18 and unmarried (although over 18 years of age may be admitted if granted entry clearance).

- that the child will be adequately maintained without recourse to public funds, that the child will be adequately accommodated without recourse to public funds,

- he is accompanying or joining his two parents (although he may accompany or join lone parent, see below),

- that the child has not formed an independent family unit and is not leading an independent life.

6.4   Children Accompanying or Joining Lone Parent

Where parents are divorced, separated or unmarried, a child can only accompany or join a parent who has sole responsibility for his upbringing; and where one parent is dead, a child can accompany or join the surviving parent.

Where a child is accompanying or joining one parent in the UK (where his other parent is alive) and the parent in the UK does not have sole responsibility of him, then his admission will only be allowed where there are serious and compelling family or other considerations which makes his exclusion from the UK undesirable. Suitable arrangements must also be made or available for his care.

6.5　　[A]　What is Sole Responsibility?

This means that the parent is principally responsible for the child's day-to-day care. This parent does not have to prove that he/she is there all the time, and the fact that he has temporarily delegated the child's care to someone else, for example, a relative, does not negate his responsibility. However, a grant of the child's custody to the particular parent is not enough as further evidence of regular contact with the child which may be substantiated by a carer or the child's school, confirming the parent's decision making role in the child's life should be provided.

Furthermore, it will be very helpful to adduce evidence of regular financial support, such as receipts of school fees or medical care which may include the payer's name; post office counterfoils, bank drafts or copies of money order; where such remittances have been made informally (though not advisable), precise dates and amounts sent, together with names and addresses of other parties involved should be forwarded.

Finally, it is worth mentioning that the longer the period of separation between the parent and the child, the more difficult it may be to prove that the parent is solely responsible for the child's upbringing.

6.6　　[B]　What is Serious and Compelling/Most Exceptional Compassionate Circumstance?

While the old immigration rule illustrates 'serious and compelling family or other considerations' by giving examples of the other parent's inability to look after the child due to physical or mental reasons, there is no closed or exhaustive list of what can amount to this phrase. Each case will, therefore, depend on its own facts and merits.

Similarly, an 'exceptional compassionate' can be anything from disablement, to inability to survive without assistance. This requirement may, however, be a difficult one to satisfy as the rules emphatically use the word 'Most' (exceptional compassionate circumstance).
Satisfying the requirement will thus depend on the fact of each case.

It is important, therefore, to seek professional advice where one is contemplating an application on this basis.

6.7   [C] What are Other Considerations that may Make Exclusion Undesirable?

It may be undesirable to exclude a child whose other parent is, for a special reason such as sickness, unable to travel with the child at the time of making the application; or to exclude a child who is physically and mentally incapable of looking after himself; or to exclude a child who is less than 12 years of age.

6.8   CHILDREN SETTLING WITH PARENTS WHO ARE SETTLED

Children can join their parents who are settled or who are coming for settlement in the UK. These children may then, or eventually be allowed to settle as well. *It is also possible for a child who is already in the UK for a temporary purpose to vary his leave, for settlement with his parents where there is a change of mind after arrival.*

The criteria to be met by children who are under the age of 18 are different from criteria to be met by those above the age of 18. Their admissions and leave to remain will, therefore, be discussed differently.

6.9   Criteria to be Met by *Children Under 18*

Children may be allowed to settle with their parents in the UK provided that:[1]

● they are under 18 years, or were given leave to enter with a view to settlement,

● they are not married or leading an independent family life,

● entry clearance is obtained (where they are seeking entry), and

●   their parent are willing to support and accommodate them without having to recourse to public funds. The accommodation is expected to be owned or exclusively occupied by the parents.

After having satisfied one of these criteria:

1.   A child may come into the UK;
   -    on the same occasion with *both parents,* or

   -    to join his settled parents.

2.   A child may come into the UK;

   -    on the same occasion with one parent where the *other parent is dead,* or

   -    to join the surviving and settled parent.

3.   A child may come into the UK;
   -    on the same occasion with *one parent,* or

   -    to join the one parent who is settled; but only where this parent has had *sole responsibility* of the child's upbringing OR where there are serious and compelling family or other considerations which make the child's exclusion undesirable, for example, where the other parent is physically or mentally incapable of looking after the child. Also, suitable arrangements must have been made for the child's care in the UK.

Example:

A child born out of wedlock, whose father is settling or settled and has had *sole responsibility* of him (even though the child's mother is alive) may be allowed to come into the UK on the same occasion with, or to join his settled father.

4.   A child may also come with one parent who is coming to settle, provided the other parent who is already in the UK is settled.

Example:

> A child is born to a married couple in Antigua. His father is now settled in the UK and the child is coming to the UK with his mother who herself is coming to settle.

5.   The rules also make provisions for a child to come on the same occasion with, or to join a parent who has been given limited leave with a view of settlement, for example, a parent who is newly married to a British or settled person.

6.   A child may also be allowed to come on the same occasion with or join his RELATIVE who is settled in the UK, provided:

-        there are serious and compelling family or other considerations which make exclusion undesirable, for example, where the child's parents are physically or mentally incapable of looking after him, and suitable arrangements have been made for his care.

As a matter of practice, the admission of children under the age of 12 years is relaxed, as it has been the Home Office's practice to regard exclusion of children of this age as undesirable.

6.10   Criteria to be Met by Children Over 18

Children in this category are expected to qualify for entry or leave to remain in their own right; they may, however, still be allowed to come or remain indefinitely with their settled parents where:-[2]

●   they live alone outside the UK in the most exceptional compassionate circumstances,

●   they are mainly dependent financially on their parents, and

●   they have no other close relatives in their country to whom they can turn to for financial support,

- there is adequate accommodation without recourse to public funds, and

- there is adequate maintenance without recourse to public funds.

6.11   MEANING OF CERTAIN PHRASES

6.12   Parent

The word *'parent'* is defined in the rules as a stepfather of a child whose father is dead; a stepmother of a child whose mother is dead; a natural father and a natural mother. Parents also include adoptive parents.[3].

6.13   Settled

One is settled for this purpose if he is ordinarily resident in the UK without being subject to any restriction on his passport or he is a person with Right of Abode, or he is a person with permanent residence visa, or a member of H.M.Forces in the UK serving overseas.

6.14   Dependence

Applicants must be able to show that they have been wholly or mainly dependent on the person they are coming to join. The immigration rules mentioned financial dependence only.

Where a settler is planning to bring a relative at some point in the future, it is advisable to keep documentary evidence of the funds he remits home for such a relative's up-keep, for example, postal order counterfoils, bank receipts/transfer documents, copies of bank draft well dated and stamped letters acknowledging receipts of such funds by recipients etc. It is also advisable to keep proof of emotional dependence and of regular contacts.

6.15   Living Alone Without Close Relatives to Turn to

Applicants must be without other close relatives in their own country to turn to and this criterion will not be met if there are other close relatives, who are willing and able to meet the financial and other needs of the applicant. Note, however, that it must be reasonable to depend on these other relative(s) rather than the sponsor.

As 'Close Relative' is not been defined anywhere in the rules, the usual approach seems to be to consider immediate relatives such as parents, siblings and children for this purpose, (a brother-in-law has however once been held to be a close relative).

Important questions will be:

-    Are they close to the applicant?
-    Are they willing and able to meet any financial or other need of the applicant?

If the answers to these questions are 'No', then one may argue that an applicant has " no close relatives to turn to".

6.16   Sponsor's Ability and Willingness to Maintain and Accommodate

The sponsor must also be able and willing to support and accommodate the applicant and any dependant who may be coming or remaining with them, without having to recourse to public funds. A sponsor who is unemployed or who is relying on states benefits will find it difficult to fulfil this criterion.

6.17   MAKING APPLICATION FOR SETTLEMENT

The following information / documents will be essential in making an application for entry clearance or leave to remain:-

- Evidence that the sponsor is settled in the UK: Certified copies of the first five pages of the sponsor's passport, together with the page showing indefinite leave to remain and the Home Office's reference number, or just the first 5 pages only, if it is a British Passport.

- The applicant's passport.

- Evidence of financial dependence:

    - Proof of remittance e.g. counter foils of Postal Order, receipts of bank payment, etc. Where money has been sent informally, precise information as to date, amount and method should be given. (We strongly advise formal methods as these carry more weight.)

- Evidence of the sponsor's financial position:

    - Wage slips
    - Letter of employment
    - Bank statements or pass books as evidence of funds.

- Evidence of suitable accommodation; stating number of rooms and number of people in the household. It may be necessary to state their age and sex. Rent book, tenancy agreement, mortgage documents can also be made available.

- Documents to show that the applicant is or lived in the most compassionate circumstances.

- Details of the applicant's other children (and close relatives) in their own country or elsewhere, explaining why each is unwilling or unable to support the applicant.

Other relevant document should also be provided, where applicable for example:

- Death Certificate,
- Medical report stating the medical condition of the relevant person, etc.
- The child's full birth certificate which may be showing the names of both parents,
- The parents' marriage certificate (where applicable),
- Documents to show that parent/sponsor has been taking interest in the child's upbringing e.g. letters between the child or his guardian and the parent or sponsor in the UK,
- document to show the incapacity of the other parent for looking after the child (where applicable),
- Evidence of sole responsibility (where applicable),
- Any other relevant documents e.g. correspondence between applicant and sponsor

---

FOOTNOTES

1	HC 395 paragraph 298
2	HC 395 paragraph 317(f)
3	HC 395 paragraph 6

Chapter 7

ADOPTION OF CHILDREN
AND SETTLEMENT

7.1 INTRODUCTION

This topic is concerned with adoption of children by those who are settled in the UK. Adoption is where a child of someone (natural parent) becomes a child of another (adoptive parent) by a *Court Adoption Order.* An adoption order therefore transfers parental responsibilities from Natural Parents to Adoptive Parents and the child will thereafter become the child of the Adoptive Parents.

For UK immigration purposes, an adopted child is treated as the child of the Adoptive Parents and this adopted child may come to the UK to settle with his adoptive parents who are settled here.

For purposes of settlement in the UK, ECO or IO would have to be satisfied that:

- there has been a *genuine transfer of parental responsibility* on the grounds of the original parents' inability to care for the child, and

- the adoption is not one of convenience arranged to facilitate the child's admission to the UK.

It should be noted that Court Adoption Order is not synonymous to genuine transfer of parental responsibility; as adoption order is for the Court while *genuine transfer of parental responsibilities* is determined by ECO or IO. It is expected therefore that ECO or IO would interview the applicant (if appropriate) and his new parents (the adoptive parents) in order to establish that there has been a genuine transfer, and even where there is no doubt that there is a Court Adoption Order, the child may still be refused an Entry Clearance or Entry where transfer is suspected not to be genuine.

For ease of understanding, this topic is discussed under the following headings:-

- Adoption outside the UK which is recognised, (Designated Country)
- Adoption outside the UK which is not recognised, (non-Designated Country)
- Adoption in the UK,
- Adoption and Citizenship, and
- Home Office Policy Concerning Adoption etc.

7.2   (A) ADOPTION OUTSIDE THE UK WHICH IS RECOGNISED (DESIGNATED COUNTRY)

Court adoption order which is granted in a designated country is recognised by the immigration authorities and the adopted child can come and join his parents in the UK after such an order, in such cases, he would need an Entry Clearance. Otherwise, a child adopted in such a designated country, who is in the UK for a temporary purpose, may apply to the Home Office and be allowed to remain with his new parents.

Designated countries whose adoptions are recognised are as follows:

7.3 Commonwealth Countries

.Anguilla	Malawi
Australia	Malaysia
The Bahamas	Malta
Barbados	Mauritius
Belize	Montserrat
Bermuda	New Zealand
Botswana	Nigeria

British Virgin Islands
Canada
Cayman Islands
Cyprus
Dominica
Fiji
Ghana
Gibraltar
Guyana
Hong Kong
Jamaica
Kenya
Lesotho

Pitcarin Island
Zimbabwe
St.Christopher and Nevis
St.Vincent
Seychelles
Singapore
Sri Lanka
Swaziland
Tanzania
Tonga
Trinidad and Tobago
Uganda
Zambia

7.4   Foreign Countries (also designated)

Austria
Belgium
China (but only where the child will be living in England or Wales)
Denmark (including Greenland and the Faroes)
Finland
France (including Reunion, Martinique, Guadeloupe and French Guyana)
The Federal Republic of Germany (including West Berlin)
Greece
Iceland
The Republic of Ireland
Israel
Italy
Luxembourg
The Netherlands (including the Antilles)
Norway
Portugal (including the Azores and Madeira)
South Africa (including Namibia)
Spain (including the Balearic and Canary Islands)
Surinam
Sweden
Switzerland
Turkey

USA

Yugoslavia (but not any of the States which now make up the former Yugoslavia)

Countries that are not in the above list should be regarded as non-designated countries.

7.5   (i)   JOINING PARENTS AFTER ADOPTION

If you have legally adopted a child from a country whose adoption orders are recognised as valid for United Kingdom law, (i.e.'a designated' country) you may apply for your adopted child to join you and remain indefinitely with you in the United Kingdom. You will need an entry clearance for this purpose, although such a child, if already in the UK for a temporary purpose, may apply for leave to remain which should be granted.

As soon as an adoption order has been issued, an application for entry clearance should be made for the child. Before entry clearance is granted, the Entry Clearance Officer will need to be satisfied that:-

1)   the adoption involved a genuine transfer of parental responsibility on the grounds of the original parents' inability to care for the child,

2)   the adoption is not one of convenience arranged to facilitate the child's admission,

3)   the child will be adequately maintained and accommodated without recourse to public funds in accommodation which you own or occupy yourselves, and

4)   that you (the new parents) are settled here, or are being admitted with a view to settlement here.

If these requirements are met, the child will normally be issued with entry clearance, and usually admitted for settlement upon arrival in the United Kingdom.

7.6   Consideration of Entry Clearance (designated countries)

Entry clearance may not be granted until all necessary information have been provided to enable a decision to be reached.   An Entry Clearance Officer is likely to make enquiries into the child's circumstances and thereafter refer the application to the Home Office. The Home Office will gather its own information about the adoptive parents, seeking local DSS advice as to whether there is any reason why an adoption order may not be granted by the courts in the UK, if an application is made there. The local DSS will normally prepare a home study report, which means a social worker will visit the adopters, as well as make police and health checks.

The necessary enquiries can be greatly expedited where your local Social Services have been able to prepare or approve a home study report in advance.   They will also be able to provide additional advice and counselling, and should therefore be contacted before you embark on a trip overseas.   A privately commissioned home study report is not usually acceptable, unless it is approved by your local authority.   The decision whether to approve such a report rests entirely with your local authority.

The DSS advice will assist the Home Office in deciding whether to allow the child into the UK, and if entry clearance is granted, the child will be allowed into the UK and will normally be granted Indefinite Leave to Enter.

7.7   Applying for Entry Clearance

Application should be made to the nearest British Diplomatic Post (usually at the home country of the child).

An application for entry clearance may be made for the child either by the new parents, or somebody acting on their behalf, although if the latter, the new parents should provide them with a letter confirming they have authority to act on their behalf.

An application may be made in person or sent by post/courier. Should you intend to send the application through, you should first check with the relevant British Diplomatic Post of their requirements for accepting such application, and whether you will be required to attend at some stage, for an interview.

When lodging the entry clearance application, you or your representative should endeavour to include original documents and, where necessary, certified translations of all the appropriate supporting documents, (a list of which is provided below). If you cannot provide an original document, a certified copy should be obtained.

A fee will usually be payable, only in local currency, when the entry clearance application is lodged; details of the current charges can be obtained from the relevant British Diplomatic Post abroad.

7.8   Documents Required to Support an Application for Entry Clearance

The following documents should be submitted with the application for entry clearance to the Entry Clearance Officer:-

a)   The completed application forms,

b)   A letter of authority from adoptive parents if somebody is acting on their behalf,

c)   A completed adoption questionnaire,

d)   The child's original birth certificate showing his/her name at birth,

e)   A completed medical report for the child, (specimen forms of which can be obtained from the British Agencies for Adoption and Fostering, 11 Southwark Street, London, SE1 1RQ).

f)   An up-to-date report completed by the overseas equivalent of (the UK) local social services, detailing the child's parentage and history, the reasons for the adoption, the circumstances in which the child was offered to you for adoption, the child's circumstances, and those of his/her parents and family,

g)   If the child is being cared for in a children's home, orphanage or other institution, the report referred to at 'f' should additionally provide the date and circumstances in which he/she came into care, and the degree of contact between the child and his/her natural parents,

h) The written consent of the child's natural parents, or those legally responsible for him/her, to the adoption, (to be valid, this must have been given freely and after the child has reached 6 weeks of age),

i) Where the child has been genuinely abandoned, i.e. his/her parents cannot be traced, a certificate of abandonment from the authorities responsible for the child's care,

j) The adoption order itself, (particularly in 'designated' country cases),

k) Confirmation of your income,

l) Details of your accommodation here, where the child would live, including who else lives there, the number of bedrooms etc.,

m) Two recent passport sized photographs of the child,

n) The appropriate fee, (details of charges available from the relevant British Diplomatic Post), payable only in the local currency.

This list should not be considered as exhaustive, or in any order of priority. Any additional documents or details which may be helpful should also be presented to the Entry Clearance Officer. Most of these documents will be required by the overseas court.

7.9   Entry Clearance Refusal

Apart from the general reasons for refusing entry clearance discussed in Chapter 1, the following additional reasons should equally be borne in mind:

● where a couple living in the UK has adopted a child of their relatives abroad, entry clearance may be refused unless the child's parents are dead or living in an exceptional difficult situation;

● where only one out of many children of the unit of the family abroad was adopted;

● where adoption was found out as mainly to bring the child to the UK for some other purpose e.g. education; or

● where the adopted child would not actually lose contact with his or her natural parents.

7.10   What happens after entry

A child whose application for entry clearance is granted to join his parents in the UK would have been granted a 'settlement entry clearance visa; therefore, upon arrival in the UK he should normally be granted leave to enter for an indefinite period.[1]

In some instances, this child may have been granted a limited period of leave to enter, for example, for a period of 12 months. This may be because one of the adoptive parents is not yet settled here.   If this is the case, an application for the child to be granted indefinite leave to remain, may be made to the Home Office at the same time as that of the adoptive parent's application.   In all instances, the child's passport should be forwarded, together with any supporting documents, and a covering letter. The child will normally be granted the same period as that of the adoptive parent.

7.11   (ii) APPLYING TO REMAIN AFTER ENTRY FOR TEMPORARY PURPOSE

An adopted child in this category who is in the UK for a short visit or any other temporary purpose may be allowed to remain indefinitely with his adoptive parents where there is a genuine change in his circumstances after such entry.

Such an application will not be subjected to entry clearance requirement although he must fulfil the following important criteria, that is, that he:-[2]

    i) has limited leave to enter or remain in the UK, and is under the age of 18;

    ii) is not leading an independent life, is unmarried, and has not formed an independent family unit; and

iii) can, and will, be maintained and accommodated adequately without recourse to public funds in accommodation which the adoptive parent or parents own or occupy exclusively; and

iv) was adopted in accordance with a decision taken by the competent administrative authority or court in his country or origin or the country in which he is resident; and

v) was *adopted* at a time when:
   a.   *both* adoptive parents were resident together abroad; or
   b.   *either* or both adoptive parents were settled in the UK; and

vi) has the same rights and obligations as any other child of the marriage; and

vii) was adopted due to the inability of the original parent(s) or current carer(s) to care for him and there has been a genuine transfer of parental responsibility to the adoptive parents; and

viii) has lost or broken his ties with his family of origin; and

ix) has been adopted but the adoption is not one of convenience arranged to facilitate his admission to or remaining in the UK.

7.12   (B) ADOPTION OUTSIDE THE UK WHICH IS NOT RECOGNISED. (NON-DESIGNATED COUNTRY)

Where a child is adopted in a country where its court adoption order is not recognised by the UK immigration authorities, this child will have to obtain an adoption order in the UK (or a designated country). If coming to the UK, Entry clearance is required for this purpose. Please read the following sub topics which are relevant: Applying for Entry Clearance; Documents for Entry Clearance; and Entry Clearance Refusal.

7.13   Consideration of Entry Clearance (non-designated countries)

Once an application for entry clearance has been made, the Entry Clearance Officer will consider both the child's circumstances and those of his/her family overseas, and then normally refer the application to the Home Office in London.

The Home Office has to be satisfied:-

i)   that the proposed adoption involves a genuine transfer of parental responsibility on the grounds of the original parents' convenience arranged to facilitate the child's admission;

ii)   that the child will be adequately maintained and accommodated without recourse to public funds in accommodation which you own or occupy yourselves;

iii)   that the adoptive parents are settled in the UK, or are being admitted with a view to settlement in the UK.

If the Home office is satisfied that these requirements are met, it will seek advice from the Department of Health, (or the appropriate territorial Health Department), about the welfare aspects of the case, and the likelihood of a court in this country granting an adoption order.   To this end, the Home Office will ask your local social services to prepare a home study report on you. The purpose of this is to assess your suitability as prospective adoptive parent, and to consider whether the proposed adoption will safeguard and promote the interests of the child throughout his/her childhood.

Once these enquiries have been satisfactorily completed, the child will normally be granted entry clearance and will usually be admitted for an initial period of 12 months.

The necessary enquiries can be greatly expedited where the prospective parents' local Social Services have been able to prepare or approve a home study report in advance. They will also be able to provide additional advice and counselling, and should therefore be contacted before you embark on a trip overseas.   A privately commissioned home study report is not acceptable, and serves no useful purpose unless it is approved by your local authority.

7.14   What happens after entry

At the port of entry, the child would normally be admitted for an initial period of 12 months. This is to enable the parents to commence adoption proceedings in the United Kingdom. Parents should lodge an application to adopt the child in the appropriate court as soon as possible after he/she (the child) arrives here. There is no minimum time limit before an application may be made to a court, although in most instances, the child will have to be living with you for at least 12 months before an adoption order may be made.

You do not have to obtain the prior permission of your local social services before placing your application with the court in the UK, although you should contact them as soon as the child arrives, as they will be responsible for supervising his/her welfare until the court here decides whether to grant an adoption order or not.

Shortly before the expiry of the child's leave to enter, you should apply to the Home Office for an extension of the child's stay. You should forward the child's passport, and a letter from the court here confirming they have received and accepted your application to adopt. If there is a long delay in the adoption application being considered by the court, it will be necessary for you to apply for further extensions in the same way. It remains your responsibility to make sure that the child has a current period of leave to remain in this country at all times. If this is not done, the child will become an overstayer and will be in breach of his landing conditions.

7.15   Applying for Leave to Remain after the Grant of an Adoption Order

If an adoption order is granted, you should again send the child's passport to the Home Office, together with a certified copy of the adoption order, your passports for confirmation of your status here, and a covering letter. The passport will be endorsed to show that he/she can remain here for at least as long as the adoptive parent who has the shorter period of leave to remain here.

However, in the majority of cases, the child is likely to be granted Indefinite Leave to Remain. If at least one of the adoptive parents is a British Citizen on the date the adoption order is made by the Court here, the child will automatically acquire British Citizenship from the date of the order. You will therefore be able to apply for a British passport for him/her from your local passport office.

7.16   (C) ADOPTION IN THE UK

Parents from designated countries have the option of obtaining adoption orders from their own country or the UK, while those from non-designated countries must obtain such orders from a UK court regardless of whether or not there is an existing order from that country.

It is possible to come to the UK for adoption and obtain entry clearance for this purpose. It is also possible for a child to enter the UK for a short visit or other temporary purpose and (after a change of circumstance) be adopted in the UK. In either cases, an application can be made for such a child to remain indefinitely with his new parents.

7.17   Coming To the UK for Adoption

To come to the UK for adoption, the child needs to obtain an entry clearance for this purpose, and although there is no provision in the immigration rules for a child to come to the UK for adoption, the Home Office may allow entry clearance to be issued as a matter or practice.

In order to allow a parent to bring a child to the UK for adoption, the Home Office will need to be satisfied that:

* the adoption will be in the best interest of the child,
* there are no obvious reason(s) why an adoption order might not be granted in the UK (If in any doubt, the child may not be granted an entry clearance),
* there is no reason under the Immigration rule why the child should not be admitted,
* and the child fulfils, or will be able to fulfil, the requirements of the Immigration rules relating to the admission of children for settlement.

Please refer to the following sub-topics which are relevant: Applying for Entry Clearance, Documents needed for Entry Clearance, Entry Clearance Refusal, and Consideration of Entry Clearance(non-designated countries).

7.18   Adoption after a Child has entered for Temporary Purpose

It is also possible for a child to be adopted whilst in the UK for a short visit or on any other temporary purpose. In this case, he does not need an entry clearance for this purpose. Also, because the child has entered the UK for temporary purpose, and possibly has a short visitor's visa which will not last until the adoption is completed, the new fact with regard to the adoption should be made known to the Home Office with a request for an extension of leave so that the adoption can be satisfactorily concluded. Such an application will be considered outside the rules.

7.19   Applying for Leave to Remain after the Grant of an Adoption Order

Immediately after such an adoption order is granted, application for leave to remain should be made to the Home Office (and in some cases, the child becomes a British Citizen automatically). For criteria to be met when applying for leave, please see Applying to Remain after Entry for Temporary Purposes. See figure7.11.

7.20   (D) CITIZENSHIP AND ADOPTED CHILDREN

Adopted children are treated as natural children of the adopters from the date of the adoption order. It is as if the child was born on this day to the adopter. For immigration purpose therefore, 'the new parents' nationality or immigration status will have a bearing on the nationality or immigration status of this child.

7.21   (E) HOME OFFICE POLICY CONCERNING ADOPTION

Since it is possible for adoption, etc., to be used to frustrate immigration enforcement, the Home Office had an internal document which is meant to deal with cases where a child is facing serious immigration problems. This document is called DP2/93 and it had two parts to it. The first part, that is, Section A deals with Marriage while the second part, that is, Section B deals with Children. You will find the relevant part of Section A in the Marriage topic (Chapter 4), while Section B is presented below. This document has now been replaced by DP3/96, and as such, the Section B below is will no longer be applicable except for cases known to the authorities before DP3/96 became operative.

The new document in place of this Section B is now referred to as DP4/96 and is also reproduced below.

7.22   Section B: CHILDREN

Part 1:   Adoption, Wardship, Custodianship and Residence Orders

This part of the instruction provides guidance on handling cases where there is reason to believe that the purpose of adoption, custodianship, wardship or residence order proceedings is to frustrate enforcement action.

Definitions

Adoption:

A child adopted by order of a Court in the UK is a British Citizen (and thus not liable to immigration control) from the date of the order if an adoptive parent is a British Citizen at that date. An adoption by order of a foreign court may not be recognised under the UK law.

Custodianship:

This represents a less final relationship than adoption and vests legal custody of the child in the adult(s) caring for him/her. Where a custodianship order is made the child's immigration status is unchanged but he should not be removed from the jurisdiction of the court while the order remains in force.

Wardship:

Children who are wards of court should not be removed from the UK without the court's leave.

Residence:

Residence orders are very similar in effect to wardship and Orders: children subject of residence orders should not be removed from the UK without the leave of the court.

Intervention

The family Court will generally attach much more weight to the child's welfare than to irregularities surrounding the immigration status of the child or a parent. Where, however, it is clear that the court proceedings are designed purely to enable the child or the parent to evade immigration control consideration may be given to instructing the Treasury Solicitor with a view to intervening in the proceedings. *There must be evidence, not just a suspicion, that there has been a serious attempt to circumvent the immigration control and decisions to intervene must be taken at not less than SEO level.*

Where intervention has been agreed the papers should be copied to the

Treasury Solicitor's office as soon as possible. Their normal practice is then to apply for the Secretary of State to be joined as a respondent, and to file an affidavit setting out the child's and/or parent's immigration history and the Secretary of State's objections.

Part 2: Abandoned Children

Enforcement action against children and young persons under the age of 16 who are on their own in the UK should only be contemplated when the child's voluntary departure cannot be arranged. In all cases removal must not be enforced unless we are satisfied that the child will be met on arrival in his home country and that care arrangements are in place thereafter. To this end, caseworkers should contact the Welfare Section of the appropriate Embassy or High Commission as well as the local Social Services Department.

If there is evidence, not just a suspicion, that the case arrangements are seriously below the standard normally provided in the country concerned or that they are so inadequate that the child would face a serious risk of harm if returned, consideration should be given to abandoning enforcement action.

Where deportation or removal remains the right course, consideration will need to be given to whether an escort is necessary on the journey.

Important Points to Note

1) A UK court will most likely not make an adoption order unless it is sure that the child's parents have agreed to the adoption or there are grounds for dispensing with parental agreement.   Where the child is from overseas, it is important that adoptive parents obtain legally acceptable evidence that the child is available for adoption.

2) It is unlawful for anyone other than an adoption agency to make any arrangements in the United kingdom for a child's adoption unless the prospective adopter is a relative of the child. If you are in doubt about whether an organisation with which you are in contact here is an

adoption agency, you may check with the BAAF. (British Agency for Adoption and Fostering), their address is in figure 7.8

3)   Medical information about the child and, about his natural parents will be required before the Home Office can consider whether to give permission for the child to enter this country for adoption. Forms for the collection of medical information relevant to adoption have been designed by the Medical Group of British Agencies for Adoption and Fostering (BAAF) and we recommend that you obtain this form and send them for completion to those who are currently caring for the child.

4)   Please note that the rules also make provision for joining or remaining with lone adoptive parent, details of which could be sought from a professional expert advisor.

7.23   DP4/96 CHILDREN

Introduction

1.   This notice provides guidance, in general terms, on the consideration of cases of those liable to be removed as illegal entrants or deported who are either children on their own here or who are parents who have children present in the UK. It supplements the advice given in DP3/96 about the consideration of marriage cases involving children with the right of abode, DP5/96 which gives guidance on consideration of cases involving children who have been resident for 10 or more years and DP4/95 which gives guidance on the use of section 3(5)(c) of the Immigration Act 1971.

Policy

2.   There is no bar to taking deportation/illegal. entry action against children of any age who are liable to such action. However, enforcement action against children and young persons under the age of 16 <u>who are on their own</u> in the UK should only be contemplated

when the child's voluntary departure cannot be arranged. In all cases removal must not be enforced unless we are satisfied that the child will be met on arrival in his/her home country and that care arrangements are in place thereafter. To this end, caseworkers should contact the Welfare Section of the appropriate Embassy or High Commission as well as the local Social Service Department.

3.   If there is any evidence, not just a suspicion, that the care arrangements are seriously below the standard normally provided in the country concerned or that they are so inadequate that the child would face a serious risk of harm if returned, consideration should be given to abandoning enforcement action. Where deportation or removal remains the right course, consideration will need to be given to whether an escort is necessary on the journey.

4.   Where deportation/removal action is being considered against a parent or parents the existence of children in the UK is a factor which must be taken into account when assessing the merits of such action. The weight to be attached to children as a compassionate factor will vary from case to case and has to be balanced against or along with other factors.

5.   In all cases the longer the child has been here the greater will be the weight to be attached to this as a factor; but the general presumption will be that a child who has spent less than 10 years in the UK would be able to adapt to life abroad. (See figure 8.6 for DP5/96 for cases involving children who have been here for 10 years or more).

Divorced and Separated Parents

6.   Deportation or illegal entry action should not necessarily be conceded where a person liable to deportation or removal as an illegal entrant, whose marriage has broken down, has access rights to his/her child (who is entitled to remain here) and seeks to remain in order to exercise those rights. He/she should be advised that such an application should be made from abroad.

Paragraphs 246-248 of the Immigration Rules provide a specific category for those who wish to enter the UK to exercise access rights to children. Entry clearance is required for this purpose. This must be obtain from abroad. Threee is a right of appeal against refusal of such an entry clearance application. Recent judicial opinion suggests that in this type of cases, there is unlikely to be a breach of Article 8 of the ECHR as "family life" has already broken down and that as there is no bar to someone applying to return to the UK for access visits, and as a right of appeal is provided for, there is no breach of Articles 13.

7.   Enforcement action should normally proceed in these cases if, notwithstanding the advice provided, the offender fails to leave. A person who then becomes the subject of a deportation order should be informed that before he/she can apply to return in accordance with paragraphs 246-248 of the Rules, he/she will need to apply for the revocation of the deportation order. Again, this must be done from abroad. Only in the most exceptional circumstances will it be right to concede a case to enable a parent to continue access visits, with agreement at no less than A/D level.

8.   It should be noted that paragraphs 246-248 of the rules apply only in cases where the parents of the child were married. It should also be noted that in cases where the parent is already the subject of a deportation order it may be unreasonable to expect him or her to return abroad to apply for entry clearance as he or she would normally be barred from re-entry for 3 years. In these cases it will be important to assess the quality and the regularity of access to the child in deciding how much weight should be attached to it as a compassionate factors.

Adoption, wardship, custodianship and residence orders

9.   The following paragraphs provides advice on the handling of cases where there is reason to believe that the purpose of one or more of the above proceedings is to frustrate enforcement action. The definition of these proceedings are:

Adoption: A child adopted by order of a court in the UK is British citizen (and thus not liable to immigration control) from the date of the order if an adoptive parent is a British citizen at that date. An adoption by order of a foreign court may not be recognised in UK law; in such cases advice should be sought from B2 Division.

Custodianship: This represents a less final relationship than adoption and vests legal custody of the child in the adult(s) caring for him/her. Where a custodianship order is made the child's immigration status is unchanged but he/she should not be removed from the jurisdiction of the court while the order remains in force.

Wardship: Children who are wards of court should not be removed from the UK without the court's leave.

Residence Orders: Residence orders are very similar in effect to wardship and children subject to residence order should not be removed from the UK without the leave of the court.

Contact Order: A court order allowing a person contact with a child and specifying the terms under which the contact is to take place.

Intervention in the above proceedings

10.   The Family Court will generally attach much more weight to the child's welfare than to irregularities surrounding the immigration status of the child or a parent. Where, however, it is clear that the court proceedings are designed purely to enable the child or the parent to evade immigration control, consideration may be given to instructing the Treasury Solicitor with a view to intervention in the proceedings. There must be evidence, not just a suspicion, that there has been a serious attempt to circumvent the immigration control and

decisions to intervene must be taken at not less than SEO level.

11.   Where intervention has been agreed the papers should be copied to the Treasury Solicitor's office as soon as possible. Their normal practice is to apply for the Secretary of State to be joined as a respondent, and to file an affidavit setting out the child's and /or parents' immigration history and the Secretary of State's objections.

12.   It should be noted that where an order has been made under the Children Act, this cannot in itself deprive the Secretary of State of the power conferred by the Immigration Act 1971 to remove or deport any party to the proceedings although it may be something to which he should have regard when deciding whether to exercise his power under the Act.

FOOTNOTES

1.   HC 395 paragraph 310
2.   HC 395 paragraph 311

Chapter 8

SIX OTHER WAYS OF ENTERING AND REMAINING

8.1 'TEN YEAR RULE'

It is important to note that there is nothing in the immigration rules called '10 year rule', but the so called 10 year rule came as a result of the Home Office's long practice in granting indefinite leave to remain to those who have lived in the UK for up to 10 years. The period of 10 years is taken from the European Convention on Establishment 1955, and the practice of its general application stems from Ministerial pronouncements, as well as letters written to MPs (Members of Parliament).

Anyone, therefore, (even where he is not a national of a country that signed the convention), who has been in the UK *wholly legally for 10 years OR wholly illegally for 14 years* may be granted indefinite leave to remain.

The practice of the Home Office in recognising the strength of connections with the UK and length of residence, combined with parliamentary statements to this effect, gave rise to legitimate expectations of consistent treatment to those who applied to regularise their stay in reliance on such a policy.

8.2 Present Practice

In one of such letters as mentioned above, the present Home Office's practice was revealed, part of which reads as follows:

'Our approach should be that where a person has 10 years or more continuous lawful residence or 14 years or more continuous residence (of any legality), indefinite leave to remain should normally be granted in the absence of strong countervailing factors. In all other cases of long residence, the strength of ties with the UK, length of the total continuous period in the UK and the proportion of it which is lawful will be the primary determining factors when deciding whether to grant or withhold leave to remain permanently'.

8.3   How the Practice Works

Someone who has been in the UK lawfully for up to 10 years may be granted an indefinite leave to remain.

Someone who has been in the UK unlawfully (overstayer or illegal entrant) for up to 14 years may be granted an indefinite leave to remain. It should be borne in mind that it is for the applicant to prove that he has been in the UK for the stated number of years; some illegal entrants may find it difficult to prove their continuous residence in the UK due to the manner of their entry.

In some cases they may not have a Passport and where they have one, there may not be any stamp showing when they actually entered the UK. Notwithstanding this problem, other evidence in form of college letters or inland revenue documents, showing their presence in the UK may be submitted.

For someone who has been in the UK partly lawfully and unlawfully, the proportion of his stay which is lawful, family ties and any other compassionate factors in his favour will be an important factor when deciding whether to grant or withhold leave to remain indefinitely.

8.4   Important Points to Note

1.   It must be noted that this Home Office Practice as discussed above is discretionary and does not give immigrants any right whatsoever, and each case will ultimately turn on its own facts.

2.   The period whilst on appeal against refusal will be counted lawful if the appeal is won, but is regarded as unlawful if the appeal is lost. This is because the Home Office distinguishes between *right to remain* whilst on appeal and leave to remain.

You have a right to remain whilst on appeal but this is not *leave to remain*.

3.   The clock for counting lawful or unlawful periods stops ticking from the date a person served with an enforcement notice, eg a notice of decision to deport.

4.   Quite apart from the long residence requirement, other helpful factors that may aid an application include:

-    FAMILY CONNECTIONS: i.e. if there are children, and other family members e.g. wife, cousins, uncle, mother, father etc. who are settled in the UK.

-    ACADEMIC &/OR EMPLOYMENT RECORD: i.e. if college principal or employer can write a good reference, stating the qualifications obtained, or duration of employment (as the case may be). Any indication showing continuous studies may also be presented.

-    FINANCIAL SOLVENCY: e.g. ownership of property and or business.

5.   Countervailing factors such as criminal convictions (apart from traffic offences) may jeopardise the chances of one's application.

6.   The whole period for which any application is being considered by the Home Office should normally count for continuous residence.

7.   Continuous absence from the UK for more than 90 days may break the chain of continuous residence, except there is an acceptable reason for this absence.

8.   People exempt from immigration control such as High Commission, Embassies and International organisation workers and their family members may not generally be expected to be granted settlement after 10 years as their stay in the UK, though lawful, cannot be counted;

although an application could be made when 14 years continuous residence is achieved.

The making of a premature application may be taken by the Home Office as an indication that the applicant no longer intends to leave the UK at the end of his temporary leave (e.g. for studies) and any further application to remain (as a student) may therefore be refused.

Also, it is not uncommon for people who are approaching 10 years of residence to have problems in varying or extending their leave to remain.

8.5   Important Documents for your Application

- All passports showing years of residence.

- College letters or certificates (if any).

- Employer's letters (if any). Though students are not expected to produce one except they have permission and have worked legally while studying.

- Marriage certificate, if married, and where the spouse is equally seeking an indefinite leave to remain.

- Proof of past and present accommodation e.g. receipts, tenancy agreements, rent book, etc.

- Evidence of funds, and

- Other necessary documents which may depend on each individual case.

Advisers are hereby referred to the Court of Appeal's decision in the case of Michael OFORI[1] which sheds further light on the approach of the Immigration Authorities and Courts under the topic.

In addition, the Home Office also now have a policy document with regard to cases where there are children when consideration is being given to parent(s). This document is referred to as DP5/96 which is reproduced below.

8.6   DP5/96

DEPORTATION IN CASES WHERE THERE ARE CHILDREN WITH LONG RESIDENCE

Introduction

The purpose of this instruction is to define more clearly the criteria to be applied when considering whether enforcement action should proceed or be initiated against parents who have children who were either born here and are aged 10 or over or where, having come to the UK at an early age, they have accumulated 10 years or more continuous residence.

Policy

Whilst it is important that each individual case must be considered on its merits, the following are factors which may be of particular relevance:

a.   the length of the parents' residence without leave;

b.   whether removal has been delayed through protracted (and often repetitive) representations or by the parents going to ground;

c.   the age of the children;

d.   whether the children were conceived at a time when either of the parents had a leave to remain;

e.   whether return to the parents' country of origin would cause extreme hardship for the children or put their health seriously at risk;

f.   whether either of the parents has a history of criminal behaviour;

3. When notifying a decision to either concede or proceed with enforcement action it is important that full reasons be given making clear that each is considered on its individual merits.

8.7 'AU PAIR'

Au Pair is an arrangement under which an unmarried person aged 17-27, without any dependant, and a national of certain countries (listed below), may come to the UK to learn English language and live for a time as a member of an English speaking family. He is expected to help in his host home for a maximum of 5 hours per day in return for a reasonable allowance and with two free days per week[2].

8.8   Nationals of Countries who may come as Au Pair

Andorra	Bosnia-Herzegovina
Croatia	Cyprus
Czech Republic	The Faeroes
Greenland	Hungary
Liechtenstein	Macedonia
Malta	Monaco
San Marino	Slovak Republic
Slovenia	Switzerland
Turkey	

8.9   Criteria to be Satisfied

The applicant must:

- not be married
- be without dependants
- be aged between 17-27
- intend to spend sometime with an English family
- intend to learn English language
- not intend to remain in he UK for more than 2 years as an Au Pair

- intend to leave the UK on completion of his stay as an Au Pair
- if he has previously spent time in the UK as an Au Pair, not be seeking leave to enter beyond two years from the date on which he was first given leave to enter the UK in this capacity.[3]

8.10   Coming for Au Pair

Where the immigration officer is satisfied that an Au Pair arrangement has been made, the passenger may be admitted for a period not exceeding[2] years with a prohibition on employment except as an Au Pair.

Where a person has previously spent time in the UK as an Au Pair, he may be re-admitted for a further period in the same capacity. This is provided that the period in which he or she will be in the UK for Au Pair purpose does not exceed 2 years from the date he was first granted leave as an Au Pair.

8.11   Important Points to Note

1.   The relationship between the Au pair (if a girl) and an English Family is not that of employer and employee, but is referred to as the 'the girl and her host'.   An Au Pair therefore receives up-keep money, entertainment allowance and pocket money, while she is expected to help with the housework and take care of any children.

2.   An au pair may stay up to a maximum period of two years.

3.   An au pair may change families provided the new arrangements continue to meet the requirements of the Immigration Rules.

4.   An au pair can apply to extend his stay if:

- he was given permission to enter the UK as an au pair; and
- he has an au pair placement; and
- an extension would not take such a stay beyond two years from the date permission to enter was first given.

Permission to remain as an Au Pair will not be granted to anyone who did not enter the United Kingdom as such. This is to say that the Immigration

Officer needs to be informed at the Port of Entry of the intention to come or seek leave to enter as an Au Pair.

5.   Nationals of Bosnia-Herzegovina, Macedonia and Turkey must obtain entry clearance from their designated British Embassy or consulate before travelling to the United Kingdom.

For addresses of Au Pair agencies you may contact:-

> The Federation of Recruitment
> and Employment Services
> 36-38 Mortimer Street
> London W1N 7RB
>
> Telephone: 0171 323 4300

6)   The new rules now make provision for both girl and boy au-pair unlike before when the provision was only for girls. Also, it is no longer possible for those who entered in another capacity to switch to this category, although one may switch from this category to another.

7)   Furthermore, it is no longer possible to aggregate the 2 year stay under this category.

8.12   LEAVE TO ENTER OR REMAIN FOR MEDICAL TREATMENT

A passenger may set out from his home country purposely for medical treatment, and a visitor already in the UK may be able to extend his visitor's visa so as to allow him to remain for treatment which must be private. Full and Semi - Visa Nationals who are already in the UK can, therefore, vary their visitor's visa for purposes of medical treatment without the need to go back to their home country for entry clearance for this purpose. Any one receiving medical treatment is treated for immigration purposes as a visitor in the UK.

The requirements to be met by a person seeking leave to enter the United Kingdom as a visitor for private medical treatment are that he.

i)   does not intend to take employment in the UK; and

ii)   does not intend to produce goods or provide services within the UK, including the selling of goods or provide services direct to members of the public; and

iii)   does not intend to study at a maintained school; and

iv)   will maintain and accommodate himself and any dependants adequately out of the resources available to him without recourse to public funds or taking employment; or will, with any dependants, be maintained and accommodated adequately by relatives or friends; and

v)   can meet the cost of the return or onward journey.

-      in the case of a person suffering from a communicable disease, has satisfied the Medical Inspector that there is no danger to public health; and

-      can show, if required to do so, that any proposed course of treatment is of finite duration; and

-      intends to leave the United Kingdom at the end of his treatment; and

-      can produce satisfactory evidence, if required to do so, of:-

the medical condition requiring consultation or treatment; and

b)   satisfactory arrangements for the necessary consultation or treatment at his own expense; and

c)   the estimated costs of such consultation or treatment; and

d)   the likely duration of his visit; and

e)   sufficient funds available to him in the United Kingdom to meet the estimated costs and his undertaking to do so.

8.13   Entry Clearance for Medical Treatment

Anyone who wishes to obtain an entry clearance for the purpose of receiving Private Medical treatment will have to satisfy the entry clearance officer :-

●   that there will be enough funds to maintain and accommodate him and his dependants in the UK. Therefore, evidence that funds have been transferred or available will have to be adduced.

●   that he has the capacity to pay any or subsequent medical bills which may arise, and if he has a sponsor in the UK, this sponsor can send to the applicant-patient some of the documents already discussed under the topic, ' How to sponsor a visitor to the UK', see Chapter 1.

●   of the arrangement for the treatment e.g. a Doctor's letter confirming:

-     this arrangement for treatment,
-     he is a private patient,
-     the nature of the ailment,
-     that the fees have been paid, and
-     the expected duration of the treatment.

It should be borne in mind that availability of treatment in the passenger's own country may not on its own be sufficient reason for refusing entry clearance or admission.

8.14   Refusal of Leave to Enter as a Visitor for Private Medical Treatment

Leave to enter as a visitor for private treatment is to be refused if the I.O is not satisfied that each of the requirements stated above is met.

8.15   Private Medical Treatment Where Applicant is Already in the UK

Anyone already in the UK as a visitor or for any other temporary purpose, may apply to remain for treatment and is expected to provide evidence of his arrangement for treatment, or the progress made regarding the treatment, i.e. a Doctor's letter confirming:

- he is a private patient,
- the nature of the ailment,
- the fees have been paid,
- the expected duration of the treatment.

8.16   Important Points to Note

i)   An applicant seeking to extend his stay as a visitor for private medical treatment will, in addition to meeting other requirements have to produce evidence from *a registered medical practitioner who holds an NHS consultant post*, of satisfactory arrangements for private medical consultation or treatment and its likely duration; and, where treatment has already begun, evidence of its progress.[5]

ii)   As suggested to us, perhaps you could ask your Doctor to confirm in his letter to the Home Office that he is an NHS Consultant.

iii) An application to enter or remain for Medical Treatment will be refused where there are reasons to suggest that treatment will be at public expense.

For consideration of an application for leave to remain, a questionnaire may be sent to the applicant which may be similar to the one below:-

1)   Evidence of the applicant's ability to support himself/herself i.e. itemised bank statements covering the last 6 months or a letter from their bank or sponsor.

2)   Please supply a letter from a *registered medical practitioner who holds a National Health Service Consultant Post* answering the following questions:

   a)   what treatment or medication is being received
        and what is the progress of that treatment?
   b)   how often, and for how long, is attendance needed
        for treatment or medication?
   c)   what is the expected cost of the treatment?
   d)   is the treatment private?
   e)   when will the applicant be fit to return home?

3)   Receipts for any private medical treatment to date.

4)   When does the applicant intend to return to his own country?

8.17   RIGHT OF ACCESS TO A CHILD RESIDENT IN THE UK.

8.18   Introduction

The new immigration rules now makes provisions for a parent granted access to a child who is resident in the UK to come to the UK to exercise such rights. This particular rule is perhaps an indication of the UK's attempt to comply with the recent rulings of the European Court about children's rights to keep in contact with their parents who reside abroad.

All applicants (Visa or non-visa nationals) need entry clearance for this purpose as the rule does not allow a visitor or a person in another temporary category to switch to this category.

8.19   Requirements to be Met

In addition to obtaining an entry clearance, the other requirements to be met by a parent seeking leave to enter to exercise access rights to his child residents in the UK are that he[6]:-

i)   produces evidence that a *Court in the UK* has granted
        him access rights to his child; and

ii)   is seeking leave to enter for the purpose of exercising
        access rights to his child; and

iii)   is either *divorced or legally separated* from the other
        parent of the child; and

iv)   intends to leave the UK at the expiry of his leave to enter; and

v)   does not intend to take employment in the UK; and

vi)   does not intend to produce goods or provide services within
        the UK, including the selling of goods or services direct
        to members of the public; and

vii)   will maintain and accommodate himself and any dependants
        adequately out of resources available to him without recourse
        to public funds or taking employment; or will, with any dependants,
        be maintained and accommodated adequately by relatives or friends;
        and

viii)   can meet the cost of the onward or return journey.

From the requirements above, it is important to explain what is meant by access.

8.20   Access

Access literally means having direct contact with someone, and under this rule, direct contact between parent and child.

The rule used the word 'access' but an understanding of the UK family law, in particular, the Children Act 1989, should assist in our definition of what access may mean under this topic.

8.21   Children Act 1989

This act defines a contact order as an order requiring the person with whom the child lives, or is to live, to allow the child to visit or stay with the person named in that order, or for that person and child otherwise to have contact with each other.

The law before the 1989 ACT used the word access which is replaced and is now known as contact order.

Contact may be direct or indirect.

8.22   Direct Contact

Contact is said to be direct when the child visits or stays with the person named in the order. It may either be visiting contact or staying contact for a certain duration, for example, once in a week or a month and may be supervised or unsupervised.

8.23   Indirect Contact

Indirect contact is where the child does not see the parent mentioned in the order. It could be telephone calls to the child at specified times sending letters, photographs, birthday cards, seasonal cards etc. to the child.

Although the rules do not categorically specify which of the two contacts as above-mentioned is regarded as access, it is suggested (based on our enquiries to the appropriate authorities) that Direct Contact would be more appropriate under this topic and access should be understood to mean direct contact.

A person granted an entry clearance for this purpose may be allowed to enter or remain for up to a maximum period of 12 months.

8.24   Documents for an Application for Entry Clearance

Documents which should be required may include:-

1)   Applicant's passport
2)   A UK Court Order (e.g. Contact Order) which details the access (e.g. weekly/monthly, supervised/ unsupervised), granted to the applicant.
3)   Birth Certificate of the child in question.
4)   Evidence of the arrangement which the applicant has made in order to exercise the right under the specific contact order granted, for example, if staying contact, that sufficient accommodation should be arranged for the child and applicant.

8.25   Important Points to Note

1)   The rule only allows a parent who is divorced or legally separated from the other parent of the child, in other words, it does not extend to a parent who was never married to the other parent.
2)   A person admitted to the UK under this category may switch to another category which does not stipulate entry clearance for the purpose, for example, to remain with spouse or as a student.
3)   There is a right of appeal against a refusal of entry clearance application.
4)   A person who entered the UK for other temporary purpose cannot switch to this category.
5)   Contact Order or the right of access must be by an order of a court in the UK not the court of the applicant's home country.

8.26   RIGHT OF ABODE

This is a special status which carries with it the complete freedom from United Kingdom immigration control. People who have this status do not need to obtain the permission of an immigration officer to enter the UK and are free to live and work here without any restrictions.

8.27   Who has a Right of Abode

The following categories of people have the right of abode in the UK:-

a)   British Citizens (by birth, naturalisation or registration),and

b)   certain Commonwealth Citizens

8.28   (a)   British Citizens

A person who is a British Citizen as discussed in chapter 15 will qualify for a Right of Abode in the UK. Please note also that although this person may also be a national of another country (as Britain recognises dual nationality), he is not precluded from claiming a Right of Abode, certificate of which can also be stamped in his other passport, that is, that of the other country he may be holding.

8.29   (b) Certain Commonwealth Citizens

A person although not a British Citizen could still have the right of abode if he is a Commonwealth Citizen and immediately before 1 January 1983:

a)   he was a Commonwealth Citizen with a parent who at the time of his birth or legal adoption was a Citizen of the UK and Colonies and had his/her citizenship by being born in the UK; or

b)   she was a Commonwealth Citizen who is a wife of a man with the right of abode.

Please consult a professional advisor for more information on Commonwealth Citizens who may have a Right of Abode.

8.30   Confirming this Status

A British passport describing you as a British Citizen will normally be sufficient evidence of your right of abode in the UK. Alternatively a British Passport in which you are described as a citizen of the UK and Colonies and which contains an endorsement that you have the Right of Abode in the UK will generally be satisfactory evidence of your entitlement to enter and live in the UK without restriction.

Where the person claiming such Right has a different passport, from those described above, an official certificate of entitlement (a small sticker) may be a fixed on his passport. Certificates are issued by the Home Office to applicants in the UK and by the appropriate British Representatives to applicants abroad).

For information concerning making an application, please contact the British High Commission abroad or the Home Office.

8.31   CONCESSION TO BRING DOMESTIC SERVANT

Outside the normal immigration rules, rich or well-to-do people may be allowed to bring their domestic staff with them to the UK. This concession is different from the provisions in the rules which allow private servants in diplomatic households to enter the UK as such. Entry clearance is required for this purpose.

Under this concession, a private servant will be permitted to enter with or join his employer without the need to obtain a work permit for this purpose. A domestic servant who is applying for entry clearance to enter with his master must   have been employed as a domestic servant for a period of 12 months prior to making such an application in the case of a master who is coming to the UK for a short visit. For a master coming for any other purposes, the domestic servant must have been employed as a domestic servant for a period of 24 months.

FOOTNOTES

1.   *1994 IMM. AR 581*
2.   *HC 395 paragraph 88*
3.   *HC 395 paragraph 89*
4.   *HC 395 paragraph 51*
5.   *HC 395 paragraph 54(ii)*
6.   *HC 395 paragraph 246*

Chapter 9

EXTENSION AND VARIATION

9.1   Extension of Leave to Remain in the UK

Where a person's temporary status is one that can be extended, an application satisfying the requirements for such extension may be made. Such extension of leave may be granted so that the applicant may remain in the same capacity if the application is made on time and the Home Office is satisfied with the application.

Extension in this sense means remaining for a further period on the same immigration status.

Factors which are commonly considered by the Home Office when dealing with such applications are:

1.   Whether there has been any breach of previous conditions or undertakings.

2.   Whether there is any need for the applicant to remain (e.g. to complete course of study or medical treatment) in that capacity.

3.   Whether one has satisfied particular requirements for the relevant rule under which the application is being made.

Where the Home Office is satisfied, the extension sought may be granted for the requested period or as the Home Office considers fit.

9.2   EXTENSION FOR VISITORS

Visitors (not those in transit) to the UK will usually be granted leave to enter for up to six months (with a prohibition on employment). Where the visa granted is not up to six months, an application for extension to increase the duration of stay to six months in the same capacity, that is, as a visitor may be favourably considered. However, transit visas can not be so extended.

There is no **provision for extension of leave over and above the initial period of six months to continue in the capacity of a visitor,** and applications for such extensions are usually refused, although there may be very few exceptional circumstances which may attract treatment outside the immigration rules.

Note, however, that visitors may still be able to vary their leave to other category with longer duration where the requirements for such category are satisfied.

9.3   EXTENSION FOR 'OTHER CATEGORIES'

Some categories of temporary leave have fixed duration which cannot be extended e.g. Working holiday, Au pair, whereas some others may continually be extended.

Where extension in a particular category is not allowed by the rules, variation may be possible if the person wishes to remain for a different purpose which will in effect allow him to remain for a longer period.

Application to vary one's status may be refused where the rules specifically require an entry clearance for that purpose prior to entry; where this requirement is not satisfied, the applicant will be expected to go to his home country to obtain an entry clearance.

9.4   ·VARIATION OF LEAVE

Visitors and others with limited leave to remain may vary their existing leave.

Variation in this sense means changing from one status to another.
This variation may, however, be in the form of an enlargement of a time limit or duration, removal of any time limit, adding, varying or revoking conditions.

Removal of the time limit is the grant of an indefinite leave and any conditions, restrictions or prohibitions in the previous leave are also removed.

The way in which an application for variation is made is important, most especially where one's circumstances change while a pending application is being considered by the Home Office. (For example, where a student whose application is pending is now married to a person who is settled in the UK).

Applicants are advised not to withdraw a pending application in such a circumstance without seeking professional advice, except perhaps there is an assurance from the Home Office that the new application will be considered favourably.

9.5   HOW TO EXTEND OR VARY YOUR LEAVE

Please note that from 26th November 1996, it is now compulsory to make a valid application using appropriate Home Office application form. **See Figure 9.16.** A valid application must be made to the Home Office before the expiration of the present visa.

Such an application should be accompanied by the applicant's passport and any other document(s) required by the immigration rules.

It is important to note that sending a passport to the Home Office without a covering letter would not suffice as valid application for an extension or variation of stay.

Where your passport is not readily available due to misplacement, loss or any other reasons, an application can still be made, (addressing the loss or misplacement or as the case may be) before the expiration of your visa. In this case you will need to state your full name, date of birth, nationality and your Home Office reference number (if known).

Where you do not know when your visa is expiring due to the absence of your passport, you should approach the Home Office with caution and professional advice should be sought immediately.

Where you need a prior approval or acceptance by another body such as the Department of Employment, an application to such a body must be made several months before your visa expires so as to avoid any delay. In some cases, it is only after such an approval or acceptance has been granted by the body that an application to the Home Office can be made for visa extension or variation.

The importance of making an application for extension or variation before the expiration of a current leave cannot but be reiterated. Where an application is made after the expiration of leave and is refused, there will generally be no right of appeal against such refusal. An application can also be refused on the basis that it was submitted late

9.6   SUCCESSFUL APPLICATIONS

Where an application is favourably considered by the Home Office, an endorsement is entered on the Passport, indicating the number of months granted and any conditions attached.

On the first occasion of variation or extension, a Home Office reference number will usually be given and written inside the back cover of applicant's passport, beginning with the first letter of the applicant's surname, and followed by up to five or six numerical figures. A married couple will usually have the same reference number.

9.7 REFUSAL TO EXTEND, VARY & CURTAILMENT OF LEAVE

While matters which may lead to curtailment of leave may also cause refusal to vary or extend, the consequences of both are different. There are, however, general considerations which apply in both cases as discussed below.

9.8 Refusal to Extend or Vary

Grounds for refusal may be for any of the following reasons:-

1. Where the applicant has failed to honour any declaration or undertaking given orally or in writing as to the intended duration and purposes of his stay.

2. An applicant, other than a person who is eligible for settlement, or who is the spouse of a person settled in the UK, may also be refused if there is a risk of subsequent difficulties in returning to his home or another country, if he is granted further leave to remain.

3. Where an applicant takes an unreasonable time to produce documents, or is unable to forward any evidence required to establish his claim under the immigration rules.

4. Failure to comply with a request to attend an immigration interview.

5. Failure, in the case of a child under the age of 18 years seeking extension or variation otherwise than in conjunction with his parent(s) or guardian (not seeking asylum), to provide, if required, a written consent, from such parent(s) or guardian.

6. Except in limited circumstances, an application to remain for a purpose for which an entry clearance is required by a person who was not admitted with such an entry clearance, is likely to be refused.

7.   Failure to comply with conditions attached to grant of leave to enter or remain.

8.   Applicant's undesirable character, conduct or associations or the fact that he represents a threat to national security.

Where variation or extension is refused, the Passport is coded by making a vertical line across the last visa stamp, as shown below.

Fig 9.9

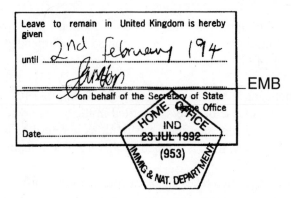

9.10   Curtailment of Leave

Curtailment is a withdrawal or cancellation of whatever is left of one's leave to remain. This may happen where a person is discovered to be in breach of his landing condition, for example, a student caught working without a work permit. The act of withdrawal or cancellation is by giving the person concerned a notice in writing (usually a notice of an intention to deport). This is also increasingly common where an application for asylum has been refused [1].

9.11 OTHER GROUNDS FOR REFUSAL TO EXTEND OR VARY AND FOR CURTAILMENT OF LEAVE

1. A person's leave may be curtailed and an application for variation or extension may be refused where false representations have been made, or material facts have not been disclosed in obtaining leave to enter or in obtaining a previous variation of leave. Such false representations or non disclosure might be by a third party or by the applicant himself. However, an innocent omission is not expected to attract such a penalty. Where a person is said to have made false representations, he may have some genuine explanation which will shed a different light on the opinion formed by the Home Office. The rules are particularly directed at people who have deliberately employed some form of deception and not otherwise.

2. Similarly, where a person has failed to comply with any conditions attached to his leave, such a person's leave may be curtailed (in which case he may be asked to leave the UK or be served with a notice of intention to deport), alternatively, where such a person has applied for a variation or extension of leave, such an application may be refused.

3. Where a person who is in the UK on temporary basis fails to maintain or accommodate himself and any dependants, and as such relies or is likely to rely on public funds, such a person's leave may be curtailed, alternatively, further extension or variation may be refused.

4. Where a person's character, conduct or association makes his continuous presence in the UK undesirable, further extension or variation may be refused.

5. Where a person is a danger to national security, or where a person ceases to meet the requirements of the rules under which he was granted leave, his leave may be curtailed, alternatively, further extension or variation may be refused.

6.   Where a sponsor of the person concerned refuses to give, (after having been requested to do so) an undertaking in writing to be responsible for his maintenance and accommodation in the UK or where the sponsor fails to honour such an undertaking, then the leave of such a person may be curtailed, alternatively further extension or variation may be refused.

7.   The absence of parental consent in writing for a child under 18 years of age where it has been required, is also a ground for curtailment of leave or for refusal of further extension or variation (this will however, not apply to a child who was admitted to the UK as an Asylum applicant).

9.12   APPLICATION FOR LEAVE OUTSIDE THE RULES

The secretary of state has abundant discretion to extend or vary leave outside the immigration rules. This means that in some cases where a certain applicant does not fulfil the requirements of a particular rule, the Home Office may, in the light of all surrounding circumstances, grant an extension or variation outside the immigration rules.

9.13   APPLYING FOR EXTENSION OR VARIATION IN PERSON

A person may visit the Home Office personally and join the long queue. It is noted that the queue outside the Home Office, Lunar House starts increasing from 6.00am. The earlier you join the queue the better. The door is opened at 8.30am but work starts at 9.00am. Ticket numbers are issued on entry and applicants will have to report at the reception desks before taking their seats.

9.14   APPLYING FOR EXTENSION OR VARIATION BY POST

Application may be made by sending all documents to the Home Office by post. You should write a letter of application indicating your reasons for seeking an extension or variation.

You can also make enquiries over the phone before addressing your documents to:

> The Under Secretary of State
> Immigration and Nationality Department
> Lunar House
> 40 Wellesley Road
> CROYDON
> CR9 2BY
>
> Telephone: 0181 686 0688

It is advisable to send your documents by recorded delivery or registered mail, and to keep the receipt until your passport and other documents are returned by the Home Office. When applying by post, you will have to quote your full name, address, date of birth, nationality and your Home Office reference number (if any). Home office reference numbers will usually be given on the first extension or variation, and these are normally noted inside the back cover of your passport.

Unless you are absolutely clear and certain of the nature and form of your application, it may be best to seek advice before making your application to the Home Office. (Please read figure 9.16.)

9.15   WITHDRAWAL OF APPLICATION

Whilst the Home Office is considering an application for extension or variation, applicants are entitled to withdraw their applications either in writing or by going to the Home Office. The Home Office may grant a 28 days visa within which the applicant is expected to leave the UK, provided this application is made within an existing leave to remain.

You are strongly advised against withdrawing your Passport as this may be regarded as withdrawing your application. If you are withdrawing your Passport, please make sure your intentions are clearly stated and made known.

Where you need to have your Passport back for any reason, it will usually be returned, but you should note that if you request the return of your passport to enable you to travel abroad, this will be regarded by the Home Office as seeking to withdraw the application.

9.16   PRACTICAL ADVICE

You are strongly advised that application for variation or extension should be made some days before the expiration of a current leave. Notwithstanding, where the visa has expired, one may still put in an application but is strongly advised to seek legal advice before doing this. It must be noted that where this application is refused, there is no right of appeal.

Whilst this application is under consideration and the Police or immigration authorities come in contact with the applicant, the fact that an application has been made should give him some form of protection and it is very unlikely that further action will be taken against him before the application is determined. However, there is no legal protection against the usual consequences of overstaying in such situations. The facts of the pending application and the surrounding circumstances will almost likely affect the way such a person is treated.

It is noted that Home Office do not treat like cases alike and most of it's decisions have always cried out for reasons. It also do frequently have little to do with justice or common sense. As such, the Home Office is unpredictable at the best times, arbitrary at the worst, commonly hiding under the familiar phrase ' each cases are treated on its own merit'.

9.17   Application Forms Introduced on 3 June 1996 - Withdrawn on 5 June 1996

On 3 June 1996, the Home Office introduced a requirement that all applications for extension or variation of leave to remain in the UK had to be made using some forms designed by them. This introduction only lasted until the 5th June 1996 as the Home Office was taken to court by the Joint Council for the Welfare of Immigrant (JWCI). *The forms have now been re-introduced.*

This rule stipulates that a *valid application* is where the applicant:

i)   uses the new application form,
ii)   fully completes the form,
iii)   signs the form, and
iv)   it is accompanied by originals of all relevant documents.

The practical implications of this rule includes the following summaries:

● in cases where an application is made at the last minute, it will no longer be possible to submit a holding application by letter and subsequently supplying all the necessary information and/or documents.

● If a last minute application is rejected as being invalid, it is likely that by the time a valid application is submitted, the applicant's leave to remain may have expired. If such an application is rejected, the applicant will have no right of appeal against this refusal.

- the form is to be signed by the applicant himself as it cannot be signed by his representative or other person acting on his behalf.

- the forms contain what looks like unintentional gaps and traps.

Applicants should also seek professional advice before completing such application forms. To obtain an application form, you can telephone:

0181 720 2233.

9.18   Your Current Address For The Home Office

Where you are dealing with the Home Office without the assistance of a legal representative, do make sure you inform them about your new address at all times. If a legal representative is assisting you, it is still your duty to inform the Home Office about your new address. Therefore, it is important that you are sure your legal representative informs the Home Office accordingly. You should remember that where your legal representative failed to inform the Home Office about your new address, any problem or embarrassment shall be yours.

The Home Office will usually send its decision to you, and any appeal documents to your last known address. If you are unable to exercise your appeal right because you have moved and did not recieve the said document because the Home Office did not have your new address, you can only blame one person, and that person is you.

FOOTNOTES

1.   *Asylum and Immigration Appeals Act, 1993 S.7*

Chapter 10

RE-ENTRY AND VISA EXEMPTION

10.1 INTRODUCTION

Visa exemption is an exemption from complying with entry clearance requirements; in other words, the passenger does not need to obtain an entry clearance before returning to the UK or as a precondition for entry into the UK.

10.2 IMPLICATION OF VISA EXEMPTION

Where a person qualifies for exemption:

a) airlines (or other carriers) should not be reluctant to bring such a person to the UK, and

b) such a person may not be refused entry into the UK for the sake of not possessing an entry clearance.

10.3 WHO IS VISA EXEMPT?

Any person who has been granted a visa for a period of more than SIX MONTHS and is returning to the UK within the period of his leave, will not be required to present a valid entry clearance on such return. For example, a student granted a 12 months visa who travels out will not be required to have an Entry Clearance before he can be re-admitted. He can leave and return anytime within this 12 months period.

10.4   APPLICATION OF VISA EXEMPTION

a)   **It is very important to note that whenever a person leaves the UK, his visa expires, that is, his leave to enter or remain lapses** [1]

This applies to persons with limited leave (e.g. students) as well as persons with indefinite leave to remain; the only exception being those who are free from obtaining leave on their return to the UK such as certain government officials and diplomats.

b)   When an exempt person other than one with indefinite leave to remain returns to the UK, a section 3(3)b stamp is usually given on entry[2] (see figure 10.12) This stamp provides that the time limits and conditions attached to the original visa are re-imposed and the old visa is thereby resurrected.

10.5   PERMANENT RESIDENTS AS RETURNING RESIDENTS & VISA EXEMPTION

A person with an indefinite leave to remain in the UK is equally affected by this visa exemption provision, but this area is divided into two.

10.6   Those Returning *Within Two* Years:

Where a person with indefinite leave to remain is returning to the UK within a period of two years, he may be re-admitted for settlement without any problem, provided he can satisfy the immigration officer that:

● he had indefinite leave to enter or remain when he left the UK;

● he has not been away for more than 2 years;

● he did not receive assistance from the public funds toward the cost of leaving the UK; and

● he is seeking admission for the purpose of settlement.

It is important to note that a person with Indefinite Leave may also be refused re-admission on the grounds of criminal convictions in any country including the UK of an offence which is punishable with imprisonment for a term of 12 months or more[3]. A passenger of undesirable character, conduct or association may also be refused re-admission. Re-admission will normally be granted where the UK is the passenger's habitual residence.

10.7   HABITUAL RESIDENCE

On grant of Indefinite Leave to Remain in the UK, the Home Office will normally issue you with a letter. In this letter is a paragraph which tells you of conditions for readmission as a person settled in the UK. In order to be considered as settled in the UK, you will have to be able to show that you are habitually and normally resident in this country, and that any absence has been of a temporary or occasional nature.

You will not be readmitted as a returning resident if you are resident overseas and you are only coming to the UK for a short period. Nowadays, habitual residence is interpreted restrictively, and therefore, returning residents are warned to be careful so that they are not treated as being resident abroad.

The test of habitual residence is whether a man's abode in a particular country has been adopted voluntarily and for settlement purposes as part of the regular order of his life for the time being [4].

10.8   Example 1

Moyo married to Mr Boyo who is a British Citizen left the UK together to Barbados, where Mr Boyo is presently working for a British firm. Moyo came to the UK without Mr Boyo for a short visit after about 18 months outside the UK. The Immigration Officer at the Port of Entry indicated to her that she is no longer considered as being habitually resident in the UK and was going to refuse her entry as a returning resident, although was prepared to grant a six month visa as visitor. Moyo protested, saying that she is still habitually resident in the UK and was in Barbados with her husband due to her husband's transfer of employment. As a result of this, she was readmitted as a returning resident.

10.9 Example 2

Mr Smith was coming back from his own country Australia after working there for the past 18 months. His children and wife live in the Australia. He also has property in Australia but nothing in the UK. He was granted a six month visa as a visitor but refused entry as a returning resident despite his previous resident status.

10.10 Those Returning *After* Two Years

Where a person has been away from the UK for longer than 2 years but can still demonstrate that he had indefinite leave to remain when he last left, and is now returning for the purpose of settlement. He may still qualify for admission as a returning resident if, for example, he maintained strong connection with the UK. It is advisable for such a person to obtain an Entry clearance before he embarks on his return journey.

Other important factors which may be taken into consideration are the *continuous existence* of the basis upon which the indefinite leave was originally granted, and the *total length of time spent outside the UK.* Furthermore, the fact that a passenger had lived in the UK for most of his life will be a strong factor in considering his re-admission as a returning resident.

A person who obtained his indefinite leave through the 10 year rule may have lost his ties with, or attachment to, the UK after such a long absence. On the other hand, a person granted Indefinite Leave on the basis of marriage who is still married, and whose wife and children are still in the UK, may not be considered to have lost his ties.

Those with Indefinite Leave will be able to avoid problems concerning re-entry in the same capacity, if they are wise enough to acquire British Citizenship (by naturalisation or registration) or if they obtain a Right of Abode (where applicable).

10.11   VISA EXEMPTION AND ITS PROBLEMS

Those who are exempt as discussed above may, to their dismay and disappointment, face gruesome scrutiny, and may also be refused entry into the UK. Unfortunately, their rights of appeal if any, can only be exercised after their departure from the UK, unless they had obtained an entry clearance before returning.

Before the introduction of visa exemption, there was a stamp commonly referred to as 'Re-entry Visa' stating that 'The holder is exempt from requiring a visa if returning to the UK to resume earlier leave before.......(date)'. The practice of stamping people's passports with this stamp had been discontinued by the Home Office as a result of the introduction of the visa exemption.

As it is not uncommon to learn nowadays that persons with valid visas are refused entry to the UK, it is becoming increasingly inadvisable for persons remaining for temporary purpose, such as students, to travel out of the UK for short breaks. The above mentioned stamp used to give the holder a legitimate expectation that he would be re-admitted to the UK, but this is no more the case.

Stamp indicating a continuation of previous leave

Fig10.12

Given leave to enter

to

Section 3(3)(b).

10.13   CASE STUDY

Dokzy, a Kenyan National, was granted a 2 year working holiday visa. After spending just 6 months out of the 2 years, Dokzy decided to visit Germany for two weeks with two friends who claimed to be British citizens. On their way back, it became apparent that these two friends were travelling with false British passports. As a member of this group, Dokzy became a suspect and was vigorously interviewed by the immigration authorities. It then transpired that Dokzy had a case pending in a Magistrates' Court for obtaining his Car Insurance with false information. Dokzy was granted temporary admission so as to appear in Court.

Dokzy was later refused Leave to Enter the UK because of this criminal case, for which he was later fined the sum of 60 pounds. He eventually had to leave the UK.

10.14   Important Points to Note

1.   There is no right of appeal against the above decision. The only remedy, if applicable, is judicial review.

2.   Except for a good cause or where it is absolutely necessary, it is important to mind how you travel in and out of the UK in spite of the so called visa exemption. *Do remember that once you leave the UK, your visa lapses temporary or indefinite.*

FOOTNOTES

1.   *1971 3(4)*

2.   *S.3(3)(b) 1971 Act*

3.   *HC 395 paragraph 320(18)*

4.   *R v Barnet Borough Council Ex.Parte Shah (1993) 2 AC 309*

Fig 10.15

ABOLITION OF RE-ENTRY VISAS

With effect from 16 May 1991 the facility for acquiring United Kingdom re-entry visas will be withdrawn.   From that date visa nationals wishing to re-enter the United Kingdom will normally need to obtain a fresh visa from a United Kingdom diplomatic post. However, this will not be necessary where a person is visa exempt or holds a valid multiple entry visa.

Visa Exemption

From 16 May 1991 anyone granted leave to stay in the United Kingdom for more than six months will benefit from a new extended visa exemption scheme.

Under the new scheme such persons will not be required to present a visa if they depart from the United Kingdom and return within the period of their original leave.   They will, however, be liable to examination at the port of entry to confirm that they qualify for re-admission.

The visa exemption scheme will also apply to persons granted indefinite leave to remain in the United Kingdom who return there for settlement after an absence of two years or less.

Visitors and others granted leave of six months or less will not be visa exempt.

Chapter 11

IMMIGRANTS AND WELFARE BENEFITS

11.1 INTRODUCTION

Immigration controls and the use of welfare benefits are intertwined. While the immigration rules do not allow immigrants to have recourse to public funds (i.e. to rely on it), the Social Security rules until recently did not seem to bar anyone who qualified from claiming.

The connection between Immigration and Social Security rules brings about THREE relevant questions:-

1. What are public funds?

2. How does a person's immigration status affect access to different types of welfare benefits, in other words, who is entitled to what?

3. How does enjoying different types of welfare benefits affect a person's immigration status?

11.2 WHAT ARE PUBLIC FUNDS?

For the purpose of Immigration rules, the term 'public funds' means [1]:-

*   Council Tax Benefit,
*   Income Support/ Job seekers allowance
*   Housing Rebate,
*   Family Credit,

Included by virtue of the Immigration & Asylum Act 1996 are:

- ❊ Child Benefit
- ❊ Housing

- Housing for homeless persons under Part iii of the Housing (Homeless Persons) Act 1985

Limited leave to enter or remain in the UK is usually with a condition not to have recourse to public funds. This is so irrespective of whether the social security rules allow the person concerned to receive such funds. It is important to note that any such recourse to public funds would be a breach of landing conditions which may have adverse immigration consequences, if found out.

Immigrants in financial difficulties must tread carefully, as solving one set of problems (i.e. financial difficulties) by claiming benefits may create another problem (i.e. Immigration difficulties).

Although other welfare benefits which are not listed above are not defined as public funds, the Home Office may nonetheless frown at applicants who claim them. While a person's application will not be refused for claiming such other benefits, a refusal based on another reason, may be found. Alternatively, the fact of reliance on such assistance (which are not public funds) may lead to negative inference that one is not able to maintain and accommodate himself.

To reinforce the effect of a claim of benefits on immigrants, part of the Immigration Rules state that ' A person's leave may be curtailed or an application for variation may be refused............ if the person has failed to maintain and accommodate himself and any dependants without recourse to public funds [2].

11.3 WHO IS ENTITLED TO WHAT?

Immigrants who have been granted an Indefinite Leave to Remain in the UK are perfectly entitled without any restrictions under the Immigration Rules to claim all that is available under the Welfare State.

Also, those whose conditions of stay do not entitle them to recourse to public funds are nevertheless free to claim the following:-

1.   UNEMPLOYMENT BENEFIT; as this is part of their National Insurance contributions (but must not drift to income support).

2.   CHILD BENEFIT for children born in the UK , (now restricted by the new Asylum and Immigration Law, 1996, see Chapter 22).

3.   FREE MEDICAL TREATMENT under the NHS is only allowed for those who have been granted leave to remain for more than 6 months, provided that the visa granted is not for the purpose of medical treatment.

4.   LEGAL AID is available to all who qualify.

5.   PENSION CLAIM is not a recourse to public funds.

6.   HOUSING, while enjoying facilities under the local authorities or Housing Associations / Trusts would not constitute recoursing to public funds, rehousing as a result of homelessness is regarded as such, (also now affected by the 1996 Law, see Chapter 22).

Apart from the inference which may be drawn from the above discussion, there are some other categories of immigrants who (though not settled in the UK) may claim any benefits to which they may be entitled.

These are:-

● Asylum seekers, or those who have refugee status, (They also have been affected by the 1996 Law, see Chapter 22.)

● E.E.A. Nationals.

In addition, the use of state education facilities for children will not constitute a recourse to public funds and should not lead to any problem provided the child is here to settle or remain with his parents who are here on temporary leave.

Finally, it is important to note that overstayers are already in breach of their landing conditions and while a recourse to public funds in such a situation will not be an additional breach, it may be frowned upon by the Home Office. A likely situation where this might have an adverse effect is where the Home Office is able to exercise its discretion to allow such overstayer to remain on compassionate grounds.

11.5   HOW DOES USING DIFFERENT TYPES OF WELFARE BENEFIT AFFECT A PERSON'S IMMIGRATION STATUS?

As earlier mentioned, having to recourse to public funds may result in an application for variation or extension being refused. Also, subsequent entry or entry clearance may be refused. The question then is, *how will the Home Office know about the receipt of public funds?* This is an interesting question which a majority of immigrants often ask, and which some do overlook. The interesting answer is that there is a growing number of officials within the welfare state agencies who are performing immigration control functions.

There is an increasing practice for those who administer the welfare benefits to question people about their immigration status. Such benefit administrators include:-

Benefit Officer: Dealing with benefit claims.

D.S.S: When checking eligibility for various national insurance benefits, and other public funds.

Hospital Clerks: When checking whether patients are eligible for free NHS treatment.

Tax Inspectors: When checking whether a person can claim tax relief for himself and or his spouse.

Housing Officers: When deciding whether to re-house a person, or treat them as homeless, or grant housing benefit.

Marriage Registrars: To be satisfied of the couple's identity, age and freedom to marry.

Education Officers: When deciding whether to award student grants.

All these officials investigate the applicant's immigration status and this has become an institutional procedure.   The role they play in immigration matters include reporting suspected offenders to the Home Office or the Police.

Sometimes, they are specially instructed to do so.   For example, benefit officers are instructed to examine passports of ' persons who appear to come from abroad' and to refer to the Home Office those who appear to be in breach of immigration conditions.

In some cases, officials are simply encouraged to do so, for example, officials may report to the Home Office where they detect a breach of immigration rules.

Some officials will also report to the Police or the Home Office without official instructions or encouragement to do so, but in response to a growing climate of opinion that it is their duty to report immigration irregularities and also because eligibility for welfare services and benefits have become more and more dependent on immigration status, or on questions of residence which are in practice often impossible to keep separate from immigration status.

There is also a growing trend towards tying welfare benefits access to residential test.   The overwhelming effect of residential test, which eventually will lead to a check on the immigration status, is to disqualify foreigners and immigrants from some benefits.

Also, the Home Office may want to know if someone has claimed benefits and thereby conduct its own investigation.

The residential test is now a widespread feature in local authorities and quite a lot of immigrants are beginning to face tedious screening and are constantly being referred, or reported to, the Home Office. Where an immigrant is so reported, his attempt to claim this benefit alone may have a serious consequence on his continuous stay or subsequent application for leave to remain in the UK.

11.5 LINKS BETWEEN GOVERNMENT DEPARTMENTS

As earlier mentioned, officials involved with immigration control now include not only immigration officers and the Police but also certain welfare workers. This is evident from the amount of transfer of confidential and personal information relating to immigrants passing round government departments contrary to the general rules of non-disclosure, and without express consent of the individual concerned. Presently, therefore, when it comes to immigrants, the normal rules about confidentiality and privacy of personal information are often disregarded.

For the above reason, it is not uncommon for the following departments of both the central government and local authorities to pass information between themselves, for example, where:-

● the Inland Revenue is tracing tax evaders,

● the General Register Office (Marriage) is watching out for marriage of convenience,

● the DSS is checking the credential of claimants (and they sometimes cross-check with the Home Office),

● the Housing Department is checking the genuiness of individual claims for housing, and

● the Department of Education is ascertaining the immigration status of applicants, including evidence of their length of stay.

The Police and the Department of Employment liaise with the Home Office from time to time.

11.6   LIABILITY OF SPONSORS

Any benefits paid to a person may be recouped from his sponsor who had earlier given an undertaking in writing to be responsible for that person's maintenance and accommodation.   For such letter of Undertaking, see figure 11.7

FOOTNOTES

1.   *HC 395, paragraph 6*
2.   *HC 395, paragraph 323 & 322(4)*

Sample of Formal Undertaking of support by a Sponspor

Fig 11.7

(RON 112)

RON112

IMMIGRATION ACT 1971

Undertaking given in pursuance of Immigration Rules

Please complete this form in block capitals

1. I, ... (name), of

    .... (address),

    Home Office Reference number ....

    Hereby declare that my date of birth is ....

*   and that I am employed as .... (occupation)

*   at .... (address)

*   my National Insurance number is ....

    : I hereby undertake that if .... (name of sponsored

    person) who was born .... in .... on place and date
    of birth of sponsored person is granted leave to enter or remain in the United Kingdom, I shall be
    responsible for his/her maintenance and accommodation in the United Kingdom, throughout the
    period of that and any variation of it.

3. I understand that this undertaking shall made available to the Department of Health and Social Security in the United
    Kingdom who may take appropriate steps to recover from me the cost of any Supplementary Benefit paid to or in
    respect of the person who is the subject of this undertaking.

Signed:

Date:

* To be completed only if sponsor
is resident in the United Kingdom.

FOR OFFICIAL USE ONLY

Certificate

I certify that this document, apart from this certificate, is an undertaking given in pursuance of immigration
rules within the meaning of the Immigration Act 1971.

Signed by ,   being a person authorised to make this certificate
on behalf of the Secretary of State

Signature:

Personalised date stamp:

Chapter 12

WORK PERMIT EMPLOYMENT

12.1   INTRODUCTION

Not everybody subject to immigration control needs a Work Permit, and also there are different types of permits which may be summarised as follows:-

1)   Work permit for certain categories of employer which we refer to as 'Work Permit Employment'.

2)   Work permit for Training and Work Experience Scheme (TWES), and

3)   Student work permit discussed in chapter 2.

The criteria for obtaining any of these permits will differ, and the immigration benefits obtainable whilst in the UK are different as well. As a general rule, a person granted work permit and leave to remain under work permit employment for up to 4 years may be granted indefinite leave to remain in the UK, although it is the practice of the Overseas Labour Service to restrict work permit to a period of less than 4 years.

The Overseas Labour Service (O.L.S) issues Work Permit in most cases, after which Leave to Remain or Enter should be sought by making an application to the Home Office.

Discussed in chapter 13 are some other categories of workers who do not need a work permit, although they may need the permission of the Home Office before they can work.

12.2   (1)Work Permit Employment

This scheme enables UK based employers to recruit or bring employees from outside the European Economic Area (EEA) to work in the UK whilst at the same time safeguarding the interests of the resident labour force. The main aim is to assist UK employers in their international development and help them overcome short term labour shortages which cannot be met locally.

Work Permits may be issued for:-

1)   those with recognised professional qualifications such as surveyors, medical doctors, dentists, nurses, etc.

2)   administrative and executive staff.

3)   highly qualified technicians with specialised experience.

4)   key workers with a high or scarce qualification in an industry or occupation requiring expert knowledge or skill.

5)   highly skilled or experienced workers for senior posts in Hotel and Catering work who have successfully completed a full-time training course of at least two years duration at approved schools abroad or who possess exceptional or uncommon skills.

6)   established entertainers or sportsmen.

7)   other people who, in the opinion of the Overseas Labour Service (OLS) will boost or enhance the national interest of the country (UK) if employed.

In addition, prospective employees falling within any of the above categories must be between 23 and 54 years old, although this age requirement may be lowered for sportsmen and entertainers who are older may still be granted this permit.

The fact that one satisfies the age condition is no guarantee that a Work Permit will be issued, as other factors will be considered. These include:-

a)   the existence of a genuine vacancy,

b)   absence of other suitable persons from the EEA to fill the vacancy,

c)   whether adequate efforts have been made by the employer to fill the vacancy from suitable people in the UK or other European Community states,

d)   the application must be for a named person and a specific post, and

e)   the need for the pay and other conditions of employment to be equal to, or as good as those offered in a similar job.

f)   where applicable, the applicant would be required to have had a minimum of two years experience.

12.3 .   Applying for Work Permit

Work permit scheme is now divided into two parts called 'Part 1' and 'Part 2'.

Where the above conditions are satisfied, an application for a Work Permit may be put forward. It is important to stress that applying for a Work Permit is the responsibility of the employer.

Part 1 applications seem to be more attractive in that they:

a)   do not need to be advertised ,

b)   are processed more quickly,

c)   are given fewer checks and the process is more streamlined.

Part 2 applications seem less attractive because the employer is expected to provide evidence of the need to recruit foreigners and not a person settled in the UK / EEA, as well as explaining:

a)   why he is unable to train or transfer an existing employee to do the job,

b)   the need to employ the overseas national, and

c)   details of actions taken to recruit or train EEA nationals to fill the post.

12.4   Part 1 Applications

These will cover:

a)   Occupations which are acknowledged by the Overseas Labour Service (OLS) as being in acute short supply within the EEA. *[Short Supply Occupations]*

b)   Senior posts in international companies which require existing employees to transfer from abroad, or posts designed to develop the careers of existing employees. *[Inter-Company transfers]*

c)   Posts at board or equivalent level, for which there are no suitable EEA candidates. *[Board or Equivalent level Posts]*

d)   New posts essential to inward investment projects bringing jobs and capital to the UK. *[Posts involving Bringing Jobs and Capital to UK]*

12.5   Clarifications of Part 1 Applications

12.6   *Short Supply Occupations

The OLS keeps a list of occupations considered by it to be in short supply in the EEA area. This list is reviewed in the Labour Market. Employers are advised to enquire from the Labour office about a specific occupation before making an application. See below for the OLS telephone number.

The OLS would normally request evidence that there are no suitable candidates available in the EEA, and although advertisement of the post is not required, the OLS may nevertheless request to know the results of any recruitment methods tried.

Work Permit will normally be issued for a period of four years but may sometimes be issued for a shorter period, with extension being granted at a later stage. Permit granted under this heading may lead to a grant of Indefinite Leave to Remain.

For recorded message of up-to-date list of occupations in short supply, please phone Overseas Labour Office on: **0114-259-4203**

12.7   *Inter-Company Transfers

Inter-company transfer is a transfer within an international company, where there is a link by common ownership between a UK company and an Overseas company.   This will also include the transfer of staff between companies which have entered into a joint venture agreement.

The Overseas Labour section may require documentation showing evidence of the link between the UK company and the Overseas company, for example, registration documents, certificate of incorporation, or letters from the company directors confirming the link.

The Inter-Company transfer is, however, divided into two categories which are:

● where the employee's experience is essential to doing a particular job. This will be applicable to senior employees of an overseas company with offices in the UK, where the employee's specialist skills, knowledge or experience are needed for the UK operation.

The OLS would normally require details of why and how the employee's experience is essential to the job. Work permits under this category can be granted for up to four years and can lead to Indefinite Leave to Remain.

● where the employee is being transferred for the purpose of developing his career. This will be applicable where an employee who is not a senior employee is coming to the UK to develop his career before returning to his home country.

The OLS would normally require details of the employee's career development objectives and the company's future employment plans for him. Work permits will normally be issued for a maximum period of three years, and it is usually difficult to extend beyond this period. It will usually not lead to a grant of an Indefinite Leave to Remain.

12.8   *Board or Equivalent Level Post

The board or equivalent level post is applicable where it can be shown that a post cannot be filled by a suitable candidate from the EEA. The overseas national must either be on the board or have a very senior position within the company.   The individual's seniority is measured by the degree of influence that his decisions may have over the company.

The company would, therefore, have to:

1)   provide proof that the position held by the employee is at board or equivalent level,

2)   give reasons why no candidate has been chosenfrom the UK/EEA area, and

3)   provide evidence of any recruitment methods tried.

Although the recruitment methods tried do not have to include advertising, but where the UK company can demonstrate that it has tried the local labour market, for example, by advertising, this may convince the OLS of the need for the overseas employee to come to the UK.

Work permits will normally be issued for a period of four years and can lead to a grant of an Indefinite Leave to Remain.

12.9   *Posts involving bringing Jobs and Capital to UK

This category requires evidence of capital investment in the UK and the creation of jobs for persons settled in the UK as well as EEA nationals. The minimum level of investment and number of jobs to be created will depend on the size of the UK operation and the nature of business. The investment must be made by an overseas company and not an individual.

Work permits will usually be issued for one year and may be extended for up to three years where the OLS is satisfied that the investment has gone ahead and appropriate people have been employed.

12.10   Part 2 Applications

These will be applicable to Overseas nationals who are considered to be key-workers, and a list of such workers can be obtained from the labour office.

Part 2 applications are less attractive compared with part 1 applications, in that:

a)   they are heavily scrutinised by the OLS,

b)   stringent conditions have to be satisfied,

c)   the post should be advertised, and

d)   the employer is expected to recruit or train an EEA national to replace any key-worker he may have in his employment.

Also, it is understood that time spent as a key-worker will usually not lead to a grant of an Indefinite Leave to Remain. Work permits will, therefore, not normally be issued for more than three years.

An application to extend a key-worker's permit up to three years (or in exceptional cases beyond three years), will have to be supported with proof of efforts to recruit a replacement from the EEA. To satisfy this condition employers are normally expected to advertise the vacancy in a national newspaper with EEA circulation or relevant trade journal. Copies of such advertisement should be sent in with the extension application form.   The OLS counld also want to see the response obtained from the advertisement. This should include the total number of respondents and full reasons why none of the UK/EEA candidates were not considered suitable for the post.

12.11   APPLYING WHILE EMPLOYEE IS OUTSIDE THE UK

The new immigration rules no longer allow Overseas nationals to switch to Work Permit employment.   Therefore, overseas nationals are expected to come to the UK with their Work Permits before taking up any appointments, although a worker who submits an application for a work permit might still be allowed leave to remain outside the immigration rules. While a non-visa national has to come to the UK with his work permit, there is no entry clearance requirement for a visa national who is in possession of a work permit at the port of entry and if refused leave to enter will also have a right of appeal exercisable whilst in the UK.

Application for a work permit is expected to be made to the OLS (Overseas Labour Service) at least six months before the employer wishes to bring the overseas national to the UK.

An application form can be obtained from:-

> The Department of Employment
> Overseas' Labour Service
> Moorfoot Sheffield
> S1 4PQ
>
> Tel:0193-784-224

For any or further information you may telephone **0114-259-4074.**

In addition to any other specific documents which may be requested by the OLS, the completed application form may be returned with the following documents:-

- evidence of the employee's qualification and experience,
- a job description,
- and letter of employment.

All documents are expected to be original copies except where it is not practicable to produce them. In addition, an employer may have to submit evidence of the advertisement made for the job, in order to prove that adequate efforts have been made to fill the vacancy with UK or EEA labour.

When a work permit is issued, it will be sent to the employer or his agent. This permit can then be sent to the Overseas national who will need it to obtain Entry Clearance at his nearest British High Commission/Embassy, if a visa national, or entry at the Port of Entry, if a non-visa national.

12.12   WORK PERMIT HOLDERS & REFUSAL OF ENTRY

Since the new rule does not make entry clearance a mandatory requirement for work permit holders, both visa and non visa nationals who are refused entry should have a right of appeal exercisable whilst in the UK.

Entry may be refused, for example;

● Where (whether or not to the work permit holder's knowledge) false representations were employed or material facts were not disclosed, either in writing or orally, for the purpose of obtaining the permit, or

● the holder's true age places him outside the age limits for employment, or

● the holder does not intend to take the employment specified, or he is not capable of doing so.

While entry may also be refused where the permit has expired, immigration officers may nevertheless admit the holder if satisfied that circumstances beyond his control had prevented his arrival before the permit expired, and that the job is still open to him.

12.13   APPLYING WHILE EMPLOYEE IS IN THE UK

Where an application for a work permit is made whilst the employee is in the UK, the OLS will not issue a Work Permit, but may recommend to the Home Office that the applicant be granted leave to remain where the OLS is willing to allow such. This recommendation from the OLS may not be followed by the Home Office as the new immigration rules do not permit a switch to a Work Permit employment. Where the Home Office refuses to extend the applicant's leave to remain, there will be no right of appeal. In any event, an application for work permit in the case of someone already in the UK should be made to the OLS   before the current leave to remain expires.

An Employee who entered the UK with a work permit or an entry clearance for that purpose, can extend his work permit or switch employment with little or no problems.

13.14   Changing Employment

The OLS issues a work permit:

- For a named employee,
- For a specific job,
- With a specific employer.

The overseas national will only be able to change employer with the permission of the OLS and a fresh work permit application will have to be made by the new employer. The OLS will normally agree to grant another work permit only where the employee will be doing the same kind of work for which the original work permit was issued. Where the overseas national is in the UK the Home Office will also need to approve the application.

If the person's employment changes within the company, the employer should obtain approval from the OLS. If the change is minor, for example, where the job title has been changed or where the employee will be working at a different address, the OLS may accept a letter from the employer or representative informing it of the change. Where the change is significant the OLS will expect a fresh work permit application to be submitted.

12.15   Extension of Work Permits

If the employer needs to employ the overseas national for a longer period than that permitted by the original work permit, he should make an application for extension to the OLS before the overseas national's visa expires.

The OLS will like to know:

1)   How much longer the overseas national is required for.
2)   Why the overseas national is needed beyond the original period.
3)   Details and supporting evidence showing the action taken to recruit or train EEA nationals.

It is advisable that an application for extension should be made 3-4 months before the expiry of the employee's visa. The person will be able to continue working whilst the application is pending.

12.16   VISA FOR WORK PERMIT HOLDER'S FAMILY

A work permit holder may be allowed to bring his spouse and any dependants to the UK. They will usually be allowed to remain with him for the duration of his leave, and where applicable, they will all be considered for Indefinite Leave to Remain at the appropriate time.

12.17   (2) Permits for Training & Work Experience Scheme (TWES)

It should be noted from the outset that the new immigration rules no longer allow a switch to this scheme, except for students who may have just completed their course of studies in the UK.

Those who intend to train or gain work experience must therefore enter the UK with a Permit for that purpose, and visa nationals are expected to obtain entry clearance in addition.

The main purpose of this scheme is to allow citizens of developing countries to come to, and/or remain in the UK for a limited period of time in order to train, or gain some work experience which may not be readily available to them in their own countries. **This training or work experience does not count towards a Work Permit (approved employment), and they are not allowed to switch to such employment.** Applicants must also have the intention to return to their country at the end of the scheme and those who enter as visitors will not be allowed to switch to this category.

Accounting, law students and a few other professionals may undertake training after passing their professional examinations.

A work permit application for training or work experience is to be made by the employer, and application forms can be obtained from the Overseas Labour Service office, (see address above).

Where the OLS is satisfied with the application, it will issue a *trainee work permit* to the employer to be forwarded to the employee.

We will now highlight the differences and similarities between the training scheme on one hand, and the work experience scheme on the other hand. While each scheme requires particular conditions to be satisfied, there are general conditions which apply to both schemes.

12.18   Training Scheme

Where the OLS considers a training programme to be satisfactory and there is no reason to believe that the applicant does not intend to leave the UK on completion of his training, he may be granted a permit, usually for a period of one year, renewable for up to 3 years. This permit may be further extended in suitable cases for another 3 years. In other words, training can last up to a period of 6 years.

Where the training involves taking examinations, proof of progress may be significant for extensions as the OLS will not normally approve continuous training beyond three unsuccessful attempts at any examination. Furthermore, the training with the employer must be continuing.

12.19   Conditions for Training Scheme

To qualify for training, the following conditions must be satisfied:[1]

i)   the training should lead to a recognised professional or specialist qualification;
ii)   the trainee must be aged 18 years or over;
iii)   the trainee must have qualifications equivalent to UK degree level;
iv)   the training should be related to the overseas nationals' qualifications;
v)   the period of training should be agreed in advance.   Where qualifications take a number of years, approval will normally be given for an initial period, which will then be extended, provided the trainee is making satisfactory progress.   A maximum of three sittings or possible sittings at any one examination are normally allowed;
vi)   training should be for a minimum of 30 hours per week excluding any time for associated study;
vii)   once the trainee has completed the agreed course of training no approval will be given for supplementary qualifications; the trainee must be engaged on the same salary and conditions of employment as an EEA trainee;
ix)   where a professional qualification is involved, the employer should be registered or approved by the appropriate professional body.

12.20   Work Experience Scheme

Where the OLS considers the work experience to be satisfactory and there is no reason to believe that the applicant does not intend to leave the UK on completion of the scheme, the employee will be issued a work permit, usually for a maximum of 12 months. A further extension may be possible so as to make a maximum of 2 years.[2] The work experience scheme provides for short term employment so as to enable the applicant to widen his occupational experience.

12.21   Conditions for Work Experience.

i)   The overseas national should be between the ages of 18 and 35. They should be employed in a supernumerary capacity and should not be filling a job, unless it is an intra-company transfer. Where the application is to fill a vacant post a full work permit rather than a trainee one is required;

ii)   the overseas national must have previous relevant experience or the appropriate academic or vocational qualifications to enable him to benefit from the work experience offered;

iii)   the work experience should be for a minimum of 30 hours a week, excluding any time for associated study;

iv)   payment is described as 'only a modest personal spending allowance'. A full wage can only be paid if the employee is coming to the UK under an exchange agreement where rates of pay are reciprocal, or if the overseas national is to be paid by an employer or organisation overseas;

v)   if the trainee is already employed by the same firm overseas and is coming to the UK to undertake work experience on an inter-company transfer, a full salary can be paid;

vi)   if the overseas national was employed by the UK company abroad in a senior position an application should be made for a full work permit.

12.22   Common Conditions for Training or Work Experience

The following conditions are of general applicability to both schemes. The training or work experience offered should be:-

-       geared towards acquiring occupational skills or qualifications,
-       of a standard recognised by the OLS.

Additionally, the applicant must have adequate knowledge of the English Language, and must be seen to be able to benefit from the training or work experience, which is not readily available in his home country.

12.23   FAMILY OF TWES PERSON

The permit holder may be allowed to bring his spouse and any dependant to remain in the UK, *but there is no provision for them to apply for Indefinite*

Leave to Remain as this will be inconsistent with the requirements to be satisfied before the trainee or the work experience candidate is granted leave by the Home Office.

Although the criteria for bringing the children of applicants under this scheme are similar to those of student's children discussed in chapter 2, the accommodation requirement provides that it must be owned or exclusively occupied by the family of the TWES person.[3]

12.24   Important Points to Note

1)   When a work permit is issued, it is granted to a particular employer for a particular job, and this should be sent to the Overseas worker who should enter the UK with it. It is also advisable to apply for a work permit 6 months before the worker is expected to take up his post.

2)   Where a work permit needs to be extended, it should be done 3 months before the worker's visa runs out. The Home Office does not usually have any objection to further grant of leave to remain once the OLS approves an extension.

3)   Where the application is in respect of employment for which a work permit or a permit for training or work experience is required (or where it is in respect of the spouse or child of a person who is making such an application) the application should be made direct to the Overseas Labour Service instead of to the Home Office as was previously the case.[4] As this is a provision in the immigration rules, then the applicant's passport is more or less deemed to have been sent to the Home Office. *This rule has been slighly amended in April 1996. Contact the OLS for more information.*

4)   Although those under the TWES scheme are not eligible for Indefinite Leave, they may nevertheless qualify to apply if their total continuous period of lawful residence is up to 10 years.

FOOTNOTES

1.	Work Permit Application Form (WP2) paragraph 7
2.	HC 395 paragraph 119 (iv)
3.	HC 395 paragraph 125 (iv)
4.	HC 395 paragraph 33

Chapter 13

PERMIT-FREE EMPLOYMENT

13.1   INTRODUCTION

This topic deals with persons coming to the UK for employment in a number of specified categories listed below who do not need work permit in order to work or establish   business in the UK. They will, however, need to deal directly with the Home Office or Entry Clearance Office rather than the Department of Employment(Overseas Labour Service). In all cases, prior entry clearance for this purpose is required.

13.2   THOSE WHO DO NOT NEED WORK PERMITS

WORKERS in the following categories may be admitted for an appropriate period not exceeding 12 months if they hold a current entry clearance granted for the purpose:

● Ministers of Religion, Missionaries and Members of Religious Orders.

● Representatives of Overseas Newspapers, News Agencies and Broadcasting Organisations.

● Sole representatives of overseas firms which have no branch or subsidiary or representative in the UK and who are coming to establish a branch or subsidiary.

● Private Servants (aged 18 or over) of members of staff of diplomats or consular missions.

● Persons coming for employment by an overseas government or in the employment of the United Nations Organisation or other International Organisations of which UK is a member.

- Teachers and Language Assistants coming to schools in the UK under the Exchange Schemes approved by the Department of Education.

- Airport-based Operational Ground Staff of Overseas-owned Airlines.

- Commonwealth Citizens with UK ancestry.

- Writers, Composers and Artists.

- Self-employed person.

- Establishing in Business under EC Association Agreement.

- Concession for Foreign Lawyers.

- Retired persons of Independent means.

- Investors

13.3   EXPLANATIONS OF THE PERMIT FREE CATEGORIES

Explained below from figure 13.4 to figure 13.52 are the categories of workers who do not require work permit from the Overseas Labour Office but will require leave to remain for the purpose from the Home Office. Entry Clearance is usually required in almost all the categories.

13.4   MINISTERS OF RELIGION, MISSIONARIES & MEMBERS OF RELIGIOUS ORDERS

For the purposes of immigration Rules:- [1]

i)   a *minister of religion* means a religious functionary whose main regular duties comprise the leading of a congregation in performing the rites and rituals of the faith and in preaching the essentials of the creed;

ii)   a *missionary* means a person who is directly engaged in

196

      spreading a religious doctrine and whose work is not in essence administrative or clerical;

iii)   a *member of a religious order* means a person who is coming to live in a community run by that order.

Under this category applicants coming to work on a full time basis, who can maintain and accommodate themselves without having to recourse to public funds, may be admitted initially for 12 months, with their leave to remain renewable every 12 months for a maximum of 4 years. Where renewal is sought, evidence of why it is necessary for such a person to continue to remain in this capacity must be provided.

The requirements[2] to be met by a person seeking leave to enter the United Kingdom as a minister of religion, missionary or member of a religious order are that:-

i)   a.   if seeking leave to enter as a minister of religion, he has either been working for at least one year as a minister of religion or, where ordination is prescribed by a religious faith as the sole means of entering the ministry, has been ordained as a minister of religion following at least one year's full-time or two years' part-time training for the ministry; or

    b.   if seeking leave to enter as a missionary has been trained as a missionary or has worked as a missionary and is being sent to the United Kingdom by an overseas organisation; or

    c.   if seeking leave to enter as a member of a religious order, is coming to live in a community maintained by the religious order of which he is a member and, if intending to teach, does not intend to do so save at an establishment maintained by his order; and

ii)   intends to work full-time as a minister of religion, missionary or for the religious order of which he is a member; and

iii)   does not intend to take employment except within the terms described above; and

iv)   can maintain and accommodate himself and any dependants adequately without recourse to public funds; and

v)   holds a valid United Kingdom entry clearance for entry in this capacity.

To obtain entry clearance for this purpose, the following documents may be required:-

- evidence of the person's qualification and experience,

- contract of employment showing wages that would be paid to him in the UK, which must be adequate for him and his dependants to live on without having to recourse to public funds,

- evidence of accommodation, and

- evidence of tasks to be performed and proof of why he is suitable for this post.

13.5   Change of employer

A person under this category can change his employment with the permission of the Home Office, but this may only be approved if the employment is as a Minister of Religion, and such a person continues to meet the requirements as above mentioned. Where a person needs to change his employment he should consider seeking advice before doing so.

13.6   Settlement and Family

A person who remains in this capacity for a period of 4 years and is still required to remain as such, may apply to the Home Office for permanent residence. He may also bring his spouse and any dependants under the age of 18 to join him at any time. His spouse and dependants may also be granted indefinite leave to remain with him in the UK.

13.7 REPRESENTATIVES OF OVERSEAS NEWSPAPERS, NEWS AGENCIES & BROADCASTING ORGANISATIONS

Persons under this category, who are on long term assignments to the UK, may be admitted initially for a period of 12 months,[3] renewable every 12 months for up to 4 years. However, such renewals are not automatic as their employers must confirm and show the need for such representatives to continue in the same capacity. *Entry Clearance is required for this purpose.*

13.8 Settlement and Family

A person who remains in this capacity for 4 years and is still required to remain as such by his employers may apply to the Home Office for permanent residence. He may also bring his spouse and any dependants under the age of 18 to join him at any time. His spouse and dependants may also be granted an Indefinite Leave to Remain in the UK.

13.9 SOLE REPRESENTATIVES OF OVERSEAS FIRMS

Representatives of overseas firms which have no branch, subsidiary or other representatives in the UK may be admitted if they obtain entry clearance for this purpose. For the entry clearance application, an applicant will have to provide proof:-

- of appointment or selection by the firm,

- why he is the most capable or best person, for carrying out the task,

- of his expertise in the firm's particular business,

- that the firm at home is functioning and trading, (presumably in profit) and

- that he is a person who can make important decisions on behalf of the firm, and

- that he is versatile in all aspects of the firm's activities and policies.

This may take the form of letter of authority or inferred from the position stated in his appointment letter.

Previous residence of the representative in the UK may also be of great assistance.

The representative should be an individual and not a firm.   Such an individual would not normally be expected to be a majority share holder in or the sole owner of, the home business.   Extension of leave to remain may be granted for a total period of 4 years.

While this sole representative would not need a work permit, other employees coming in from overseas to work in the newly established branch will need a work permit.

13.10   Settlement and Family

If the sole representative remains in this capacity for a period of 4 years, and his employers still require him to continue in this capacity, he may apply to the Home Office for permanent residence.   He may also bring his spouse and any dependants to join him at any time.   His spouse and dependants under the age of 18 years may also be granted an indefinite leave to remain in the UK.

13.11 PRIVATE SERVANTS IN DIPLOMATIC HOUSEHOLDS

A person who is a servant in the household of a member of staff of a diplomatic or consular mission who enjoys diplomatic privileges and immunity within the meaning of the Vienna Convention on Diplomatic and Consular Relations, or a member of the family forming part of the household of such a person, may be granted leave to enter for a period of 12 months. This initial 12 months may be extended for a total period of 4 years.   This person must also obtain an entry clearance for this purpose.

13.12   Requirements to Be Met[3]

An applicant must;

a)   be aged 18 or over
b)   intend to work full-time as a private servant
c)   not intend to take employment other than as a private servant
d)   be able to maintain and accommodate himself and any dependants adequately without recourse to public funds.

13.13   Settlement and Family

A Person who remains under this category for a period of 4 years and is still required to remain as such by his employer may apply to the Home Office for permanent residence. He may also bring his spouse and any dependants to join him at any time. His spouse and dependants under the age of 18 years may also be granted an Indefinite Leave to Remain in the UK. This is a new provision in the present immigration rules.[5]

13.14   OVERSEAS GOVERNMENT EMPLOYEES

For the purpose of this rule,[6] an overseas' government employee is a person employed by:

● an overseas government

● the United Nations Organisation

● an international organisation of which the UK is a member.

A person under this category must have a valid entry clearance for this purpose and will initially be admitted for a period of 12 months renewable up to a total period of 4 years, provided his employer still requires him to remain as such.

13.15   Settlement and Family

A person under this category together with his spouse and children under the age of 18 may be granted Indefinite Leave to Remain after remaining as such in the UK for a total period of 4 years.

13.16   TEACHERS AND LANGUAGE ASSISTANTS

A person seeking leave to enter under this category must hold an entry clearance for this purpose, and should be granted initial leave [7] of 12 months which is renewable for a total period of 2 years, if he:

a)   is coming to an educational establishment in the UK **under an exchange scheme approved** by the Education Department or administered by the Central Bureau for Educational Visits and Exchanges or the League for the Exchange of Commonwealth Teachers,

b)   intends to leave the UK at the end of his exchange period,

c)   does not intend to take employment except in the terms of this paragraph,

d)   is able to maintain and accommodate himself and any dependants without recourse to public funds,

e)   holds a valid UK entry clearance for entry in this capacity.

Please note that employment under this category is for a maximum period of 2 years and does not lead to a grant of an Indefinite Leave to Remain.

13.17   AIRPORT-BASED OPERATIONAL GROUND STAFF OF OVERSEAS-OWNED AIRLINES

A member of the operational ground staff of an overseas owned airlines who is being transferred to the UK to take up a duty at one of the UK international airports as:

    a)   a station manager
    b)   security manager
    c)   technical manager,

and intends to work full-time for the airlines as such, may be granted leave to enter for an initial period of 12 months, renewable for a total period of four years. Entry clearance is required for this purpose.[8]

13.18   Settlement and Family

A person under this category together with his spouse and children under the age of 18 may be granted an Indefinite Leave to Remain after having remained under this category for up to 4 years, provided he is still required by his employer to continue in this employment.

13.19   COMMONWEALTH CITIZENS WITH UK ANCESTRY

A commonwealth citizen who is able to prove that one of his grandparents was born in the UK and Islands, may be granted leave to enter the UK for a period not exceeding four years in order to come and work. Such a person would not need a Work Permit in order to come to the UK to work.

13.20   Requirements for Entry Clearance

The requirements which have to be satisfied by an applicant for leave under this category are that:-[9]

    a)   he is a Commonwealth Citizen, (for the list of commonwealth countries see chapter 3), and

b)   he is aged 17 or over, and

c)   He is able to provide proof that one of his grand parents was born in the   UK and Islands. The applicant would also have to show his connection with the grandparent and would therefore, need to provide:-

   i)   his grandparent's birth certificate, or

   ii)   his grandparent's marriage certificate where applicable, (for example where there has been a change of name due to marriage).

   iii)   his parent's birth certificate.

   iv)   his parent's marriage certificate, where applicable (for example, where there has been a change of name due to marriage).

It is important to note that the Immigration Appeals Tribunal has held that in the case of illegitimate children, paternal grandparents (i.e. the father's parents) do not count, in other words, it is the maternal grand parents of an illegitimate child that count. [10]

d)   he is able to work and intends to take or seek employment in the UK (since it is the ability to work or intention to take or seek employment that matters. The applicant does not need to have secured employment before.

e)   he will be able to maintain and accommodate himself and any dependants adequately without recourse to public funds.

f)   he produces a valid UK entry clearance for entry in this capacity.

13.21   Leave to Enter or Remain for Spouse and Children

The spouse and children of a person in this category may be granted leave to enter or remain in the UK for a period not in excess of that granted to him, for which the requirements to be met are discussed in chapters 4 and 6 respectively.

13.22   Settlement

A person under this category together with his spouse and children under the age of 18 years may be granted Indefinite Leave to Remain provided he has spent a continuous period of 4 years in the UK in this capacity and satisfies requirements a - e above. *[There is no requirement that such a person should be in employment at the time of the application or even during the course of the four years. However, due to the fact that eventual grant of Indefinite Leave is discretionary, it would be advisable to be in gainful employment at the time of the application].*

13.23   WRITERS, COMPOSERS AND ARTISTS

Entry clearance is mandatory for this purpose. If admitted, they are granted 12 months leave to enter, renewable every year, for a maximum period of 4 years.

While extension of leave to remain is granted every 12 months, this will only be allowed if there is satisfactory evidence that the person is maintaining and accommodating himself and any dependants from the proceeds of his self employment as a writer, composer or artist, without having to recourse to public funds, and without having to resort to employment for which a work permit is required.

13.24   Who is a Writer?

A writer is a person who writes books, articles, etc. especially as an occupation. It may be easier for someone whose publications are many or widely known to be able to prove that he is a writer by occupation.

13.25   Who is a Composer?

A composer is one who structures, creates, puts together, or produces musical or literary work.

13.26   Who is an Artist ?

An artist is a person who practices in art, especially in painting, drawing or sculpture. It has not been made clear if someone who sings as well as composes music is an artist or an entertainer who needs a work permit.

Therefore; where one will be carrying out some of composition and recordings, or life performances, it would be advisable to check with the Home Office if a work permit is required.

13.27   Criteria for Entry Clearance

Entry clearance will only be granted to applicants who can show that they:-

-       have established themselves outside the UK as writer, composers or artists primarily engaged in producing original work which has been published (other than exclusively in newspapers or magazines), performed or exhibited for its literary, musical or artistic merit; and

-       do not intend to do work other than in the related field; and

-       will be able to maintain and accommodate themselves and any dependants from their own resources, including the proceeds of their work without having to recourse to public funds.

13.28   Settlement and Family

A person who remains under any of the three categories in figure 13.23 above for up to 4 years may apply to the Home Office for permanent residence. He may also bring his spouse and children under 18 years to join him at any time. His spouse and dependants may also be granted indefinite leave to remain in the UK.

13.29   SELF- EMPLOYED PERSONS

The rules define business as an enterprise of:- [11]

i.   a sole trader; or
ii.   a partnership; or
iii.   a company registered in the United Kingdom.

Where the applicant wishes to **establish** himself in a business or join as a partner or as a director in an existing business or to be self-employed, an entry clearance is needed for this purpose.   Leave to enter may initially be for a period of 12 months, renewable for a total period of 4 years.

In applying for an entry clearance, there are common conditions which apply to those taking over or joining as a partner or director, and those who are establishing a new business, and at the same time, there are specific conditions which apply to them respectively.

13.30   Common Conditions for Entry Clearance

These include showing or providing:-

- evidence that the applicant has £200,000 in his control, held in his own name and not by a trust or other investment vehicle.

- proof that this money is to be put into the business,

- proof that the level of his financial investment is proportional to his interest in the business (in the case of partnership),

- the applicant's ability to bear his share of the liabilities arising from the business,

- that the business will be able to occupy him on full time basis,

- and that there is a genuine need for the applicant's services or investment in the UK.

13.31   Special Conditions: Taking Over or Joining as a Partner or Director in an Existing Business

In addition to the common conditions stated above, the applicant will have to produce:-

i)   a written statement of the terms on which he is to take over or join the business; and

ii)   audited accounts for the business for previous years; and

iii)   evidence that his services and investment will result in a net increase in the employment provided by the business to persons settled here to the extent of creating at least 2 new full-time jobs.

Also, the proposed partnership or directorship must not be a disguised employment, and the applicant will not be expected to supplement his income from the business by taking up employment of any kind, or have recourse to public funds.

Finally, the applicant must be bringing money of his own into the business. This money can be from any source (including money already in the UK).

13.32   Special Conditions: Establishing a New Business

In addition to the above common conditions, the applicant will have to produce evidence:-

i)   that he will be bringing into the country sufficient funds of his own to establish a business; and

ii)   that the business will create full-time employment for at least 2 persons already settled in the United Kingdom.

13.33   Settlement and Family

A person who remains under any of the above mentioned categories for up to 4 years may apply to the Home Office for permanent residence. He may also bring his spouse and children under 18 years to join him at any time. His spouse and dependants may also be granted an indefinite leave to remain in the UK.

13.34   ESTABLISHING IN BUSINESS UNDER EEA AGREEMENTS

This is   another category of business people intending to establish themselves in business under the provision of EEA Agreements,   where there is no minimun financial investment but other criteria which are similar to the provisions for self employed person.

This topic concerns the nationals of the following countries:- [12]

Hungary,
Poland,
Slovakia,
Bulgaria,
Romania, and
Czech Republic .

Please note that there is a slight difference in the treatment of the Hungarian nationals as against the treatment of the others.

A person from *Poland , Slovakia, Bulgaria, Romania* and *Czech Republic* can establish a UK registered company, be a partner in a firm or be a sole trader; whereas a person from *Hungary* can only establish a UK registered company.

Entry Clearance in this capacity is required, but unlike business people from other countries outside the EEA, *there is no financial requirement;* in other words, they can establish in the UK once they have **sufficient funds** to set up their business.

● Where a Polish, Hungarian , Slovakian, Bulgarian, Romanian or Czech is establishing a UK registered company, he will need to show that:-

i)   he will have controlling interest in the company;

ii)   he will be actively involved in the promotion and management of the company;

iii)   the company will be registered in the UK and be trading or providing services in the UK; and

iv)   the company will be the owner of the assets of the business.

● Where a Polish, Slovakian, Bulgarian, Romanian or Czech is in partnership or a sole trader, he will need to show:-

i)   that he will be actively involved in trading or providing services on his own account or in partnership in the UK;

ii)   that he, or he together with his partners will be the owner of the assets of the business; and

iii)   in the case of a partnership, that his part in the business will not amount to disguised employment.

Other requirements to be met by all applicants are: -

i)   that the money he is putting into the business is under his control and sufficient to establish him in business ;

ii)   that until his business provides him with an income he will have sufficient additional funds to maintain and accommodate himself and any dependants without recourse to employment (other than his work for the business) or to public funds;

iii)   that his share of the profits of the business will be sufficient to maintain and accommodate himself and any dependants without recourse to employment (other than his work for the business) or to public funds; and

iv)   that they do not intend to supplement their business activities by taking or seeking employment in the UK other than their work for the business.

A person who is able to satisfy the above requirements should be admitted for a period not exceeding 12 months with a condition restricting his freedom to take employment, and he may be granted further extensions for a maximum period of 4 years.

13.35   Extension of Visa for a Person who is Established in a UK registered Company

A person who wishes to extend his leave to remain under this category will have to show:-

i)   that he is actively involved in the promotion and management of the company;

ii)   that he has a controlling interest in the company; and

iii)   that the company is registered in the UK and trading or providing services in the UK.

13.36   Extension of Visa for a Person Established as a Sole Trader or in Partnership

A person who wishes to extend his leave to remain under this category will have to show:-

i)   that he is actively involved in trading or providing services on his own account or in partnership in the UK;

ii)   that he, or he together with his partners, is the owner of the assets of the business;

iii)   in the case of a partnership, that his part in the business does not amount to disguised employment; and

iv)   the current financial position of the firm or business in the form of audited accounts for the business.

An extension of stay in order to remain in business with a condition restricting his freedom to take employment may be granted for a period not exceeding 3 years provided the Secretary of State is satisfied that each of the requirements listed above is met.

13.37   Settlement and Family

A person who remains in this capacity for 4 years, together with his spouse and any dependants under the age of 18, may apply to the Home Office for permanent residence. An application to remain as such will be considered in the light of all relevant circumstances, including his conduct, character and continuity of his business, provided that he:-

i)   has spent a continuous period of 4 years in the UK in this capacity and is still so engaged;

ii)   has met all requirements stated above throughout the 4 years; and

iii)   submits audited accounts for the first 3 years of trading and management accounts for the 4th year.

13.38   CONCESSION FOR FOREIGN LAWYERS

The Home Office has for a long time operated a concession outside the immigration rules which allows overseas Solicitors, Barristers and Legal Consultants to come to the UK in order to set up a Law Practice without the need to invest the required amount of   £200,000. **Entry Clearance is**

needed for this purpose and an applicant will usually be granted 12 month's leave to enter, renewable for a total period of 4 years after which an application for Indefinite Leave to Remain may be granted.

Although the amount needed does not have to be up to £200,000, a *sufficient amount* of money to set up in practice, accommodate and maintain any dependants would be expected.

Applicants will also have to obtain the appropriate **letter of confirmation** from the Law Society that they can practice in the UK. This process may involve confirmation from the equivalent governing body in the applicant's home country confirming applicant's qualifications, experience, and suitability to practice in the UK.

13.39   Letter of Confirmation

In order for the Law Society to assess a foreign lawyer's application, it will require the following documents and information (with certified English translations where appropriate).

1)   a)   A letter or certificate from the relevant Home Bar or Law Society or State Authority regarding the foreign lawyer's professional qualifications: for example, a certified extract of the Roll of the Supreme Court. Should the applicant be a member of more than one Bar, then certification is required from each.

     b)   A letter of recommendation of good standing, signed by the authorised officer of the lawyer's state authority, Bar or Law Society: for example, a certificate of admission and fitness to practise. Should the applicant be a member of more than one Bar, then a letter is requested from each.

     c)   A brief curriculum vitae, including particulars of any previous employment, whether as a lawyer or otherwise, as well as date and place of birth.

In the case of membership of a firm of lawyers outside the UK, the curriculum vitae should state the name and address of the firm, whether the applicant is a partner or associate and the length of time the applicant has been associated with the firm.

d)   A signed undertaking in the prescribed form by the applicant to the secretary-general of the law Society that he will observe the standards of conduct which apply to a solicitor of the relevant UK jurisdiction.

e)   Where the lawyer intends to practise in the UK.

f)   The names and addresses of three British referees.

All referees must be professionals and at least one of the referees should be a solicitor admitted in the relevant UK jurisdiction in which the applicant proposes to practise. (Each individual lawyer seeking Law Society consent needs to supply separate referees).

2)   After examining the documentation, the Law Society will write to the Entry Clearance Office stating whether or not there is any objection to the application being granted. The Law Society will, at the same time, notify the applicant or the applicant's representative that it has written to the Entry Clearance Office, in order to enable the applicant to forward any remaining supporting documentation to the Entry Clearance Office.

3)   Presently, a non-refundable fee of £146.88 (inclusive of VAT) is charged. The cheque should be sent with the application, made payable to 'The Law Society'. Please telephone the Law Society for more details.

13.40   Documents Necessary for Entry Clearance Application

-       Evidence of qualifications,

-       Letter from the Law Society confirming theirconsent to the applicant being allowed to come to the UK to practice,

15.9   ABANDONED CHILDREN

New born infants found abandoned in the UK will qualify for British citizenship though they will have to be registered as such.

15.10   CUKC'S

Those people holding CUKC Passports (Citizens of UK and Colonies) who had failed to register as British Citizen before the end of 1988 can obtain an indefinite leave to remain, and may then Naturalise in order to become British citizens.

15.11   OVERSEAS BRITISH

Those who are British Dependent Territories Citizens(BDTC), British Overseas Citizens(BOC), British Protected Persons(BPP), and British Nationals (Overseas)(BNO) can register as British on fulfilling some conditions which are discussed below.

List of Overseas British Countries, that is, BDTC, BOC, BPP and BN, can be obtained from the Nationality Section of the Home Office.

15.12.   Registration

British Citizenship by registration is basically divided into two. The two different types of registration are for people under 18 years old on one hand, and other applicants, on the other hand.

15.13   APPLICATION FOR REGISTRATION OF A CHILD UNDER 18

15.14   Registration as of Right will apply to:

i.   A child born in the UK on or after 1st of January 1983, who is not a British Citizen at birth but·one of whose parent(s) later becomes a British citizen or becomes settled in the UK.

NOTE: where the child is born out of wedlock, it is the mother's status that counts.

ii.   A child born in the UK on or after the 1st of January, 1983 who is not a British citizen at birth, but who lived continuously in the UK for 10 years with an absence of not more than 90 days in any year (if any).

iii.   A child born outside the UK on or after the 1st of January 1983 by parents who are themselves British Citizens by descent.

15.15   Registration at Home Office's Discretion will apply to:

D.   i.   A child born outside the UK before the 1st of January, 1983 to a woman who was British (bearing in mind that where the father was British pre-January 1983, the child himself is British).   The child's father must give his consent for the Registration if the child was born within wedlock, except, where there has been a divorce, legal separation or where the father is deceased; in which case, this consent may be dispensed with.

ii.   A child adopted outside the UK by British Citizens (those adopted in the UK will be British from the date of adoption).

iii.   A child born outside the UK to a parent whose father (i.e. the child's grandfather) is in Crown Service, designated or

European Community Institution Service.

iv.   A child born outside the UK to a parent in designated or Community Institution Service.

v.   A child born to a parent who had renounced and subsequently resumed British citizenship.

E.   Any child the Home Secretary considers for registration solely and absolutely at his discretion.

Application under Home Office's discretion must give details of all the child's criminal convictions except those which are regarded as 'spent'. Spent means that it will be ignored.

In calculating the 'spent' period, it is the prison sentence that counts and not the actual time spent in prison, and suspended sentence will be counted as if a prison sentence had been imposed/served.

A sentence of more than two and a half years imprisonment can never become spent.

Examples of sentences and 'spent' periods for convictions

Fig 15.16

Sentence	Conviction becomes spent after	
Imprisonment or youth custody Over 6 months - 2 1/2 years	10 years	
	7 years	all halved
Imprisonment or youth custody up to 6 months		if person under 17
Fine	5 years	when convicted.
Community service order	5 years	

Absolute discharge	6 months
Borstal	7 years
Detention centre	3 years
Probation order	1 year or when order expires, whichever is longer.
Conditional discharge	
Bound over	
Care order	
Supervision order	

Order for custody in remand home	1 year after the order expires.
Approved school order	
Attendance centre order	

Hospital order with or without a restriction order	5 years, or 2 years after order expires, whichever is longer.

If a person is sentenced to more than 2 1/2 years in prison, the conviction can never become 'spent'.[1]

15.17   OTHER APPLICANTS

A person who falls within the following categories may also put in an application to be registered as British citizen:

- British Overseas Citizen,

- British Subject (S.31 of British Nationality Act 1981: please refer to this Act),
- British Protected Person; provided,
  they meet the '5 year residence' requirement, that is, the applicants must:

- have been in the UK at the beginning of the 5 year period;

- have not remained outside the UK for a period exceeding 450 days out of this 5 years;

- have, in the last 12 months immediately before the application, been free from restrictions on length of stay in the UK;

- have not remained outside the UK for a period exceeding 90 days during the last 12 months of the 5 years; and

- have not at any time in the 5 year period been in breach of immigration rules;

OR

If they have, at any time been in Crown Services, showing that they have:

- a responsible post,

- given outstanding service,

●   some close connection with the UK, and

●   proof and explanations of any special circumstance which they feel
     the Home Secretary should take into account when considering the
     application.

15.18   FILLING OF THE APPLICATION FORM FOR CHILDREN UNDER 18

Application forms can be obtained from:

> Nationality Office
> 3rd floor India Building
> Water Street
> LIVERPOOL
> L2 0QN
>
> Telephone: 0151 237 5200

Completed application forms and documents, together with the fee should
be sent to the above address.

* The current fee is £120.

15.19   Important Points to Note

●   Parents' or Guardians' consent is compulsory for the application.

●   An application will not be valid unless it has been signed and dated
     by the parent(s) or guardian(s).

●   Full fees must be paid at the time the application is being forwarded.

●   Documents to be sent with the application may include evidence:

-    that the child was born IN or OUTSIDE the UK; usually his Birth
     certificate;

- that his parent(s) is British or settled in the UK, e.g. Passport or Birth Certificate, or Registration or Naturalisation certificate of parent(s);

- that parents are married, proof of the marriage; or of divorce, or of death, and

- that the child is adopted (if he is); the adoption papers, together with any other facts and documents which may be relevant to the application.

- where the applicant will be in need of any of these documents within 6 months of making the application, he may not enclose them, but must give an explanation in writing. The applicant will be asked to send these documents when the application is ready for consideration.

- Presently, it takes roughly between 6-9 months to arrive at a decision on any application.

● It should be noted that applications which are of right have little or no problem, but those which fall within the Home Secretary's discretion may be refused. Unfortunately there is no right of appeal against such refusal although one can always re-apply.

● A Certificate of Registration will be issued where the application is successful, and once registered, one is eligible to apply for a British Passport.

Figure 15.20 is an example of Certificate of Registration.

15.21   FILLING THE APPLICATION FORM FOR OTHER APPLICANTS

Application forms can be obtained from the address shown in fig. 15.18

Completed application forms and documents, together with the fees, should also be sent to this address.

Figure 15.20

HOME OFFICE

British Nationality Act 1981

Certificate of registration

as a

BRITISH CITIZEN

The Secretary of State, in exercise of the powers conferred by the British Nationality Act 1981, has registered the person named below as a

BRITISH CITIZEN

Full Name

Name at Birth if different

Date of birth

Plascce and country of birth

Issued on the direction of the Secretary of State
HOME OFFICE LONDON

Certificate No.

Date

Reference No.

Section 1(3)
BRITISH CITIZEN

This certificate does not certify the accuracy of the personal particulars, which are those supplied by the person who made the application.

Any unauthorised alteration may render this certificate invalid.

019930

15.22   Important Points to Note

● An application will not be valid unless it has been signed and dated by the applicant.

● Full fees must be paid at the time the application form is being forwarded.

● **Documents** which are likely to be required may include evidence:

- that the applicant is a British Dependent Territories citizen, or British subject, or British Protected person. Therefore, any of the following documents may be forwarded as and where appropriate; passport, naturalisation or registration documents, the applicant's birth certificate and or parents marriage/birth certificates.

- Proof of 5 year residence (where appropriate to the application); letter(s) from employers, educational establishments, or D.S.S, National Insurance Contribution or P60 and any other documents which may show that the applicant has lived in the UK during the 5 year period.

- Proof of Crown Service; a letter from the establishment where the applicant is or was serving, showing details of the post held, length of service and any other relevant points which may be of help to the application.

● Presently, it takes roughly between 6-9 months to get a decision on any application.

● A certificate of Registration will be sent if application is successful, and once registered, one becomes eligible to apply for a British Passport.

15.23   Naturalisation

This is a means by which foreigners of full age and capacity can acquire British citizenship. **The first important criterion for naturalisation is the attainment of a settled status, that is, to have indefinite leave to remain in the UK.**

Other criteria for naturalisation will depend on whether indefinite leave to remain is acquired through [2]:
- Marriage to a British Citizen,
             or
- By other means (referred to as "Other Applicant").

15.24   [i]SPOUSE OF A BRITISH CITIZEN

15.25   Essential Criteria

An applicant under this heading must:

- be 18 years of age or over,
- be of a sound mind,
- be of good character,
- be married to a British citizen up until the date of application,
- at the date of application, be resident in the UK and should not be subject to any time limit,
- meet the '3 year residence' requirement, that is, the applicant must [3]:

    - have been in the UK at the beginning of the 3 year period;

    - not have remained outside the UK for a period exceeding 270 days out of the 3 years;

    - not have remained outside the UK for a period exceeding 90 days, during the last 12 months of the 3 years;

    - not have, at anytime in the 3 year period, been in breach of the immigration rules.

15.26   Important Points to Note

1.   *Time spent* in the UK *which does not count* towards residence is:

● a period when exempt from immigration control, for example, while as a diplomat, or
● a period of imprisonment following a conviction, see figure 15.16

2.   Where a person does not fulfil all the requirements due to any special circumstance, an application may still be made but he will have to explain this special circumstance.

3.   **It is Marriage to a British Citizen that counts (and not to a person with Indefinite Leave to Remain).** For a person who is married to someone who has Indefinite Leave to Remain, an application should be made under the 'other applicants category'.

15.27   [ii] OTHER APPLICANTS

15.28   Essential criteria

The applicant must:

● be 18 years of age or over;
● be of a sound mind;
● be of good character;

● have sufficient knowledge of the English Language (or Welsh or Scottish Gaelic), although this knowledge does not have to be perfect, it must be sufficient to fulfil duties of a citizen and to mix easily with people. If the applicant is unable to speak due to a disability, communication by writing, or British sign language, will be sufficient. (The elderly and those who are physically or mentally handicapped do not have to meet this language requirement);

● intend to live in the UK;

- not be subject to any time limit on his leave in the UK in the last 12 months prior to the date of application;

- meet the '5 year residence' requirement, that is, the applicant must [4]:

    - have been in the UK at the beginning of the 5 year period;

    - not have remained outside the UK for a period exceeding 450 days out of this 5 years;

    - have in the last 12 months immediately before the application, been free from restrictions on length of stay in the UK;

    - not have remained outside the UK for a period exceeding 90 days during the last 12 months of the 5 years;

    - not have at anytime in the 5 year period, been in breach of immigration rules.

15.29   Important Points to Note

1. *Time spent* in the UK *which does not count* towards residence is:

    - a period when exempt from Immigration Control for example, while a diplomat, or
    - a period of Imprisonment following a conviction.

2. *An application can only be made a year after the settled status has been acquired.*

15.30   Differences Between the TWO Categories

15.31   A.   Residence Requirement

In the case of 'Other applicants' they must have been in the UK for 5 years without an absence in excess of 450 days, while in the case of "spouse", it is 3 years with an absence not in excess of 270 days (if any).

15.32   B.   Language

In the case of 'Other applicants' the applicant must normally have sufficient knowledge of English (or Welsh or Scottish Gaelic) language, while as a ''spouse'', you do not have to satisfy this requirement.

15.33   C.   Intention to live in the UK

'Other applicants' are not required to fulfil this criterion, while ''spouses'' must fulfil this.

15.34   D.   Time to Make an Application

'Other applicants' can only make an application a year after they have been granted indefinite leave to remain, while ''spouses'' can make their application from the date they obtain such leave to remain, provided the total aggregate period spent in the UK is up to 3 years.

It is important to note that a person who is divorced from his British spouse can only make an application other than as a spouse (i.e. under the 'other applicants' category).

Good character is a criterion which must be satisfied by all applicants, therefore, criminal record or bad association will count against any application.

15.35   GOOD CHARACTER REQUIREMENT

15.36   Criminal Record

Generally, a person who has been convicted of a serious offence cannot be regarded as a person of good character, therefore, all applicants must give details of all criminal convictions, **except** those which may be regarded as 'spent'.

Certain convictions may be regarded as 'spent' after a period of time from the date of conviction if the person has not been convicted again in that period. 'Spent' means that it will be disregarded when considering the application. See above for periods of 'spent convictions'.

In calculating the spent period, it is the **prison sentence** that counts and not the time served; and a suspended sentence shall count as if it were a prison sentence.

15.37   Bad Associates

Applicants with few or no convictions, but who are strongly suspected of engaging in crime or are known associates of criminals, will normally be refused.   Although financial irresponsibility, serious insolvency or bankruptcy, commercial malpractice etc. might bring about a refusal, financial incompetence, unemployment or receipt of social security benefits, defects of temperament etc. are not in themselves sufficient to justify a refusal.

15.38   FILLING THE APPLICATION FORM

Application forms can be obtained from the Nationality Division in Liverpool, and completed forms and documents, together with appropriate fees should be forwarded to the same address given above.

* Current Application fee is: £150 (£120 for spouse of a British citizen).

15.39   Important Points to Note

Applications must be supported by **two referees,** and each must have known the applicant for at least 3 years, and must:

- be a British citizen
- be 25 years of age or over,
- not be related to the applicant
- not be related to the other referee,
- not be applicant's solicitor or agent, and
- not have been convicted for an imprisonable offence during thelast 10 years.

- Application will not be valid unless it has been signed and dated.

- **Documents** which are likely to be required, may include evidence of:

  - Age and name; e.g. birth certificate or passport,

  - residence in the UK during the qualifying period; e.g. letters from employers, school or other educational establishment, department of social security showing national insurance contributions, P60 forms or letter from the Inland revenue,

  - any other relevant documents, including marriage certificate if a spouse.

Presently, it may take between10-15 months to get a decision on any application. **The decision to grant a Certificate of Naturalisation is totally at the Home Office's discretion.**

- There is no right of appeal against refusal, but one can always re-apply.

- The Home Office may ask the Police or other representatives to interview an applicant at his home.

- Where the application is successful, a Certificate of Naturalisation will be issued and with this, one becomes eligible to apply for a British Passport.

Certificate of naturalisation is similar to Certificate of Registration. (see figure 15.20)

Although one can not appeal against the Home Secretary's decision to refuse to grant a certificate of registration or naturalisation, and he does not have to provide any reasons for such refusal, however, closer attention should be paid to the on going case of Mr Mohamed Al Fayed who has won at the Court of Appeal against the Home Secretary's refusal to grant him British Citizenship on the grounds that no 'reasons' were given.

15.40   CITIZENSHIP AND ADOPTED CHILDREN

Adopted children are treated as natural children of the adoptive parents from the date of the adoption order. For nationality or immigration purposes, therefore, the 'new parents' nationality or immigration status will have a bearing on the nationality or immigration status of this 'new child'.

The following points will be helpful, taking the date of adoption to be any date after the 1st of January 1983:

1.　Where the adoptive parents were British on the day of adoption and the adoption took place in the UK, the child becomes a British citizen automatically.

2.　Where the adopters were British on the day of adoption and the adoption took place outside the UK in a country whose adoption is recognised, the child can be registered as British citizen on application. This application can be made from the British Embassy of the child's country or in the UK after his entry.

3.　Where the adoptive parents had permanent residence on the day of adoption and the adoption took place in the UK, the child may benefit from the new parents' permanent residence, and may naturalise to become British.

4.　Where the adoptive parents had permanent residence on the day of adoption and the adoption took place outside the UK, the child will have to be sponsored to join his parents in the UK. He may subsequently benefit from the new parents' permanent residence, and may naturalise to become British.

15.41   LOSS OF BRITISH CITIZENSHIP

British citizens may lose their citizenship, and such loss will largely depend on how it was acquired in the first place. Though, there are several ways of acquiring British citizenship, all these can be put under two headings for this topic.

15.42   (i). Where British Citizenship is by Birth

Children born in the UK and who acquire British Citizenship from the date of birth, including few others who acquire British citizenship without the need to register or naturalise (e.g. Adopted child where the adoptive parents are British) may lose their British citizenship by:

-   Declaration of Renouncement

15.43   (ii). Where British Citizenship is by Registration or Naturalisation.

The Home Office can revoke a Registration or Naturalisation certificates, therefore, deprive someone of his British Citizenship, where:

● registration or naturalisation has been obtained by fraud, or false representation or concealment of material facts,

● the person has been disloyal to the Country, or

● the person has, during any war with the UK, traded unlawfully with the enemy country, or

● the person is sentenced to an imprisonment of more than 12 months within five years of the date of registration or naturalisation.

It is important to note that before revocation is carried out, there is a right of Inquiry for the person involved before a specially-appointed committee of inquiry.

FOOTNOTES

1.   *Rehabilitation of Offenders Act 1974*
2.   *British Nationality Act 1981, S.6 & Sch.1*
3.   *British Nationality Act 1981, S.6(2) & Sch.1(3)*
4.   *British Nationality Act 1981, Sch.1*

Chapter 16

INDEFINITE LEAVE TO REMAIN

16.1   INTRODUCTION

This topic is primarily concerned in bringing together topics or sub-topics which lead to the final conclusion of remaining indefinitely in the UK. Indefinite Leave to Remain and Permanent Residence are synonymous.

Basically, indefinite leave to remain may be obtained through the following ways:

16.2   i. By Birth

{a}   A child born in the UK after 1st of January 1983 to a non-settler does not become a British citizen automatically. Where such a child has not been in the UK for up to 10 years, and an application for registration to become a British citizen has not been favourably considered, an application for permanent residence can be made for him if he intends to travel out of the UK.

{b}   Also a child born in the UK to a non-settler mother where the child's father is British, may apply for Indefinite Leave to Remain . [1]

16.3   ii. Marriage

Spouses of British citizens, persons with Right of Abode or persons with indefinite leave to remain in the UK may be granted permanent residence. A 12 month visa is usually granted in the first instance (Probationary period), subsequent to which indefinite leave may be granted. Marriage to nationals of the Economic European Area (EEA) may also lead to permanent residence after 5 years.

16.4   iii. Long Residence

A person who has remained in the UK legally for a period of 10 years, or illegally (including overstayer) for a period of 14 years, or combination of both for a period of between 10 and 14 years may be allowed to remain indefinitely in the UK. The grant of such leave is at the discretion of the Home Office.

16.5   iv. Four Years in Employment

Those granted leave to remain:

a)   as Writers, Composers and Artists.

b)   in Approved Employment.

c)   in 'Permit free employment' such as;

    i)   Ministers of Religion.

    ii)   Missionaries and Members of Religious Orders.

    iii)   Representatives of Overseas Newspapers.

    iv)   Representatives of News Agencies.

    v)   Representatives of Broadcasting Organisations.

    vi)   Representatives of Overseas Firms.

    vii)   A person employed by overseas government (but not a member of the diplomatic staff) or in the employment of the United Nations Organisation or other International Organisations of which the UK is a member.

  viii) Operational Ground Staff (not other staff) of Overseas Owned Airlines.

d)   in their own established business, including those allowed to remain as partners in a firm.

e)   in Self Employment.

f)   as Persons of Independent Means.

g)   Investors.

These categories of persons, together with their spouses and children under the age of 18 who are unmarried may be granted indefinite leave to remain if they have remained as such in the UK for a period of 4 years.

Immigration rules state that their application for permanent residence will be considered in the light of all the relevant circumstances, and in the case of a person in employment whether the employer wishes to continue to employ him; and in the case of a self employed person, whether he wishes to remain in business.

16.6   v.   Refugees

A person who has been granted the status of refugee and has remained in that capacity for up to 4 years together with his family, should be granted an indefinite leave to remain in the UK. An asylum-seeker granted exceptional leave to remain, renewable, and if so renewed for a period of 7 years, together with his family, should also be granted an indefinite leave to remain in the UK.

16.7   vi.   E.E.A. Nationals and Residence Permit Holders

EEA nationals who have been granted a 5 year residence visa and have worked in the UK continuously for 4 years may, together with their family members, be granted indefinite leave to remain.

16.8   vii. Where Grandparent of a Person was born in the UK

A Commonwealth citizen who is aged 17 or over, and can prove that one of his/her grandparents was born in the UK, may be granted an entry clearance to take up or seek employment in the UK. Having remained in the UK for a period of 4 years as such, he may be granted an indefinite leave to remain.

16.9 viii. Those Joining Settled Relatives in the UK

Those who are allowed to join their settled relatives in the UK may eventually be allowed to remain permanently. Although there is no provision in the rules for adults to come to, or remain in the UK with children who are underage either because they are born here or they need the care and attention of their parents, an application outside the immigration rules may be considered. Please seek advice before making such an application.

16.10 ix. Private Servants in Diplomatic Households

The new immigration rules now make provisions for Indefinite Leave to Remain for Domestic Servants of Diplomatic Households.

16.11 x. Home Secretary's Discretion Outside the Rules

The Home Secretary, as earlier mentioned, has abundant discretion within or even outside the immigration rules, to grant any person deemed to be so entitled an indefinite leave to remain in the UK. The main reason for mentioning this point is the fact that there are many policies which Home Office officials follow, and any application made outside the normal immigration rules should be made carefully. Expert advice should also be sought before such application is made.

16.12 LOSING YOUR INDEFINITE LEAVE TO REMAIN

It is not quite difficult to loose one's permanent residence and, for this reason, we strongly advise those who may qualify for **Naturalisation** to apply for it at the earliest opportunity.

You may lose your indefinite leave to remain in the following ways:-

16.13   (a). Staying Away for More Than 2 Years

A person who stays away from the UK for more than 2 years may find it difficult to enter and or remain in the UK. Although such a person may be granted entry, he may have to face rigorous questioning. The basis on which the indefinite leave was granted in the first instance may then become relevant. Therefore, a person who acquired his indefinite leave through marriage may find the subsistence of the marriage an important factor, together with full explanation as to why he had stayed for such a long period of time.

16.14   (b). Change of Habitual Residence

A person who is considered as having changed his habitual residence in the UK, whether or not he has been away for less than two years, may not be re-admitted as a returning resident, although may be allowed to enter as a visitor or for any other temporary purpose. *Anyone who has been away for less than two years, considered at the airport to have changed or lost his UK habitual residence, and possibly granted entry as a visitor or in a temporary capacity, may nevertheless apply to the Home Office so that his indefinite leave may be restored. Please seek professional advice where you find yourself in this situation.*

16.15   (c) Indefinite Leave Through Fraud

Where it is later discovered by the Home Office that the indefinite leave was obtained through fraud (fraud here covers any type of deception), such leave may be withdrawn.

16.16   (d) Reason of National Security

Non-British citizens, including a person who has an indefinite leave to remain, may be refused entry into the UK if the Home Secretary directs that their exclusion from the UK is conducive to the public good in the interests of national security.

16.17   (e)   Criminal Convictions

A person who commits criminal offence which is punishable with imprisonment of a term of 12 months or more whilst in the UK may be recommended by the Court for deportation.

Also, a person who may have an Indefinite Leave to Remain, may be refused re-admission on the grounds of criminal convictions in any country, including the UK, of an offence which is punishable with imprisonment for a term of 12 months or more. Equally, a passenger of undesirable character, conduct or association, may also be refused re-admission.

Contrary to general belief, indefinite leave is not as definite as it sounds as this leave can be revoked for reasons of criminal convictions or public good. Also, whenever you leave the UK, your Indefinite Visa lapses and your readmission is at the discretion of the Immigration Officer at the port of entry. For this reason, therefore, it is wise to secure permanent residence by becoming a British Citizen at the earliest opportunity by way of Naturalisation.

FOOTNOTES

1.   *HC 395 paragraph 308*

Chapter 17

ASYLUM SEEKERS AND REFUGEES

17.1   INTRODUCTION

It is noted that quite a large number of people do not know the difference between an asylum seeker and a refugee. An asylum seeker is a person who is seeking leave to remain for protection from his home country and whose application may be pending at the Home Office for consideration. When an application for asylum is considered favourably by the Home Office, this person is granted leave to remain as a refugee.   The words asylum seekers and refugee are used interchangeably.

17.2   WHO IS A REFUGEE?

A refugee is a person who:

OWING TO A WELL FOUNDED FEAR OF BEING PERSECUTED
for reasons of;

-    Race,
-    Religion,
-    Nationality,
-    Membership of Social Group or Political Opinion, who is outside his country of nationality and is unable to, or owing to such a fear, is unwilling to avail himself of his country's protection, or who, not having a nationality (i.e. stateless) and being outside the country of his former habitual residence, is unable or unwilling to return to it OWING TO SUCH FEAR.[1]

In simple terms refugees are people seeking protection in other countries because they fear persecution in their own country for reasons stated above. Certain rights and protection are afforded refugees as a result of the Geneva Convention of 1951 relating to the Status of Refugees (as amended by the Protocol to the Convention 1967), and the United Kingdom has adopted the practice of treating anybody granted asylum as a refugee with the rights and protection emanating from the said Convention.

17.3   WELL FOUNDED FEAR

Well founded fear is the recognised type of reaction which a reasonable bystander will expect from persons in the claimant's situation or position. This fear must be verifiable and newspaper cuttings, photographs, documents and other helpful pieces of information may be useful to substantiate or prove the fear. This fear must be linked to a real likelihood of persecution. While the asylum seeker has to prove that there is a real likelihood of such a persecution, he is not bound to demonstrate that such a persecution will occur. It will be sufficient to show that there is a serious possibility of persecution.

17.4   PERSECUTION

The word 'persecution' will include any form of Oppression, Harassment or Maltreatment, and these will cover a wide variety of activities. The fact that the persecuting body or organisation seek to justify their activities would not necessarily defeat the applicant's claims.

Therefore, it may be possible to recognise such persecution in times of civil war where unlawful means are being used or where atrocities are being perpetrated against a particular ethnic or religious group, although mere hardship due to war is not on its own a good ground. A good example is the case of the Tamils sent back to Sri Lanka after the Secretary of State had rejected their asylum claim because he considered that the death or destruction feared was a consequence of civil war.[2]

The adjudicator found on the evidence that there was a history of racial discrimination and hatred by the Sri Lankan Army, who in turn perpetrated atrocities against civilians creating risks of persecution for reasons of race, religion or political opinion.

The case was decided in favour of the appellants and the government was eventually asked to return them to the UK.[2] Persecution does not necessarily have to be threatened or perpetrated by the government. It will be enough where a particular group within the populace is the oppressor and the Government tolerates their oppressive acts or turn a blind eye to them. Furthermore, an impending persecution would still be acknowledged even where the applicant could have relocated in another part of his country or country of residence **where such a relocation exercise will be unreasonable.**

17.5   PROSECUTION

Although, prosecution (especially for common law offences) would normally not be regarded as persecution, it may be regarded as such where a fair trial is likely to be denied or where there is evidence that the prosecution is being conducted for political reasons.

17.6   REFUGEES AND COMMON PROBLEMS

One major source of concern is that a lot of people will not be able to leave their countries of origin as quickly as necessary (for purposes of seeking asylum) even where there is genuine fear of persecution, because of the penalties for carriers who bring in passengers without entry clearance[3] . Even though the immigration authorities have declared that carriers will not be penalised if the passenger is subsequently accepted as a genuine refugee, how many carriers will like to run that risk? Compounding this problem is the fact that there is no provision for applying for entry clearance as a refugee.

Furthermore, it is not uncommon for carriers to be owned by National Governments and, for asylum seekers to be fleeing from this same governments. How then will such carriers bring such people on explanation that they are coming to the UK as asylum seekers?

Finally, the transition from arrival in the UK to the grant of asylum is not an easy task. Growing discontent among UK residents as well as abuses perpetrated by bogus asylum seekers have not made the journey for asylum-seekers any easier.

17.7 SEEKING ASYLUM AT PORT OF ENTRY

Changes in the immigration rules make it mandatory for cases to be referred to the Home Office where a person claims asylum at the port of entry or where he or she appears likely to be eligible for asylum as a result of what he says. Asylum will not be refused if the only country to which the applicant can be removed is one to which he is unwilling to go owing to a well founded fear of persecution for reasons of race, religion etc.

Until an asylum application has been determined by the Secretary of State, no action will be taken to require the departure of the asylum applicant or his dependants from the United Kingdom. (There are now, however, limitations to this statement of the law introduced by the new Asylum and Immigration Law, 1996, see chapter 22 for such limitations.)

A considerable amount of time may be needed to establish the fear of the applicant and it is not uncommon for such an applicant to be detained initially at the port and subsequently at a refugee camp or detention centre. Where application for asylum is being considered by the Home Office, temporary admission may be granted. Where the applicant is detained but temporary admission is not granted, a bail application can be made.

Where the application for asylum is successful, the applicant is granted leave to remain.

17.8   SEEKING ASYLUM AFTER ENTRY

Since fear of persecution may develop at any time, it is not uncommon for people to apply for asylum after having gained entry through other temporary means. This may either be because the event leading to the fear is new or because they have only just decided to put in their applications. The fact that such an application was not made on entry should not of itself be a reason for refusal. Just as those making their application at the port of entry, applicants who are already in the UK will have to be formally identified so that investigations of their claims may be conducted. Applicants will also be interviewed in connection with their claims.

An application can be made to the Home Office in writing or in person and applicant will be required to produce the following documents:-

17.9   Proof of Identity

Applicant's passport(s) and, if applicable, passports of the applicant's spouse, children and any other dependants.

Where an applicant's passport is unavailable, other documentary evidence to establish identity (name and date of birth) and nationality are needed, for example, ID/membership cards, birth/marriage/school certificates are needed.

17.10   Proof of Accommodation

An applicant will have to show proof of where he is currently living (not correspondence address) and such proof should show applicant's full name and address, for example, recent bank statements, building society book, medical card, housing benefit book, tenancy agreement, driver's licence, telephone/electricity/gas bill etc.

Where the applicant is living in someone else's house, he will have to provide a letter from his householder/host confirming his permission for the applicant to stay at that address, together with this person's proof of accommodation which shows his full name and address, preferably from the above list of documents.

17.11   Proof of Entry

The Home Office would like to know from an applicant how or in what manner he entered the UK; and while some people may have travelled to the UK with their own passports, it is noted that there are some categories of people who may have entered the UK, sometimes with British or EC passports, in which case there would not be any record of their entries.

17.12   Passport Photographs

The applicant will also have to give to the Home Office his recently taken 3 coloured passport photographs and, where applicable, those of his spouse, children and other dependants. .

Where the application for asylum is successful, the applicant is allowed to remain as a refugee. Where the application is, however refused, there would normally be a right of appeal.

17.14   CRIMINAL CONDUCT AFFECTING REFUGEES

Where, after admission into the UK or grant of refugee status, an asylum-seeker or refugee is discovered to have committed a war crime, crime against humanity or any serious non-political crime, he may lose the protection afforded under the Convention and may be expelled from the UK.[4]

It is very important to give accurate information while answering questions about one's personal details in the asylum questionnaire. Such questions will include the applicant's Age, Nationality, Family background, Marital Status, Political Affiliation, number of children and dependants, together with the reasons for fear of persecution as claimed.

It is equally important to give the right details of one's spouse and children as they may benefit from the final grant, if the application is successful.
In considering the application, the Home Office will be particularly interested in establishing;

259

- whether you had problems obtaining your passport or leaving your country,

- whether you support any political party or religious organisation, stating the names or founders, aims and objectives, branches and your position in the group,

- why you chose to come to the UK in spite of your stop over in a third country, and the reason why you did not claim asylum in this other country,

- whether or not you or any family members were detained or harassed in country of persecution, requesting details of dates and place of detention, how you or the person detained were released, and whether or not you or the person were charged or sentenced to any terms of imprisonment,

- your educational qualifications, including dates of institutions attended,

- your employment records, including dates, position held, and names and addresses of employers,

- whether or not you are a member of an organisation in the UK, providing details of such organisation and rallies you may have attended,

- whether or not you have any criminal convictions abroad or in the UK,

- whether or not you have completed or eligible for military service in your country, and

- the genuineness of your fear of persecution.

The Home Office's acknowledgement which identifies the applicant normally states that he should not engage in employment (paid or unpaid). If, however, the application has not been resolved within six months of its making, the applicant may then apply to the Home Office for a work permit.

This acknowledgement is also very important as it must be produced when the applicant applies for welfare benefits, (see figure 17.28).

17.16   RECOGNITION OF REFUGEE STATUS

Once recognised as a refugee, a person should be given a UN identity document known as travel document. Furthermore, the Convention requires that refugees should be given similar treatment accorded to nationals of the country granting asylum. Current UK practice therefore is to treat refugees in the same manner as those who have indefinite leave to remain, as regards employment, housing, education, health care as well as welfare benefits.

Also, a refugee is entitled to bring his family members to the UK, and he becomes eligible for indefinite leave to remain once he has spend 4 years as a refugee.

17.17   TRANSFERRING REFUGEE STATUS FROM ONE COUNTRY TO ANOTHER

Although there is no right for a refugee to have asylum transferred to a Country in which he is temporary resident in the European Countries, member states of the Council have an agreement on transfer of responsibilities. They have provided for transfer of responsibility but only after 2 years of continuous and lawful residence in one country which is not for the purpose of study, training, medical treatment or a period of imprisonment.

17.18   DUAL NATIONALS

A person who is a citizen of two countries will not qualify for asylum in the UK if he fears persecution in one of his countries of nationality, but without a valid reason based on a well founded fear, has not sought the protection of his second country of nationality.

17.19   THIRD COUNTRY REFUSAL

An application for asylum is expected to be made at the first safe country where the passenger arrives. Where an applicant is found to have come to the UK through another country which is considered safe, his application may be refused for this reason and the applicant may be referred back, and removed to, this other country. However, where the applicant has close relatives in the UK, his application may be considered and may not be refused for the same reason as mentioned above. 'Close relatives' will include spouse, parents and children.

17.20   Important Points to Note

1.   Asylum will usually be granted on merit where the only country to which the asylum seeker could be removed is one where persecution is feared, or where there are risks that any other available country to which such a person may be removed will return him, or facilitate his return to the country of persecution.

2.   Where an application for asylum is refused, the applicant may be removed to a country from which he embarked, including the country from which he feared persecution. Right of appeal against the asylum refusal or against destination may be possible.

3.   A person without a current permission to take employment may apply to the Home Office for such permission if his asylum application has not been resolved within six months. Also, the present Standard Acknowledgement Letter (SAL) being issued by the Home Office is valid until a decision has been taken on the application. Where an application is refused, the Home Office now request the return of the SAL.

4.   While the application is pending, applicants are usually requested to attend the Home Office for identification purpose and for fingerprinting. On this occasion, a document informing the applicant not to work (though he may recourse to welfare benefits) is usually given. Three passport photographs are requested.

- Confirmation from the Law Society of the applicant's ability to practice in the UK,

- Evidence of financial means to establish a new legal practice in the UK,

- evidence of maintenance and accommodation and for any dependants without having to recourse to public funds, or do any other work except in the practice.

13.41   Other Useful Information

An Entry Clearance Officer will, in the course of the interview, like to know what will become of the applicant's practice in his home country and details of his future plans regarding his practice in the UK and at home.

Note that foreign lawyers under this category do not have a right of audience in the UK court except such rights as derived from European Union law or Commonwealth custom. This is because they are not admitted as Solicitors in the UK. *Those wishing to qualify as Solicitors would have to re-qualify by way of 'Qualified Lawyers' Transfer Test.* This test is for those who have a right to remain and work in the UK.

A foreign lawyer who needs the permission of his Home Bar to practice abroad will be asked to provide a copy of the authorisation from the Home Bar to practice abroad. Details of any requirements imposed by the Home Bar should also be included.

While this category concerns registration or approval by the Law Society in the UK, anyone interested in becoming a Barrister in the UK may contact the General Council of the Bar.

For further information about the letter of confirmation from the Law Society (or the Bar Council), the following addresses and telephone numbers are provided:-

The Law Society   **The General Council of the Bar**

50 Chancery Lane   3 Bedford Row
London WC2A 1SX   WC1R 4DB
Tel: 0171 242 1222   Tel: 0171 242 0082

13.42   Settlement and Family

A person who qualifies under this category, together with his spouse and any dependants under the age of 18 should be granted leave to enter for a initial period of 12 months. Their leave to remain may be extended for another three years after which an application for indefinite leave to remain could be made.

13.43   RETIRED PERSONS OF INDEPENDENT MEANS

A person seeking admission into the UK as a retired person of independent means must have entry clearance for this purpose.[13] There has been slightly change in this area compared with the old rule.

13.44   Conditions for Entry Clearance

The conditions for entry clearance are that:

i)   is at least 60 years old;

ii)   has under his control in the UK a disposable income of his own of not less than £25,000 per annum;

iii)   is able and willing to maintain and accommodate himself and any dependants indefinitely in the UK from his own resources with no assistance from any other person and *without taking employment* or having recourse to public funds;

iv)   can demonstrate a *close connection with the UK*; and

v)   intends to make the UK his main home.

Minimum age is now set at 60 years. This is in recognition of the fact that younger people are more than likely to want to establish themselves in employment or business. This means that a person may not retire on health grounds under the age of 60 and be allowed to enter or remain in this capacity except possibly outside the immigration rules. Previously income disposable income was fixed at £20,000 pounds per annum or capital of £200,000 pounds, but now the immigration rules specify £25,000 pounds disposable income only.

A passenger with an entry clearance for this purpose may be admitted for an initial period of 4 years. Where the period is less than 4 years, extensions which may bring the total period to an **aggregate** of 4 years may be possible.

'Aggregate' means sum total of period spent in the UK.

13.45   CLARIFICATION OF VARIOUS TERMS AND PHRASES

13.46   *Without taking Employment:-*

'Taking employment' as mentioned above covers paid employment as well as self-employment; therefore, while establishing a business may be permissible, the day to day running of such a business would have to be carried out by other people.

While investment in property generating income may be acceptable, buying houses which involve property management by the applicant may not be acceptable as such management function will be construed as work. A person in this category who wishes to engage in business will have to delegate the day to day running of such business.

13.47   *Close Connection with the UK:-*

'Close Connection' will be interpreted in the light of the circumstances of each individual case. Close connection includes having close relatives in the UK and a period of previous residence by the applicant may , on its own, constitute a close connection.

13.48   Settlement and Family

A person in this category, together with his spouse and children under the age of 18 may be granted an indefinite leave to remain after having remained in the UK for an aggregate period of 4 years and has made the UK his main home.

13.49   INVESTORS

This provision is new in the present immigration rules[14] and it appears to be aimed at boosting the flow of capital form abroad by self-sufficient persons coming to the UK to invest. Entry clearance is required for this purpose. A 12 months visa will initially be granted. This is renewable for a total period of 4 years. There is no age requirement. **Professional advice should be sought when making an application under this category.**

The requirements to be met by such an investor are that he:-

i)   has money of his own under his control and disposable in the UK amounting to no less than £1 million; and

ii)   intends to invest not less than £750,000 of his capital in the UK by way of UK, in UK government bonds, share capital or loan capital in active and trading UK registered companies (other than those principally engaged in property investment and excluding investment by the applicant by way of deposits with a bank, building society or other enterprise whose normal course of business includes the acceptance of deposits); and

iii)   intends to make the UK his main home; and

iv)   is able to maintain and accommodate himself and any dependants without taking employment (other than self-employment or business) or recourse to public funds.

v)   holds a valid UK entry clearance for entry in this capacity.

13.50   Type of Investment

An Applicant can invest in:-

● **Unit Trust** provided £750,000 is invested in companies which meet the requirements of the Investors Rules.

● **Private Companies** where he has share holdings or loan certificates in the form of legal documents, of not less than £750,000 .

Please note that applicants may not invest the required sum of £750,000 in Property or Off-Shore Companies, Banks or Building Societies, although they may invest extra capital in these organisations.

13.51   Employment

An Applicant in this category may not be allowed to work as an employee of any company including that where he invests the required money, although he may be allowed to engage in business or self-employment, for example as a non-executive director. He may also be allowed to inject capital other than the said £750,000 in another business.

13.52   Settlement and Family

A person who has been in the UK under this category for a period of 4 years, together with his spouse and children under the age of 18 may be granted Indefinite Leave to Remain provided he continues to fulfil the above requirements.

FOOTNOTES

1. *HC 395 paragraph 169*
2. *HC 395 paragraph 170*
3. *HC 395 paragraph 137*
4. *HC 395 paragraph 152*
5. *HC 395 paragraph 158*
6. *HC 395 paragraph 160*
7. *HC 395 paragraph 110*
8. *HC 395 paragraph 178*
9. *HC 395 paragraph 186*
10. *C(an infant) 1976.........AR 165*
11. *HC 395 paragraph 200 & 210*
12. *HC 395 paragraph 213 , 214, 218 & 219 as amended with effect from April 1996.*
13. *HC 395 paragraph 263*
14. *HC 395 paragraph 224*

Chapter 14

CHILDREN BORN IN THE UK

14.1   INTRODUCTION

All children born in the UK before the 1st of January 1983 are British by birth, unless they are:-

● Children born to certain members of diplomatic or consular missions in the UK.

UK means England, Wales, Scotland and Northern Ireland (excluding the Republic of Ireland).

As the principle of citizenship by birth was abandoned on the 1st of January 1983, a child born in the UK from that date can only be a British citizen if at least one of his parents is:

● British, or

● 'settled' in the UK or

● where the child is born out of wedlock, to a British or settled mother.

14.2   WHERE PARENTS ARE MARRIED

Where the parents are married the status of either of the parents can confer citizenship on the child. For example, if the mother has permanent residence at the birth of the child, and the father has a student visa, *the child is a British citizen.*

14.3   WHERE PARENTS ARE NOT MARRIED

Where parents are not married, the nationality or immigration status of the mother is the one that counts. Therefore, even if the father is a British citizen or settled and the mother is on a temporary visa (e.g. as student), *the child is not a British citizen.* However, the new immigration rules allow an application to be made for Indefinite Leave to Remain for such a child where this child is under the age of 18, unmarried, not leading an independent life and has not formed an independent family unit, where his father is a British citizen.

But where the mother is a British citizen or settled at the birth of the child, and the father is not, *the child is a British citizen.*

14.4   Other Relevant Points

Although the United Kingdom recognises dual nationality, some countries do not. It is therefore important for parents to be familiar with their home country's law about conferring or denying Citizenship on children born abroad. This is because where both parents have permanent residence in the UK and they still keep their home country's passports (e.g. Indian passport) or nationality, although their child is British by birth, the law of their home country may not confer its nationality on the child.

14.5   IMMIGRATION STATUS OF
NON-BRITISH CHILDREN

A child born in the UK after 31st of December 1982 who is not a British citizen at birth will be subject to immigration control. However, such a child will be allowed to remain in the UK without asking for permission to do so, and there is nothing illegal about their so remaining.

Problems can only arise if:

● the child's parents are being deported or removed, or

●   the child leaves the UK for any reason, and later seeks to re-enter.

Therefore:

1.   Where the parents are being deported, the child may be deported at the same time. But where one parent is being deported, the child may be allowed to remain, if the remaining parent is willing to, and capable of, looking after him.

2.   If the child leaves the UK, he will be subject to entry control on returning, and might not be re-admitted. However, the rules for the re-entry of such a child are slightly different from those affecting children born abroad. For this reason, therefore, the admission of this child born in the UK is not dependent on:

-   meeting maintenance and accommodation requirements,

-   neither do both parents need to be present in the UK.

14.6   Children Born in the Republic of Ireland

A child born in the Republic of Ireland is not affected by the above. In other words, children born in the Republic of Ireland are born Irish regardless of their parents nationality or immigration status, although their citizenship should be formalised by way of registration which can be done at any time. What is needed for such registration is the child's Birth certificate.

An example is the case of someone   who is a student in the UK. Since she did not need a visa to travel to Ireland she went and had her baby there, and she returned to London with a European (Irish) Passport for her child.

It should also be noted that parents of a child born Irish can apply to remain with their child in Ireland, provided they are not a threat to the state because of criminal propensities. This is so not withstanding their immigration status in the UK or in Ireland and they are generally allowed to remain.

14.7   Practical Approach

Parents of a non-British child born in the UK who, at the end of their temporary stay, are returning home finally, may consider an application for leave to remain for this child most especially where the child has reached the age of 7 years. This visa can be stamped on a separate passport for the child. The child does not have anything to lose by applying for Indefinite Leave to Remain and where this is refused, it does not take or diminish the child's right, now or in the future. You may wish to seek advice before making an application as suggested.

Alternatively, an application for registration of the child could be made as the child will probably fulfil other requirements for registration except the 10 year residence requirement. The Home Secretary has the discretion to consider such application favourably, and the child does not lose anything even where this application is refused. Such a child can re-apply once he fulfils the 10 year residence requirement. [See chapter 15 for discussion on Registration]

Also, where a child is born out of wedlock and the mother is on temporary visa (e.g. as a student) but the father is a British citizen or has a Right of Abode in the UK, this child can apply for Indefinite Leave to Remain which is usually granted. It is also possible to make such an application outside the immigration rules where the father only possesses indefinite leave to remain.

14.8   Criteria to be Met for Re-entry

Where a child who has no settled status seeks re-admission to the UK, he would normally be granted leave to enter for the same period as his parents, if there is evidence that he:

●   is under the age of 18, and

●   is not leading an independent life, is unmarried, and has not formed an independent family unit, and

- he was born in the UK, and

- he has not been away from the UK for more than 2 years.

14.9   Important Points to Note

1. Where a child is seeking re-entry and the parents have or are granted leave of different duration, the child may be granted leave for whichever period is longer, except that if the parents are living apart, the child may be granted leave for the same period as the parent who has his day-to-day responsibility.

2. A child born in the UK out of wedlock to a British father who is seeking re-entry, may be granted permanent residence where this father has *responsibility* for him.

3. Where parental rights and duties are vested solely in a Local Authority and the child qualifies for admission or is already in the UK, indefinite leave to enter/remain should be granted.[3]

4. Where a child's parents have no leave to remain, the child may not be allowed to come to the UK. A child may, however, be allowed in for a period of 3 months:

    -    where both parents are in the UK and

    -    it appears unlikely that they will be removed in the immediate future (e.g. parents on appeal for refusal of an application, as opposed to appeal against an Intention to Deport), and

    -    there is no other person outside the UK who could reasonably be expected to look after him.

14.10   'PARENTS' RECOGNISED FOR IMMIGRATION PURPOSES

'Parent' for this purpose include:

- Step mother or father where his own father/mother is dead (therefore if his natural father or mother is still alive, the child may not be able to join, or come with his step-parent).

- Natural parent(s) even if the child is born out of wedlock.

- An adoptive parent but only where a child was adopted in accordance with a decision taken by the competent administrative authority or court in a country whose adoption orders are recognised by the United Kingdom.

- Any person to whom there has been a genuine transfer of parental responsibility on the grounds of the natural parents' inability to care for the child. (Step father/mother who would have been recognised but for the fact that the child's father/mother is still alive(see above), may come within this paragraph, though strong and cogent evidence must be adduced).

14.11   HOW THESE CHILDREN CAN BECOME BRITISH CITIZENS

Children born in the UK (although not British at birth) will be eligible for British Citizenship if one of the following situations arise:

1.   Where the child is born out of wedlock to a British or settled father and a non-British mother, the child will become British from the date of the parents marriage.

2.   Where the parents (or the mother, where unmarried) acquire indefinite leave after the birth of the child, the child may be registered as a British Citizen.

3.   Where the child is adopted in the UK by a British couple, the child is a British citizen.

4.   Where the child lives in the UK from the age of 0-10 years and has not been absent for more than 90 days in any of the 10 years, he is entitled to register as a British citizen. The Home Office also has the discretion and may choose to register a child who, on application, has been absent for more than 90 days in any one year; or who has not yet attained 10 years of age. ·

FOOTNOTES

1.   *HC 395 paragraph 308*
2   *HC 395 paragraph 308*
3   *HC 395 paragraph 305*

Chapter 15

ACQUIRING BRITISH CITIZENSHIP

15.1   INTRODUCTION

There are few ways of acquiring British citizenship; and it is also important to note that although British citizenship can be acquired by birth, not all children born in the UK are British citizens. Some people may also have to either Register as British or Naturalise to become British.

It is also worth mentioning that UK recognises dual nationality/citizenship; therefore, a person may be a British Citizen as well as a citizen of another country where the law of the other country allows for this.

British citizenship can, therefore, be acquired in the following ways:

15.2   BY BIRTH

The legal sources of British Citizenship are contained in the British Nationality Act of 1981 which abolished citizenship by birth in the UK. Children born in the UK after commencement of this Act, that is from the 1st of January, 1983 will only become British citizens if at least one of their parents is British or settled in the UK (or where the child is born out of wedlock to a British or settled mother). However where the mother is not British nor settled but the father is, the parents' subsequent marriage will give the child the status of a British Citizen.

15.3   Example:

Gillian who is from New Zealand gave birth to Dalroy in the UK. Dalroy's father, Mr Vandross, is a British Citizen. As Gillian and Mr Vandross are not married at the time of Dalroy's birth, then Dalroy is not a British Citizen.

It is also possible for a child to trace entitlement to British citizenship through a parent who had died before his or her birth, as 'parents' include the parent of a child born posthumously (i.e. born after the death, for example, of the father).

A child born in Britain but to non-settlers will have to register as a British at the appropriate time.

15.4   BY DESCENT:

The law provides for automatic transfer of citizenship for just one generation, except for those working abroad on Her Majesty's service. Persons born abroad after 31st of December 1982 are British Citizens if their father or mother is British at the time of their birth (or if the mother is British, where birth was out of wedlock). A child under this category is, thus, classified as British citizen by descent.

Parents who are British citizens by descent cannot normally transfer their citizenship to children born abroad, unless these parents are abroad on Her Majesty's service. British citizens by descent include those who have obtained citizenship by virtue of birth abroad to parents who are themselves British citizens by descent. Children born outside the UK and whose parents are British citizens by descent will have to register as British.

15.5   Example:

Mr and Mrs Kwegan who are both British by birth in the UK, went to the USA where they gave birth to Darlina. Darlina is a British citizen by descent and does not have to register as British. Where Darlina is not on Her Majesty's service, her children born outside the UK will have to register to become British.

For registration of such children, either of the following set of requirements must be fulfilled, taking Sophie as Darlina's child'

15.6 *i. WHERE THE APPLICATION IS MADE IN THE CHILD'S 1st YEAR*

- One of Sophie's grandparents Mr and Mrs Kwegan   must be British (which they both are).

- Sophie's parent(s) Darlina is a British citizen by descent.

- Darlina must have been in the UK for up to 3 years immediately before the birth of Sophie (with an absence, if any, of not more than 270 days).

15.7 *ii WHERE THE APPLICATION IS MADE AFTER THE CHILD'S 1st YEAR*

The additional requirements to the above three are:

- Sophie should be under 18 years old.

- Darlina and Sophie must have been in the UK for up to 3 years immediately before the date of application (with an absence, if any, of not more than 270 days).

15.8 ADOPTED CHILDREN

Children adopted in the UK will become British citizens if the adopting parents are British by the date of the Order. However adoption Orders made in foreign countries in favour of adopters who are British may make the adopted children eligible for registration as British citizen.

5.   A person refused asylum may be served at the same time with a notice of enforcement action, for example, notice as an illegal entrant or notice of intention to deport. Where this has happened, you will note in chapter 4 that once an enforcement action has commenced, application to remain on the basis of marriage will highly likely be refused.

17.21   FINGERPRINTING OF ASYLUM SEEKERS

Police and immigration officers are empowered to request any person who has made a claim for asylum, either at the port of entry or where already in the UK (together with his dependants) to be fingerprinted.

Police officers are now empowered to arrest without warrant, any person who should be fingerprinted but has failed to turn up after an invitation for such printing within a reasonable time e.g 7 days[5] . Such a person may then be detained until he is fingerprinted.

It is also important to note that failure to provide one's fingerprints may be taken into account when the Home Office is making a decision on the applicant's application.

17.22   REFUSAL OF ASYLUM APPLICATIONS
AND APPEALS

Asylum applications would normally be refused for reasons which include the following:-

●   where there is no well founded fear of persecution,

●   failure to make application at the first safe country,

●   where a person has committed a war crime or a crime against humanity,

263

- where the persecution which existed before fleeing ceases to exist,

- where a person of dual nationality failed to avail himself of the protection of his other country, and

- for reasons of national security.

Other factors which may lead to refusal of application include:-

- A failure, without reasonable explanation, to make prompt and full disclosure of material factors, either orally or in writing, or otherwise to assist the Secretary of State to the full in establishing the facts of the case may lead to refusal of an asylum application. This includes failure to comply with a notice issued by the Secretary of State requiring the applicant to report to a designated place to be fingerprinted, or failure to complete an asylum questionnaire, or failure to comply with a request to attend an interview concerning the application.

In determining an asylum application, the Secretary of State will have regard to matters which may damage an asylum applicant's credibility if no reasonable explanation is given. Among such matters are:-

a)   that the applicant has failed to apply forthwith upon arrival in the United Kingdom, unless the application is founded on events which have taken place since his arrival in the United Kingdom;

b)   that the applicant has made false representations, either orally or in writing;

c)   that the applicant has destroyed, damaged or disposed of any passport, other document or ticket relevant to his claim;

d)   that the applicant has undertaken any activities in the United Kingdom before or after lodging his application which are inconsistent with his previous beliefs and behaviour and calculated to create or substantially enhance his claim to refugee status;

e)	that the applicant has lodged concurrent applications for asylum in the United Kingdom and in another country;

f)	that the application is made after the applicant has been refused leave to enter under the 1971 Act, or has been recommended for deportation by a court empowered by the 1971 Act to do so,

g)	or has been notified of the Secretary of State's decision to make a deportation order against him or has been notified of his liability for removal.

If the Secretary of State concludes for these or any other reasons that an asylum applicant's account is not credible, the application will be refused.

The actions of anyone acting as an agent of the asylum applicant may also be taken into account in regard to the matters set out above.

Where an application for asylum is refused, either at the port of entry or where the application was made while already in the UK, there may be a right of appeal exercisable whilst the applicant is in the UK which must be exercised, commonly, within 10 days of the refusal notification. Their right of appeal is exercisable whilst in the UK regardless of circumstances of entry.

Please note that under the new social security rules, benefits (such as Income Support, employment and housing benefits) will no longer be paid to asylum-seekers appealing against a decision refusing their applications or to anyone who makes an asylum application having entered the UK for another reason.

## 17.23	EXCEPTIONAL LEAVE TO REMAIN

Where the Home Office recognises a person's fear of persecution but thinks that this risk of persecution will not remain for too long, or for any other reasons, it may grant such a person an Exceptional Leave to Remain. This person may be issued with the Home Office travel documents.

Exceptional leave is usually given on a year to year basis, and unlike refugee status, it does not carry with it any settlement at the end of 4 years. A person given an exceptional leave will have to wait for 4 years before he can be allowed to bring his family, while an indefinite leave may be granted after 7 years.

A person who has been granted this exceptional leave would have had his application for asylum refused and may have a right of appeal. Where his application is so refused, but there has been a grant of exceptional leave, he can still put his claim forward once again in order to upgrade his new status to that of a refugee.

Finally, a person with exceptional leave to remain will be treated as a person who has full refugee status as regards employment, housing, education, health and social benefits.

17.24   SECOND ASYLUM APPLICATION

It is possible to apply for asylum more than once. This is allowed because a person's fear for persecution can occur any time, and different reasons may prevail on different occasions.

Where a second or repeated application is made, the Home Office will treat this application as a fresh application to be considered on its own merit. However, the basis of new application must be quite distinct from the first one.

However, the Home Office, in considering whether to treat further material, representations or information as a fresh claim, it will disregard any material which:

- is not significant;
- is not credible; or
- was available to the applicant at the time when the previous application was refused or when any appeal was determined.

17.25   Example

Where the basis of claim for the 1st application is on the basis of Religion, the Home Office should treat a 2nd application on the basis of Politics as a fresh application. This second application will also go through the normal process, including a right of appeal, if applicable.

17.26   TRAVEL DOCUMENT

Travel document is issued by the Home Office and is meant to replace your passport which is rendered invalid as a result of your new status. It is more or less a passport valid for travel to all countries except your own country, but not everyone qualifies for it.

17.27   Who is entitled to a Travel Document

A travel document may be issued to a person who is lawfully resident in the United Kingdom and who:-

- Has been accepted in this country as a refugee under the terms of the 1951 United Nations Convention relating to the Status of Refugee or;

- Has been accepted as a Stateless person or;

- Is permanently resident in this country, and:

    * can show that he has been formally and unreasonably refused a passport by his own national authorities, or;

    * entered this country on a non national travel document which has expired.

- Has been granted exceptional leave to remain following an unsuccessful asylum application and:

    * The initial grant of exceptional leave to remain was made after the implementation of the Asylum and Immigration Appeals

Act 1993 (26 July 1993), or

* The initial grant of exceptional leave to remain was made before 26 July 1993 and he can show that he has been formally and unreasonably refused a passport by his own authorities.

17.28   Applying for a Travel Document

You will probably need the following documents:-

* Your passport(s) or travel document you held when you entered the UK (and those of your children, if applicable).

* Your police registration certificate, if applicable.

* If your name has changed since you entered the UK or since the issue of your last travel document, evidence confirming this change i.e. Marriage Certificate, Adoption Order, Deed Poll.

* Postal Orders for the correct fee made payable to 'The Accounting Officer, Home Office'. Cheques are not accepted.

* Two photographs (plus 2 photographs of each child included.)

If you cannot send the correct documents, you should try and provide proof of your lawful residence in the UK. These may include:

- Letters from past employers
- Letters from Government Departments

- Birth/Marriage Certificates

- Rent or Mortgage books

- Letters from your bank

All these documents are expected to cover all the time you have lived in the UK.

17.29   Fees Payable

No application will be considered unless it is accompanied by the correct fee. The respective fees are:

● Those people formally accepted as Refugees and
Stateless Persons - £18.

● All others £67 .

These fees will not be refunded if the application is unsuccessful.

For further information, you may telephone Home Office (Travel Documents) on: *0181 760 2345*

17.30   Settlement and Family

A person who is granted exceptional leave to remain for a total period of 7 year may be granted Indefinite Leave to Remain. Also, a person, granted a refugee status may be granted the same after 4 years as a refugee. Their wives and dependent under 18 years old may also be granted permanent residence.

17.31   CEASING TO BE A REFUGEE

A person who has been granted asylum in the UK may lose this status on,

● acquisition of new nationality or by voluntary re-acquisition of his old nationality,

● voluntary re-establishment in the country of persecution,

● voluntary acquisition of passport from the Embassy or Consulate Office of Country of persecution as opposed to acquisition of Convention Documents which will be given to refugees for short visits.

Actual cessation of refugee status will not automatically mean repatriation as the refugee may have been granted Indefinite Leave to Remain in the UK.

17.32   Mixed Appeals

Perhaps this is one other advantage available to asylum appellants which must be stressed. The rules allow asylum seekers who are appealing against the Home Secretary's decision to refuse their asylum application to be able to appeal against any other decision where there is usually no such right.

FOOTNOTES

1.   *Article 1 Geneva Convention relating to status of Refugees 1951 (as amended by the protocol to the convention 1967)*

2.   *Sivakumara (House of Lords)*

3.   *Immigration Carrier's Liability Act 1987 (also Carrier's Liability Order 1991 SI*

4.   *Article 1(f) Geneva Convention relating to status of refuges*

5.   *Section 5: 1993 Act*

Fig 17.33

Immigration and Nationality Department

Lunar House 40 Wellesley Road
Croydon CR9 2BY
Telephone: 071-760

HOME OFFICE

ind

HO Reference:

Name: ....

Forename: ....

Date and place of birth: ....

Nationality: ....

Passport number: ....

Date and place of arrival: ....

....

Address in UK: ....

....

....

Accompanied by:
(Please notify any
change in address)   ....

....

Signature: ....

The above named has applied for asylum in the UK and this is under consideration. The applicant may not take employment paid or unpaid. Permission to take employment may be granted if the application for asylum has not been resolved within a period of six months. Any application to take employment should be accompanied by this acknowledgment, which will be endorsed accordingly.

Signature: ....   IND & I Stamp

NI Number: ....

This form must be surrendered to the Immigration Department on completion of consideration of asylum claim or departure from the UK.

Chapter 18

APPEALS

18.1   INTRODUCTION

Immigration law allows those aggrieved or dissatisfied with entry clearance or immigration officers' decisions to appeal against such decisions. But some appeal rights will only be exercisable after the passenger or appellant has left the UK, even though the appeal hearing is still going to take place in the UK.

Those who have to appeal whilst still in their home country will not be granted visa to come to the UK to attend the hearing, but may have contacts in the UK who will represent them or instruct legal representatives on their behalf.

Those who remain in the UK to present their appeal are not in breach of any landing conditions, neither are they to be regarded or treated as overstayers. *The effect of the appeal is to freeze the position of their stay in the UK pending the determination of their appeal, its withdrawal or when the appellant leaves the UK (as the case may be).* Notice of refusal of application and of his right of appeal (where applicable) will normally be handed, or sent, to applicant's last known address or his Legal representative.

Right of appeal is the right to be heard by an independent body or different tribunal apart from the decision maker.

18.2   WHAT YOU MAY APPEAL AGAINST

Subject to certain exceptions and qualifications, appeals can be made against the following cases:

- refusal of entry clearance
- refusal of leave to enter
- refusal to vary leave to remain
- refusal to extend leave to remain
- inclusion/addition of condition such as one prohibiting employment
- curtailment of leave to remain
- refusal to remove conditions attached to leave to remain
- decision to deport
- refusal to revoke deportation order
- the validity of directions to remove an illegal entrant
- removal to a particular country or destination.

Where appeal rights are to be exercised back in one's home country, the necessary papers should be submitted to the British Consulate or High Commission, while those whose rights are exercisable in the UK should have their papers filed with the:

> Appeals Section
> Home Office
> Lunar House
> CROYDON
> CR9 2BY

(or as may be directed by the appeal papers)

When an appeal is lodged, an acknowledgement letter confirming that the appeal has been lodged will be sent to the appellant. Where such an appellant is in the UK, this paper is proof that he can remain in the UK pending his appeal.

Any restriction or prohibition on working ceases to exist once on appeal, though it may be advisable not to work in certain instances, particularly where the chances of success in appeal are bright negative inferences can be drawn if found working.

18.3 WHAT YOU CANNOT APPEAL AGAINST

There is no right of appeal against the following:-

1)   A Refusal of entry clearance, or entry (leave to enter) for:

- Visitors,

- Prospective Students, and

- Students who are accepted on a course for less than 6 months duration, and their dependants, *unless they have valid entry clearance when they seek entry.*

2)   A refusal of entry clearance or entry (leave to enter) on the grounds that the applicant or any person whose dependant he is:-

- 'does not hold a document' which is required by the immigration rules, or

- does not satisfy age or nationality requirements as stipulated by the immigration rules, or

- seeks entry for a period exceeding that permitted by the immigration rules.

3)   A refusal to vary leave or extend leave on the grounds that the applicant or any person whose dependant he is:-

- does not hold 'a document' which is required by the immigration rules because it ' has not been issued', or

- does not satisfy age or nationality requirement as stipulated by the immigration rules, or

- has requested for the variation or extension which will allow in the duration of the person's leave to exceed that which is permitted by the immigration rules, or

- has not paid a fee required by law.

A person who has no right of appeal against refusal may be issued a notification of an intention to deport where it is found out that he has not embarked.

18.4   APPEAL RIGHTS WHICH ARE EXERCISABLE OUTSIDE THE UK

It is possible to appeal against:-

● refusal to grant entry clearance.

● refusal of entry where the passenger arrives without an entry clearance or work permit

● refusal to revoke a deportation order.

● the validity of directions to remove someone as an illegal entrant.

● Home Secretary's certificate regarding safe 3rd country (asylum matter).

For some reasons, Immigration Law does not allow appeal against certain decisions, though where there is no such right of appeal, judicial review may be available.

Equally, those whose appeals are exercisable from outside the UK but are given temporary admission, may also be able to apply for Judicial Review in very limited circumstances whilst in the UK.[1]

It is important to note that leave to apply for Judicial Review is commonly refused where the aggrieved person still has rights of appeal, whether in or outside the UK.

18.5   Example:

Mr Shah, who has been in the UK for the past 6 years as a student travelled home to Pakistan. He had up to six months left of his student visa, but on his return to the UK he was refused entry to resume his studies. He was nevertheless granted a temporary admission for 7 days. As Mr Shah still has a right of appeal exercisable outside the UK, Judicial Review may not be entertained.

18.6   THOSE WITH NO RIGHTS OF APPEAL

There will be no right of appeal against the following decisions:-

- where the Home Secretary personally makes the decision to make someone a prohibited immigrant.

- curtailment of leave for reason of National Security or other Political reasons.

- a decision to deport for reasons of National Security or other Political reasons.

- where the Home Secretary personally decides that the departure of an immigrant from the UK is conducive to the public good.

- variation of leave where the applicant seeks variation after the expiry of an existing leave.

- refusal to extend 'packing up time'. Packing up time is the period of 28 days which the Home Office usually gives to whoever is refused further extension or variation, and those who withdraw their application before it has been decided.[2]

- where the making of a deportation order is on the recommendation of a Court (not Immigration Tribunal), but there is a right of appeal to a higher Court (Crown Court or Court of Appeal) against this recommendation itself.

18.7   TIME LIMIT FOR APPEALS

Anyone appealing against the decision of the Home Office, Immigration Officer or Officer or Entry Clearance Officer must do so within a certain period of time stipulated in the appeal documents, otherwise, you will lose your right of appeal. To guide against loosing your right of appeal, it is important that you provide the authorities with your forwarding address at all times. The following time limits may be applicable:

- *3 months period:* for appeals from overseas against refusal of entry clearance or certificate of entitlement

- *28 days period:* against refusal of leave to enter, refusal to revoke a deportation order and against the validity of directions for removal.

- *14 days period:* applies to the remainder of appeals especially refusal of extension or variation.

- *7 days period:* applies to asylum application refused.

- *5 days period:* applies to asylum appeal hearing from Adjudicator for leave to the Tribunal.

- *2 days period:* applies to asylum application refused under the fast track procedure see chapter 22.

Please note that time Begins To Run from the date of decision or action in most cases, and the appeal papers should reach its destination before the time runs out. Appeal papers should be sent by recorded delivery. These papers must be signed to make them valid.

18.8   MERITS AND PRESENTATIONS OF APPEALS

An appeal lodged within the required time limit will be assumed to be valid. An appeal may either be to the Home Office, an Adjudicator or Immigration Appeals Tribunal (I.A.T). The offices of the Adjudicator and Tribunal are referred to as appellate authorities. Where an appeal is to the Home Office it will, as soon as practicable, prepare what is called an explanatory statement of facts which should set out the facts they are relying upon, that is, a summary of their side of the case. When you lodge your appeal, the receiving authority will formally acknowledge by sending a letter to the appellant.

The appellate authorities will:

i)   send to the appellant a copy of the said explanatory statement,

ii)   as soon as it is practicable, fixed a date for the hearing of the appeal, and

iii)   notify the appellant and the Home Office of the date, time and place of the hearing.

18.9   Merits

It is important to weigh the merits of a case as soon as possible. This is because as you may already know, representation at the appeal can be expensive where you are not representing yourself or where you are not being represented by a charitable organisation. Legal Aid is not available for hearings at the Immigration Appeals Tribunal.

The best way of weighing up your case is by substituting your mind for the mind of an immigration officer and reason the way he would reason. Be frank with yourself and try as much as possible to be objective. The whole idea of weighing the merits of your case at the earliest opportunity is basically to make sure that you do not waste your precious money on a useless case.

It is admitted that considering the merit of your case to decide whether or not it is worth pursuing may not be an easy one. The difficulty may be as a result of your little knowledge of the immigration rules. It is, therefore, advisable to seek professional advice on these matters.

In some cases, representations to the Home Office with additional information, explanations or clarification (as the case may require), may result in the grant of the leave in question. This will mean that the appeal will no longer be necessary.   In fact, there is nothing wrong in putting forward to the Home Office those information and or documents you intend to rely upon at the appeal.

18.10   Presentation of Appeals

Representation can be made in writing where this will be appropriate in a particular case.

Representation in writing may be inexpensive but may not be as effective as oral representation where witnesses and oral evidence can be tested in examination.

All appeals are listed for hearing at 10:00am although the case may not be called until much later. Adjournment requests will rarely be allowed except agreed with the Home Office presenting officer or where one has a very good reason for seeking this adjournment.

At the appeal hearing you may present the case yourself or be represented by a legal representative. The Home Office will be represented by someone from their Presenting Office, whose duty is to present cases at appeals. You may be questioned by your representative and the Home Office presenting officer may also question you. Where the case is complex or where a person is not familiar with immigration rules and procedures, it is advisable to employ a legal representative to make a good presentation of your appeal. You should assist your representative by telephoning him to remind him of the hearing date, as well as working with him in the preparation of the appeal.

Appeals will be heard in most cases in the first instance by one person referred to as an adjudicator, while a panel tribunal panel consists of three persons. Appeals from the adjudicator's decision are usually heard by the tribunal. An Adjudicator or the Tribunal's determination, that is, the decision to allow or dismiss the appeal is usually sent by post2 to all parties except in certain asylum cases where determinations of the Immigration Appeals Tribunal are rarely given on the same day of the hearing.

There is no legal aid for oral representation at the Immigration Appeals Tribunal (that is, at the Adjudicator or the Tribunal hearings).

Lastly, where all rights of appeals have been exhausted, or where appeal rights do not exist at all, or where appeals have been lost, representations may still be made to the Home Office, albeit, outside the immigration rules.

8.11   Appeal From an Adjudicator to the Tribunal

Where the Appellant loses his case before an adjudicator, he may apply for leave to appeal to the Tribunal, and where leave is granted, he will another opportunity to present his case once again, otherwise, the only legal remedy available would be Judicial Review. Likewise, the Home Office do the same where it loses an appeal, but will rarely apply for leave for judicial review.

18.12   APPELLANTS AND NEW APPLICATIONS

An appellant who wants to remain on a different basis from the application that has been refused cannot use this new circumstances at the appeal hearing . Therefore, a person who is on appeal against a refusal of an extension, for example, as a student, but is now married to a person settled in the UK cannot put forward or argue this new circumstance (the marriage) before the Adjudicator.

The best approach is to put forward this new fact to the Home Office well before the date of the appeal hearing. Three copies of such representation may be made, one to the Home Office, one to the presenting officer's unit of the Home Office, and the last one to the Appellate Authorities, together with a letter requesting for the appeal to be adjourned while the Home Office considers the new facts provided in the representation. An adjournment may be granted, but where this is refused, the appeal might be dismissed and the appellant will technically, thereafter, be overstaying, unless a right of appeal to the Tribunal is being exercised.

Where the Home Office decides on the new application favourably, it will write to the applicant-appellant, requesting for the withdrawal of the appeal. It is very important to get an unequivocal and unambiguous letter from the Home office to this effect, stating its intention clearly before an appeal is withdrawn. If an appeal is simply withdrawn before the Home Office has reached a decision to grant the appellant leave to remain, the appellant becomes an overstayer.

Applicants and appellants are strongly advised to seek expert assistance in such cases.

18.13   JUDICIAL REVIEW

Judicial review is the High Court procedure to challenge the validity of a decision of a body exercising public administration, including immigration authorities. Most immigration authorities' decisions whether of an entry clearance officer, an immigration officer, an adjudicator, a tribunal or even a criminal court carrying out immigration functions, are potentially subject to judicial review.

Judicial review is possible except where the law makes express provision to the contrary, or the case itself lacks merit. The ground for judicial review may be illegality, irrationality or procedural impropriety (that is, where the E.C.O, I.O or the appellate authorities were wrong in law, or there has been procedural defects).

Full legal aid may be granted where the case is considered by the Legal Aid Board to have merit.

18.14   Applying for Judicial Review

It is very important to have a good case as Legal Aid may not be granted if the case is considered otherwise. Pursuing Judicial Review privately is expensive. Barrister's opinion may be needed, so that once it suggests a meritorious case, leave of the High Court may be sought, and where given, full hearing of the case should be possible.

In order to minimise costs and time, it is strongly advised that should there be an unfavourable opinion from the barrister, appellants may have to discontinue with the pursuit of Judicial Review.

The courts have indicated that Judicial Review applications should not be entertained where existing appeal rights have not been exhausted .

18.15   SEEKING YOUR MP's (Member of Parliament) ASSISTANCE

A member of Parliament (MP) can intervene on behalf of a person as the last resort (i.e. where there is no right of appeal or any appeal pending), and this intervention may be:

● where all legal avenues have been exhausted, or

● in port refusal case (though legal remedies have not been taken or exhausted).

The MPs who may be able to intervene is the local MP for the applicant or his sponsor's constituency.

Usually, MPs will only like to intervene where there are justifiable reasons for them to do so, or where there are exceptional compassionate circumstances, or new and compelling evidence which may not have been available at the time the person's application was being determined by the immigration authorities.

Where an MP's intervention is successful, the person's removal will usually be deferred.

For details of your local MP, you may telephone the House of Commons on:

(0171) 219 3000

18.16   Important Points to Note

1.   Where someone is refused an extension or variation, there is no longer any leave on which to remain. Nevertheless, such a person will not be an overstayer as the appeal process freezes his position as well as gives him a 'stay' pending the outcome of the appeal, or its withdrawal, or when the appellant leaves the UK. Therefore, so long as the appeal is pending variations or extensions of visa will not usually be granted except the appeal is withdrawn; although further representations in line with the application upon which the appeal is being brought may still be forwarded to the Home Office and may be favourably considered.

2.   Appeals are heard at different centres which include Thanet House (at the Strand), or at York House (Feltham) near Heathrow Airport, Wood Hall (in Wood Green), Banbury, Belfast, Birmingham, Cardiff, Glasgow, Gravesend, Leeds and Manchester. Those who want to exercise their rights of appeal should do so within the stipulated time.

3.   Anyone apprehended by the police or immigration officers and detained after a notice of intention to deport is served on him, but who has a fixed address, may be given a temporary release. Otherwise, a bail application could be made to an adjudicator. Temporary release or bail is necessary in this case as it may take few months before his appeal is heard.

4.   Appeal against intention to deport is not usually a very easy one, and whether or not a person has a good case may depend on how long he has been in the UK before he is served with the notice of intention to deport. A person who has been in the UK for less than 7 years can only argue in such an appeal that there is no power in law to deport him. For those who have remained for 7 years or more, several points may be argued, including strong ties with the UK, see chapter 21.

5. Most appeals are heard in the first instance by an adjudicator and a further appeal may be made to the Tribunal only if the leave (permission) is granted to do so. Where a child born in the UK is included as a deportee, the appeal is to be heard by the Tribunal.

6. Legal Aid is not available for appeals at the Tribunal but may be available to pursue your case in the Court of Law; also, advice at Solicitor's office engaged in legal aid work may be free if the appellant qualifies under the **Green Form Scheme.**

After an appellant may have exhausted his rights of appeal within the immigration framework (i.e. appeal to the Adjudicator and or the Tribunal) a further safe guard is provided. This process may be cumbersome and expensive, but where the case has merit, it may be a good course to pursue. This is by going to the court of law, starting from the High Court for Judicial Review, and further appeals may proceed to the Court of Appeal and to the House of Lords in some cases.

8. When your address changes, make sure you notify the Immigration Appeals Tribunal (as well as the Home Office), and where you require an interpreter, make sure you inform the Tribunal as early as possible. Always quote your appeal reference number as well as your Home Office reference number in all correspondence to the Tribunal.

18.17   MIXED APPEAL FOR ASYLUM APPELLANTS

Where an asylum seeker is refused leave to enter or remain, he may be able to appeal against this decision. In the appeal forms to be completed are two columns for grounds of appeal, one with regard to the asylum basis, while the other is for any non-asylum ground.

Therefore, where this person is appealing against refusal of asylum, he should provide grounds and appeal against the Home secretary's decision which has nothing to do with asylum if appropriate.

18.18   Example

A person declared an illegal entrant who is married to a person settled in the UK will not have a right of appeal if his application for leave to remain on the basis of marriage is refused. However, if he is appealing against his asylum application which is refused, he can appeal against the refusal of leave to remain on the basis of marriage at the same time, which will be heard by a Special Adjudicator.

18.19   Asylum Appellant Not Covered by 'Mixed Appeal'

The additional appeal right as available under the mixed appeal will not be available to a person:

- where a deportation order has been made against him on the ground that it is conducive to public good,

or

- where the Secretary of State has issued a 3rd Country Certificate in respect of his application for asylum and that certificate has not been set aside upon appeal.

FOOTNOTES

1. *Secretary of State for the Home Departm.*
    Exparte Swati (1986) 1 ALL ER 717

2. *Immigration (Variation of leave) order 1976*
    s1 1976/1572 as amended by s1 1989/1005

Chapter 19

OVERSTAYERS AND ILLEGAL ENTRANTS

19.1   WHO IS AN OVERSTAYER?

Any person admitted to the UK for a limited period who then remains beyond the time limit granted, without an extension or variation is usually described as an overstayer.

This description will also fit a person whose application for variation or extension has been refused, but who continues to remain in the UK without any form of authority.

The description will equally fit a person whose appeal has been unsuccessful and has decided to go 'underground'.

19.2   CONSEQUENCES OF OVERSTAYING

Overstaying is a criminal offence triable in the Magistrates court. This offence is however rarely prosecuted as the immigration authorities prefer to remove such an offender either by deportation or supervised departure.

A person who has overstayed his leave has no right to be considered for an extension or variation as there is no subsisting leave to vary or extend. Therefore, while consideration may be given to an application made by such a person, a refusal will not attract a right of appeal.

Notwithstanding the above, where an applicant has plausible, genuine or compassionate explanation, the Home Office has a discretion to grant an overstayer leave to remain. This should not be an encouragement of any kind as subsequent applications to enter the UK by such a person may be adversely affected by the previous overstaying.

Another effect of overstaying is to render the person liable to deportation.

An overstayer may be held in detention pending his removal and deportation, although it is not unusual for such a person to be granted temporary release, especially where an appeal against such intended deportation is pending. Alternatively such a person may be granted bail by an adjudicator.

19.3   WHO IS AN ILLEGAL ENTRANT?

An Illegal Entrant is a person:

- who enters or seeks to enter the UK in breach of a deportation order, or

- who enters or seeks to enter the UK by evading immigration controls, or

- who enters or seeks to enter the UK by employing some deception or sharp practice on entry clearance officer(s) and or immigration officer(s) *(Illegal Entry by Deception)*, or

- who is subject to immigration control and has entered from Ireland without possessing the required leave *(Entry through Ireland)*.

The *third* and *fourth* points deserve further explanation.

19.4   Illegal Entry by Deception

It is important to note that a person granted leave to enter the UK may subsequently be declared an illegal entrant, not withstanding that there may have been a considerable time lapse between the date of deception and discovery.   Once it becomes known to the immigration authorities that deception was initially employed in order to gain entry into the UK, a person may be so declared.   It is, therefore, possible for someone who has overstayed his leave, or who has leave (visa), to be so declared.

Also, the fact that the deception used was exercised by a 3rd party on behalf of the applicant will not avail the person from being so declared.

Examples of Fraudulent or Deceptive activities will include;

- where one travels with a British or any Passport not belonging to him or any false travel documents.

- where one gives false information so as to facilitate his entry.

- where one's main intention of coming into the UK was discovered to be different from what was indicated to the immigration officer at the port of entry.

- where one deliberately withholds or conceals information which would have been relevant to the grant or refusal of an entry clearance or entry. This area has led to some controversy because it is arguable that mere silence, especially where the immigration officer did not ask the appropriate questions should not be termed as deception.

As earlier mentioned, most people who are commonly declared illegal entrants (because of deception) are those who may have overstayed their leave, or those caught working without permission, or those who put in fishy applications, (for example where people in transit apply for leave to remain as a student) and are called, or subsequently interviewed, on which occasion their original intention for coming transpires.

19.5   Entry from Ireland without Leave

A person is allowed to travel within the common travel area, that is, between the Isle of Man, Channel Island, Republic of Ireland and the UK, without the need to obtain visa to go to these countries provided he has visa to enter one of them. A person without a visa, that is, an overstayer is not free to travel as such.   Since there is no immigration barrier between these countries, everyone is theoretically free to travel without any problem. Infact, you do not need your passport either, to travel. Anything to identify you, e.g., Drivers Licence, may suffice. However, an overstayer in the UK who travels to Republic of Ireland, for example, would be treated as an illegal entrant when he returns to the UK if his travel is known to the authorities. It is very unlikely for the authorities to know except perhaps the passenger mentioned this in the course of an interview.

19.6   CONSEQUENCES OF ILLEGAL ENTRY

A person declared an illegal entrant will be liable to removal (and not deportation) from the UK.

While illegal entry is also a criminal offence, the immigration authorities usually opt for removal as opposed to prosecution.   Also while an overstayer, who is not declared an illegal entrant, may exercise his right of appeal against the Home Office's intention to deport, removal of illegal entrants is usually a quicker exercise without any right of appeal whilst in the UK.

19.7   'ILLEGAL IMMIGRANT'

While this term is commonly used, it is only a colloquialism commonly used by a lot of people (including arresting or detaining Police Officers), for those who have overstayed or people who may eventually be declared as illegal entrants.

19.8   CASE STUDY

1.   Singh (an Indian National) wanted to come to the UK to study. He was told by his friends that a student entry clearance is usually very difficult to obtain as conditions to be satisfied are quite numerous. Singh therefore entered the UK as a visitor in March 1996 and was granted a 6 months visa.

To facilitate his entry, Singh told the Immigration Officer at the port of entry that he was married with two children, and that he owned a shoe factory in New Delhi.   Meanwhile, Singh came into Britain with some UK College prospectus.

Shortly before his visa ran out, Singh sent his Passport to the Home Office with other necessary documents to support his application for a student visa. But before his application could be processed at the Home Office, Singh was caught by the Police working with a Cleaning company.   He was subsequently interviewed by an immigration officer.

Part of the Questions asked and Answers provided are as follows:

I.O   :Do you have a wife anywhere?
Singh   :**No**

I.O   :Have you ever been married?
Singh   :**No**

I.O   :How many children have you?
Singh   :**None**

I.O   :When did you decide to study in the UK?
Singh   :**Sometime in 1995**

I.O   :Why did you not tell the Immigration Officer at the port
            of entry that you were coming to the UK to study?
Singh   :**I thought it would be more difficult to enter if I had told
            him I was coming to study**

The immigration officer came to the conclusion that Singh was an illegal entrant.

2.   Singh's case may be contrasted with that of Toxi (from Zimbabwe) who was similarly faced with the question of illegal entry.

      Toxi wanted to come to the UK to study. He was also aware of how difficult it could be to obtain an entry clearance for this purpose.

Toxi thereupon took his time to decide on what to do. In the meantime Toxi was granted admission to the Harare University and his father decided to give him a holiday treat to the UK.

In March 1996, Toxi told the interviewing entry clearance officer that he was going to London for a short visit. On getting to the UK, Toxi obtained a College prospectus with the aim of securing a place. Toxi also secured a job at a supermarket as a security officer. Subsequently, the supermarket was burgled and Toxi being the security officer on duty, reported this to the Police. A series of interrogations took place during which Toxi was himself questioned vigorously by the Police and it transpired that Toxi did not have any right to work. He was later interviewed by an Immigration Officer.

Part of the Questions asked and Answers provided are as follows:

I.O: When did you decide to study in the UK?
Toxi: **5 months before coming to the UK**

I.O: Why did you not tell the Entry Clearance Officer or the Immigration Officer at the port of entry that you were coming here to study?
Toxi: **I thought it would be more difficult to gain entry if I told them I was coming to study, and I was not sure that I would be staying here as I had secured admission in Harare University**

I.O :Will you be forwarding a student application to the Home Office very shortly?
Toxi :**I probably will.**

Toxi was declared an illegal entrant as it was claimed that he failed to declare his genuine intention from the outset.

While Singh's situation may seem to be a clear cut one, Toxi's declaration as an illegal entrant seems challengeable.

19.9   Practical Advice

Questions asked and answers provided during an entry clearance application or at the port of entry are the tools the immigration authorities use in deciding whether someone is an illegal entrant or not. It is, therefore, our advice that such questions and answers, as much as one can remember, should be written down as soon as it is practicable for you to do so.

Chapter 20

IMMIGRANTS, POLICE AND EMERGENCY SITUATIONS

20.1   INTRODUCTION

Immigrants should know that the police share powers in the enforcement of immigration law with immigration officers. The demarcation lines are not particularly drawn so that at times there may be confusion, which becomes compounded when the police stray beyond their function of dealing with criminal conduct and turn their attention to the administrative function of immigration officers.

It is, therefore, important to make a clear distinction between the powers to examine an immigrant under the administrative powers of the immigration law exercisable by immigration officers, and the general powers afforded to the police to INVESTIGATE and PROSECUTE immigration problems classified as crime. Different consideration apply to both and they are examined below.

20.2   IMMIGRANTS' DUTIES TO THE POLICE & IMMIGRATION OFFICERS

Immigrants facing examination under the immigration law are under a duty to answer questions, and to produce documents required of them by an immigration officer, by showing who they are and in the case of persons seeking entry, why they should be granted leave to enter.

Furthermore, there is no right of silence and right of access to a solicitor may be dispensed with.

By contrast, when the police are interviewing anybody in connection with their general duties to detect and prosecute crime, there is no obligation on an immigrant to answer any questions (though such refusal to answer may lead to adverse inferences), and if the immigrant is arrested on suspicion of an offence, the Police and Criminal Evidence Act 1984, and the Codes of Practice will apply. This includes and encompasses the rights of suspects to a Solicitor.[1]

20.3   FUNCTIONS OF THE POLICE RELATING TO IMMIGRATION

20.4   Investigation

It is part of the common law duty of the police to investigate crime and prosecute offences where there is sufficient evidence or reasonable suspicion. All immigration offences attracting criminal sanctions are thus capable of being investigated by the police. Where such investigation is being conducted, the Police and Criminal Evidence Act and it's code of practice will apply accordingly.   Although telling lies to a police officer may constitute an offence, an immigrant commits no offence if he refuses to answer questions put to him by the police.

20.5   Powers of Arrest[2]

The law specifically gives a police constable power to arrest without warrant and may prosecute anyone who has, or whom he, with reasonable cause, suspects to have COMMITTED or ATTEMPTED to commit the following offences (only a few important ones are mentioned here):-

a)   if contrary to the law, he knowingly enters the UK in breach of a deportation order or without leave (illegal entrant).

b)   any person knowingly concerned in making or carrying out arrangement for securing or facilitating the entry into the UK of anyone whom he knows or has reasonable cause for believing to be an illegal entrant.

c)   if, having only a limited leave to enter or remain in the UK, he knowingly either:

- remains beyond the time allowed by the leave (overstayer)
OR
- fails to observe a condition of the leave (e.g. not to work).

d)   if, without reasonable excuse, he fails to observe any restriction imposed on him as to residence or as to reporting to the police or an immigration officer (e.g. on grant of temporary release following an arrest).

e)   any asylum applicant who fails to comply with, or attend for finger printing requirements.

20.6   Other Relevant Points

1.   Offences of Harbouring;
It is an offence for anyone knowingly to harbour anyone whom they know or have reasonable cause for believing to be either:

- an illegal entrant, or

- an overstayer, or

- in breach of condition not to work.

Harbouring means to provide a lodging for, or to shelter.

2.   Any employer who employs an immigrant without proper documents (e.g. Work Permit) may be caught by the rule of harbouring. Such employer must have known or have reasonable cause for believing that the immigrant has not got proper documents, otherwise, he will not be guilty. The Immigration & Asylum Act 1996 now makes it a punishable offence to employ an immigrant who has no right to work in the UK. See Chapter 22.

From the above discussion, it is apparent that the police powers are exercisable on suspicion of an offence based on reasonable suspicion. What constitutes reasonable suspicion is a matter of fact and degree, and the fact that a person is black or brown or sounds foreign is not enough for enquiry into his immigration status. Regrettably, whenever foreigners come into contact with the police, mostly in road traffic situations or even as victims of crime, the police tend to ask them for their passports. This should not be the case.

Reasonable suspicion must, therefore, have some concrete basis which can be considered and evaluated by an objective third party.

As the police have the right to request someone to identify himself, any document which shows the immigrant Name, Address and Date of Birth should suffice, (e.g. British Drivers Licence). Unfortunately, police officers commonly request foreigners to produce their passport without giving them other options of identifications. The police may however be perfectly entitled to request for a passport if they have reasonable suspicion that the suspect has or is about to commit an immigration offence; it is our view that only on this basis should a police officer justifiably request for a passport without giving options for any other forms of identification.

Lastly, it is also not uncommon for your so called relatives or friends to alert the Police or
immigration authorities about your immigration situation in the UK.

For extended powers of the Police and Employers liability, see the new Asylum and Immigration Law 1996 {Chapter 22}.

20.7   RIGHTS OF IMMIGRANTS ON ARREST BY POLICE

An arrested person has:

- a right to notify someone of his detention,
- a right to consult privately with a Solicitor,

- a right to inform his High Commission or Consular Office, and
- a right to remain silent when questioned.

A police officer, thus, has no right to an explanation of a person's immigration history, and cannot cancel, withdraw or curtail the leave given to any immigrant nor can he declare that an arrested person is an illegal entrant.

Also, where there is no statutory power for police officers to enter a premises by force without a warrant for the purposes of search or arrest, it is uncommon for police officers to pretend that they are investigating other crimes such as burglary in the first instance so as to gain entry into a premises. Alternatively, the police will be very polite and this is when a suspect becomes a 'Govnor', or better still, may come with investigating Immigration Officer(s).

20.8   POLICE AND HOME OFFICE ENQUIRIES

The Home Office occasionally delegates to the police the tasks of interviewing persons in connection with Immigration and Nationality applications. Such enquiries may be to establish the whereabouts of a person, to question a married couple as to their intentions, to examine the adequacy of accommodation of a sponsor in the UK, or to examine applicants for naturalisation. Though, there is no obligation to answer any question in such situations, failure to do so may put an application at risk of rejection, where necessary information is not forthcoming.

The Home Office may also use the police to effect personal service of notices of refusal to vary leave where it is considered desirable, but they rarely do this.

20.9   OVERLAP OF DUTIES

20.10   Police & Immigration Officers

There is mutual co-operation and exchange of information between the police and the immigration service. Details of convictions against Non-British Citizens are routinely supplied to the Home Office computer. This may be necessary to assist the immigration officers when considering leave to enter for someone who has a criminal record, or for the Home Office, where it might wish to exercise its powers to deport.

Frequent operational links are made between immigration officers and the police who may provide necessary information about immigrants which they may have on their computers.

There are also arrangements for immigration officers to be called in by the police whenever an immigrant whose immigration status is suspect has been apprehended by them; Police cells are usually used for detaining such people pending an immigration officer's enquiries into the suspect's immigration status.

The expected maximum period for detention in a police cell for immigration matters is currently five (5) working days; where the police is holding someone on behalf of the immigration authorities, the 24 hour rule for detention does not apply. Detained immigrants may be kept in prison, but where no further detention is authorised, they may be released without charge or restriction, on police bail or by the immigration authorities on what is called TEMPORARY RELEASE, with restriction on Residence and/or to Report weekly or monthly at a local police station or an immigration office. Where further detention is authorised and the immigrant exercises his right of appeal, an application for bail may be made to an adjudicator. In such a case, sponsor(s) may be needed.

To request for temporary release/admission, the sponsor may be required to provide his details such full name, address, date of birth, relationship with the detainee and his immigration status in the UK. Such a sponsor may also be interviewed to establish his relationship with the detainee.

Please note that the new Asylum and Immigration Law 1996 now provides that detainees can apply for bail even where there is no pending appeal [3] .

20.11 MAKING A BAIL APPLICATION

An application can be made orally but commonly appreciated in writing. Where an application is made in writing, it should contain the following particulars:

-   the full name of the Applicant;

-   the address of the place where, and the purpose
    for which, the applicant is detained.

-   whether an appeal is pending;

-   the address where he would reside if his application
    for bail were to be successful;

-   the amount of the recognizance in which he
    would agree to be bound; and

-   the grounds upon which the application is made and, where a
    previous application has been refused, full particulars of the
    change in circumstance which has occurred since that refusal.

Such request is to be made to the Immigration Appeals Tribunal nearer to where the detainee is being detained.

Any one contemplating making an application should find out from an Immigration Officer at his detention centre with regard to the details of which branch office of the Immigration Appeals Tribunal he should write to.

Surety will be required by the Adjudicator, and a hearing date is usually fixed as a matter of urgency. In most cases, an application for bail will be heard within 7 working days of requesting for a date.

20.12   Criteria for Surety

A surety is a person who accepts responsibility to produce the suspect as and when required. For a person to be accepted as surety:

● he is expected to be a British Citizen, a person who has permanent residence, or someone with good immigration history, and

● he must have a clean record (i.e. no criminal records or convictions), and

he may be required to have money or property worth up to £4,000 (if one person) OR £2,000 each where two people are responsible. Please note that the adjudicator may fix any amount of the recognizance. For example, a sum of £27,500 has been accepted in the past.

20.13   REGISTRATION WITH POLICE

Commonwealth citizens are not required to register with the police, but a majority of foreign nationals admitted for more than 3 months for employment or 6 months for other purposes, and their spouses and children over 16 years are required to register with the Police.[4]

Registration involves going to the local police station and giving detailed particulars including:

● name,

● address,

● marital status,

● details of employment or occupation (if any), including employer's

● name and address,

● a photograph, and

● registration fee.

Subsequent change of address, or marital status etc. should be reported to the police within 7 days. The police will issue a Certificate of Registration to such a registered person.

20.14   Important Point to Note

1.   Driving is the most common way of bringing one's self to the attention of the authorities, especially committing driving offences such as driving without valid driver's licence, M.O.T, road tax, or over-speeding, jumping the light and other petty criminal matters such as evading transport fares,   keeping bad company or associates, may lead to further or other investigations which can   reveal a person's immigration status.

We strongly advise against falling into, committing, or engaging in, any offences.

2.   It is important therefore to have a good adviser, most especially before an interview at the police station as it is very easy to make you an illegal entrant which will facilitate your removal.

20.15   Dealing with Emergency Situations

Situations may arise where someone, such as a   friend or relative may require immediate and urgent assistance to deal with an immigration problem. These may occur at the Port of Entry or when arrested by an immigration or police officer. The event may also happen to be on a weekend when the assistance of Solicitors or Legal Representative may not be readily available. It is important, therefore, to be familiar with the general guidelines which may assist immigrants in such a difficult situations. This sub-topic is designed to assist pending the intervention of an experienced legal representative.

20.16   Initial Steps to Take if Assisting Friend or Relative

● Obtain as much information concerning his problems as soon as possible from the Police or Immigration Officer concerned, and where possible, from your friend or relative,

● Obtain your friend's full name and his alias, date of birth and nationality,

● Obtain the telephone number of the officer, or the department in charge of his case,

● As the immigration department will usually issue Home Office reference or Port reference number as soon as possible, obtain this from them or from your friend, it will assist to trace your friend's file with the authorities. Such numbers would usually have been noted on papers served on your friend by the immigration authorities.

● Ask for photocopy of documents and interview notes relating to the case from your friend or immigration officer,

● When in contact with police or immigration officer, always ask for the officers name and write down what was discussed, as much as possible, for future reference,

● Where a passenger is due shortly to arrive at a port of entry, details, including the arrival terminal should be obtained.

● You may also need to have information which your relative may have provided the British Consular (or Entry Clearance Officer) in his home country.

It is important to talk to your friend or relative first and seek to know what information he may have given the Police or immigration officer. Where possible, do not discuss his case with any officer using your little knowledge of his past immigration history which may complicate matters for him. You may contact the Police or Immigration Officer, possibly, to obtain some background information from them.

Where a person with emergency problems is not in detention or custody, he can assist himself by taking the necessary steps mentioned above, but should perhaps say as little as possible until he is able to consult with his legal representative.

Where a person with emergency problems is in custody or detention, his anxiety for immediate release may blur his sense of judgement and reasoning. Such a person should not provide information in the absence of his legal representative or before obtaining advice.

A person who is standing as a sponsor, particularly where the immigration authorities are considering releasing a detained person, may be asked:

- his full name,
- address/ type of accommodation,
- telephone number,
- immigration status in the UK,
- employment,
- his relationship with the detainee (and how close),
- together with any other relevant information.

20.17   Appeals

Where someone has a right of appeal, he will usually be provided with some documents. These will provide reasons for refusing leave or decision to deport, together with forms to be completed. He may also be presented with a paper requiring his signature, disclaiming his right to appeal against their decision.

A person in detention may be so vulnerable that he may sign such a disclaimer form without consulting a Solicitor. Since the appeal rights should be lodged within a certain time, commonly, 14 days, it may be necessary to seek advice before taking action regarding filling or signing any form.

Where you have to complete and send off your appeal forms because time is against you, make sure you complete and sign these forms.

You may also write your reasons why you disagree with the decision, adding that further grounds may follow. Send off all these documents by recorded delivery and see your legal representative with copies of everything you have sent off as soon as you possibly can.

20.18   CASE STUDY

Mr Alpha from Russia was apprehended by the Police after committing a traffic offence. He was asked to identify himself by providing documents, for example, his driver's licence, instead he said 'I am British and my name is Charles'.   The officers concerned conducted a search of the vehicle involved and found a letter addressed to a Mr Alpha.

Mr Alpha was taken to the police station for further questioning and was later escorted to his home address where a Russian passport bearing Mr Alpha's photograph was found. The name on this passport was Mr Alpha. An immigration officer attended the police station to interview Mr Alpha, subsequent to which he was declared an illegal entrant liable to be removed to Russia.

Mr Alpha's girlfriend, Omega decided to visit him at the Police station. Omega was asked to identify herself which she did with an expired travel pass bearing her photograph. The police officer involved noticed the fact of the expiration and asked Omega in an informal manner how she was going to get back home. Omega answered 'by public transport'. The officer then noticed that Omega was wearing a pair of bathroom slippers which made him doubt that she would be travelling back in public transport as it was an extremely cold day.

This officer then asked Omega how much she had on her for her fare back home. Omega kept mute and could not produce any money.

Another officer walked into the station and commented that he had seen a car at the end of the road without a tax disc. The officer dealing with Omega jokingly said 'it's not your car, is it?'   Omega became tense and uncomfortable. The officer took a closer look at the keys on Omega. One of them was for an Audi. The car outside was also an Audi.

The keys were taken off Omega, tested on the car, giving the officers access. On searching the car, the officer noticed some documents with Omega's name, the same name on the travel pass. The officers returned and requested for Omega's driving documents, which she said was at home.

Omega was escorted home, her room turned upside down, and her property thoroughly searched. No driving documents were found. Omega's passport was later discovered and she was found to have overstayed her leave.

It was then time for Omega's interview by an immigration officer. Guess what................?

BE CAREFUL! YOUR CAR CAN DRIVE YOU BACK HOME.

FOOTNOTES

1.   *S.58 Police and Criminal Evidence Act 1984*

2.   *Immigration Act 1971 S.24/25*

3.   *Immigration and Asylum Act 1996, Paragraph 12 Sch.2*

Chapter 21

DEPORTATION

21.1   INTRODUCTION

Deportation is the process whereby a Non-British Citizen or a person without a Right of Abode is compulsorily removed from the UK and excluded from returning, for an Indefinite Period.

Therefore, where a person who has leave to remain is served with a *'notice of a decision to deport'*, the notice operates to freeze the leave.

Some Non-British Citizens, for example, Diplomats[1], Irish and E.E.A Nationals are not usually deported except in extreme cases.

21.2   REASONS FOR DEPORTATION

The Home Secretary may decide to deport a person for the following reasons:

1.   Breach of Landing Conditions e.g. Overstaying, Working without a Work Permit etc.

2.   Where the Home Secretary deems deportation to be conducive to the public good.

3.   Where a Court of Law recommends deportation after a conviction for an offence punishable by imprisonment.

4.   In some cases, where a member of the immediate family is being deported, other members can be deported as well [2].

21.3   DEPORTATION FOR BREACH OF CONDITIONS

Leave to enter may have been granted for a limited period, and this may in addition be with a condition restricting or prohibiting employment. Failure to observe this condition (or any other conditions), or remaining in the UK beyond the leave given, makes a person liable to deportation. This may also be a criminal offence punishable by fine and or imprisonment. A person convicted of such a breach may also be recommended for deportation by the sentencing Court.

In considering whether deportation is the course where someone has contravened a condition (e.g. working) or, has remained without leave (e.g. an overstayer), full account will usually be taken of all the relevant circumstances known to the Home Office including his age; length of residence in the UK, strength of connections with the UK; personal history including character, conduct and employment record, domestic circumstances; previous criminal record, compassionate circumstances, and any other representations which may be forwarded on his behalf.

21.4   DEPORTATION CONDUCIVE TO PUBLIC GOOD

Deportation may be conducive to public good:-

1.   Where a person is suspected of criminal and immoral activities.

2.   Where there is a criminal conviction but no recommendation for deportation is made.

3.   Where the character, conduct or association of a person is considered undesirable, in other words, it impinges on the public domain or there is sufficient threat to public order.

4.   Where the Home Office has been misled, for example, into granting an Indefinite Leave to Remain. An illustration is where false representation as to marital status, or as to continuous existence of

cohabitation have been made at a time when the parties were 'living together', but separately.

5.   Where it is in the interest of National Security.

In considering whether deportation is the proper course where public good is concerned, full account will usually be taken of all the relevant circumstances known to the Home Office including age; length of residence in the UK; personal history including character, conduct and employment record, domestic circumstances, the nature of any offence, previous criminal record; compassionate circumstances, and any other representations forwarded on the person's behalf.

21.5   DEPORTATION RECOMMENDED BY COURT

Where a person who is charged with a criminal offence either in connection with his immigration status (e.g. overstaying etc.), or unconnected (e.g. theft), is found guilty of the offence which is punishable by imprisonment, deportation may also be recommended by the court.

A recommendation for deportation can only be appealed against as an appeal *against sentence* in the criminal court appeal system and not through the immigration appeal system.   The only exception is where there is a subsequent claim for asylum and the claim is unsuccessful; such a claimant will be able to appeal against Destination.

Furthermore, the Home Office is not compelled to deport just on the basis of the Court's recommendation, though it normally will. When the court so recommends, the immigrant will usually be detained pending the decision of the Home Office, unless he is released, after making such recommendation, by an appeal court, or by the Home Office.

It is important to note that recommendation for deportation is usually exercised judicially, and should be concerned with the criminal behaviour rather than the enforcement of an immigration policy. Therefore, a minor offence such as non payment of a parking ticket should not normally merit a recommendation for deportation.

As stated above, deportation does not follow as a matter of course on such recommendation. The Home Office will only deport after it has taken into account all the relevant circumstances known to it, including: age, length of residence in the UK; strength of connections with the UK; personal history; including character, conduct and employment record, domestic circumstances, nature of the offence for which the person was convicted, previous criminal record; compassionate circumstances and any representations forwarded on the person's behalf.

21.6   Two Existing Safeguards

● No court may recommend a person's deportation unless the accused has been given not less than 7 days notice in writing, informing him of the likelihood of being recommended for deportation.

● Such a person recommended for deportation may still appeal to an adjudicator against the intended destination and, to a higher criminal court, against sentence.

21.7   DEPORTATION OF FAMILY MEMBERS

Where a person is or has been ordered to be deported, his spouse and any children under 18 years (including the spouse's children by another person) may be deported; and if a person is or has been ordered to be deported, his children under 18 years may also be deported. The power to deport children covers the children that have been adopted, including children born out of wedlock, but EXCLUDES children:-

● whom the husband and wife have given up for adoption,

● who are above or just under 18 years, and have spent some years in the UK, who have left home on taking employment, and

● have established themselves on an independent basis, and

● who are less than 18 years but are now married.

In considering whether deportation of a family altogether should be made, full account must be taken of all relevant circumstances known to the Home office, including: length of residence in the UK, any ties which the wife or children have with the UK otherwise than as dependants of the principal deportee (e.g. where parents and family members of wife reside in the UK), the ability of the wife to maintain herself and children in the UK, or to be maintained by relatives or friends without having to recourse to public funds now and for the foreseeable future and any compassionate or other special circumstances.

In the case of children of school age, the Home Office will usually take into consideration the disruptive effect of removal on their education and whether plans for their care and maintenance in the UK if one or both parents were deported are realistic, together with any other representation which may be forwarded on their behalf.

21.8   Limitation on Family Deportation

However, there are limits on family deportation. Where a man or woman ordered to be deported leaves the UK and EIGHT WEEKS have elapsed since his departure, his or her family may no longer be deported if the deportation order against the principal deportee does not include their names[3].

The rule states that family deportation documents shall include the names of all the family members as being jointly and severally liable to deportation. Once this is not done from the outset, or within 8 weeks of the departure of the principal deportee, such other members cannot be deported.

21.9   Important Points to Note

1.   A person who has been divorced from his spouse cannot be deported along with him as a family member.

2.   Even if the spouse is deported, once the marriage is dissolved, he/she will cease to be subject to the order and he is then free from this deportation order and will be free to come into the UK without revocation of this order.

3.   Where a spouse qualifies for settlement in his own right, for example, following four years in approved employment, he will have a valid claim to remain notwithstanding the expulsion of his spouse and his deportation will not normally be contemplated.

4.   Where the person is living apart from his spouse (the principal deportee), the Home Office will not normally include him and any children who may be living with him in the deportation order.

5.   When children who have been deported alongside their parents reach the age of 18 years, they will cease to be subject to the deportation order and will then be free from this deportation order and they will be free to come into the UK without the revocation of this order.

21.10   APPEALING AGAINST INTENTION TO DEPORT

The most important thing in this area are the grounds of appeal which may be forwarded or presented and these grounds may be classified into two categories.

21.11   {a} Limited Grounds (restricted rights)

Those who have been in the UK **for less than seven years** may only appeal against the legality of such decision i.e. whether or not the Home Office has the power in law to deport them (the answer to which is usually Yes)[4,] although judicial review may be considered in appropriate cases.

21.12   {b} Unlimited Grounds (unrestricted rights)

Those who have been in the UK **for 7 years or more** may rely on unlimited grounds of appeal, including their long residence, family ties, compassionate circumstances [5] etc.

21.13   DEPORTATION OF A MINOR

With the exception of;

● deportation of a child whilst deporting members of his family, and

● a child after attaining the age of 17, convicted of an offence for which he is punishable by imprisonment and for which the court recommends deportation, CHILDREN UNDER THE AGE OF 18 ARE NOT USUALLY DEPORTED ON THEIR OWN.

21.14   DETENTION PENDING DEPORTATION OR REMOVAL

● anybody who has been notified of a decision to deport;

● a person who has been declared an illegal entrant;

● a person whose actual deportation order has been signed;

may be detained pending removal from the UK. Alternatively, the immigration authorities may allow temporary release with restrictions as to residence and/or reporting restrictions.

Where an immigrant is served with a Notice of Decision to deport is detained, the first 5-7 days may be spent at a Police station, thereafter, he is likely to be transferred to a detention centre, for example, Hamondsworth near Heathrow, Beehive at Gatwick, or a local prison pending appeal against the decision to deport him or his removal to a particular country; such a detainee may make application for bail to an adjudicator.

21.15   Important Points to Note

1.   Where no appeal is lodged against an intention to deport, or where an appeal is dismissed, the Order for Deportation is usually submitted to the Home Secretary for signature. It is important to note that where this has happened, that its revocation, (subsequent to which leave to

remain can be allowed) may happen only where there are serious compelling or strong compassionate circumstances for such a person to remain at the Home Office's discretion.

2.   An application for revocation of deportation order is expected to be made whilst the person is outside the UK, with a right of appeal against refusal. Although revocation while this person is still in the UK may also be considered favourably on the basis of *serious and compelling or strong compassionate circumstances,* an unfavourable decision attracts no right of appeal.

21.16   DIFFERENCE between REMOVAL and DEPORTATION

Those who are found or declared as illegal entrants in the UK are subject to removal from the UK, while others, for example, overstayers, may be deported. Those being removed can only appeal against the reason for their removal from outside the UK, but they may appeal against destination whilst still in the UK. Those subject to deportation may appeal in the first instance against the Home Office's intention to deport them, as well as against destination whilst still in the UK.

21.17   Additional Points to Note

Those being deported will initially be notified of the Home Office's intention to deport as well as of their rights of appeal. Where they appeal against the decision to deport, they should appeal against destination (if need be) at the same time.

Also, it is not definitely clear which of the two i.e. Deportation or Removal, is the lesser of two evils.

With deportation, the order may be revoked after 3 years on application before the person may be allowed back into the UK, whereas people removed may, in theory, appear to stand a better chance than those being deported. However, in practice, those removed, although there is no provision to bar their re-entry, the Home Office practice suggests that their entry will also be a difficult task.

Lastly, a person who enters in breach of a deportation order (i.e. while the order is still in force) is an illegal entrant, whereas, those removed cannot be so declared provided they entered without deception or fraud on the new occasion.

21.18   REVOCATION OF DEPORTATION ORDER

The effect of a deportation order is to INVALIDATE any leave to enter or remain in the UK while the order is in force. A deportation order comes into force on the day it is signed rather than when it is served, and in the following cases, the Order will cease automatically:-.

1.   Where the person becomes a British Citizen, or

2.   Where the person was a spouse under family deportation order, but   is now divorced from the principal deportee, or

3.   Where a child deported under family deportation order, later attains 18 years of age or becomes married.

Apart from the above situations, a deportation order continues in force until such time as it is revoked by another order known as Revocation Order. Though revocation of a deportation order does not entitle the deportee to re-enter the UK, it however makes him eligible to apply for admission.

21.19   APPLICATION FOR REVOCATION

Applications for the revocation of a deportation order will be carefully considered in the light of the grounds on which the order was made and of the case made in support of the application. The interest of the community, including the maintenance of an effective immigration control are to be balanced against the interests of the applicant, including any circumstances of a compassionate nature.

In certain case, for example, where an applicant has a serious criminal record, continued exclusion for a longer term of years may be appropriate. In other cases, revocation will not normally be authorised UNLESS the situation of the person has been materially altered either:

- by a change of circumstances since the order was made, or

- by fresh information coming to light which was not before the court that made the recommendation, or the tribunal, or the Home Office.

The passage of time since the person was deported may also in itself amount to such a change of circumstances as to warrant revocation.

No application for revocation will be allowed (except in the most exceptional circumstances) until after a period of 3 years since the making of the deportation order.[6]

21.20   Important Points to Note

1. As a general rule, *three years must elapse* before an application for revocation can be entertained.

2. In the most exceptional circumstances, an application for revocation may be considered within a shorter period.

3. There is no guarantee that the Order will be revoked either before or after the said 3 years, but there is a right of appeal against refusal where the application for revocation is made from outside the UK.

4. Application for revocation should be made either to the:

    - Entry Clearance Officer at the nearest British Consul or Embassy, or
    - The Home Office in Croydon.

21.21   OTHER FORMS OF EXIT

Apart from Removal and Deportation, there are two other ways of departing from the UK. These are voluntary and supervised departures.

21.22   Voluntary Departure

The following people may be able to opt for this type of departure:

● A person who has been served with a notice of intention to deport but not detained.

● A person liable to deportation who is unsuccessful in any appeal or representation, but whose deportation order has not been signed and he is not detained.

● A person who is overstaying but not known to the authorities.

● A person who may have been declared an illegal entrant but granted a temporary release.

Voluntary departure is where someone takes his passport, buys a ticket and departs from the UK on his own accord. At least, one cannot require a person to leave who has already left. So a deportation order will not normally be signed against someone otherwise liable to it, if he has left before the signing of the order.

One good thing about voluntary departure is the fact that this person may still be able to come into the UK, though he may face gruesome questioning by an Entry Clearance Officer (where entry clearance is needed before coming), or by an immigration officer at the port of entry, where his circumstances in the UK before departure is known; For instance, a person whose application for variation or extension is refused would have had his passport coded, and the gap between the expiration of his visa and his departure from the UK will bring suspicion of an immigration irregularity.

21.23   Supervised Departure

Supervised departure is where a person may, in certain circumstances, leave the UK while being closely monitored by the immigration authorities. This method is just a bit less harsh compared with deportation. With supervised departure, it is the actual departure that is of paramount importance to the immigration authorities and this is the reason why the immigration authorities will like to see the person off to the plane, just like someone who is being deported.

Anyone who is being detained for immigration matters, but against whom a deportation order has not been signed, can generally depart in this way.

21.24   Practical Advice

It is always better to tackle the Home Office before Deportation proceedings commence. Where such proceedings seem inevitable, the person involved should seek professional advice before any interview or filling of any forms or questionnaires. Where possible, depart voluntarily.

FOOTNOTES

1.   *S.1 1972 / 1613*
2.   *Immigration Act 1971, S. 3 (5)(c)*
3.   *1mmigration Act 1971, S.5 (3)*
4.   *Immigration Act 1988, S.5(i)*
5.   *HC 395 paragraph 364*
6.   *HC 395 paragraph 391.*

Chapter 22

NEW ASYLUM AND IMMIGRATION ACT 1996

22.1 INTRODUCTION

The implications of the new law are much wider than have been highlighted by the news media. The sweeping changes affect asylum seekers and employers, create new immigration offences, increase police powers, and take away re-housing and child benefits from certain immigrants. To effect these new provisions, the Home Secretary is empowered to publish supplementary provisions in other documents which would be referred to under each appropriate sub-headings discussed below. The following sub-headings shall be discussed:-

a)   Fast Track for Asylum Application/Appeal.

b)   Removal to Safe Third Countries.

c)   New Immigration Offences and Increased Penalties.

d)   New Powers to the Police.

e)   Restrictions on Employment.

f)   Re-housing and Child Benefit.

22.2 a} FAST TRACK FOR ASYLUM APPEAL

The fast track appeal has been in existence since 1993 but only for claims considered as 'without foundation'. This fast track procedure is now applicable to the vast majority of asylum appeals.

Please note also that in practice, most asylum applications are now being dealth with as fast as possible. Therefore, it is not strange for consideration of an application and its subsequent appeal process to last less than two months.

An asylum seeker whose application is refused will usually have a Right of Appeal; this appeal will fall under the fast track prodedure, where:

1.   the appellant is from or to be sent to a country designated (identified) by the Home Office as a country in which it appears that there is in general no serious risk of persecution. This means that where the Home Office has identified a country to be a safe country, an asylum appellant who is to be removed to such a country will be subject to a fast track procedure.   The list of such designated countries is contained in what is known as white list, the latest of which was published on 8 February 1996 in which **Bulgaria, Cyprus, Ethiopia, Ghana, India, Kenya, Pakistan, Poland, Romania and Tanzania** have been declared to be safe countries. The white list is designed to be flexible so that countries could be added or subtracted according to the changing situations, the key criterion for a country to be included is not its human rights record but the volume of asylum claims it generates and the rate at which the Home Office refuses them.

2.   a claim does not show a fear of persecution by reason of the appellant's race, religion, nationality, membership of a particular social group or political opinion.

3.   although a claim shows a fear of persecution, the fear is manifestly unfounded,

4.   although a claim shows a fear of persecution, the circumstances which gave rise to the fear no longer subsist,

5.   the asylum application is made at a time after the appellant has been refused leave to enter the UK, for example, as a visitor,

6.   the asylum application is made at a time after the appellant has been notified of a decision to make a deportation order against him,

7.   the asylum application is made at a time after the appellant has been notified of his ability to be removed as an illegal entrant or one who entered the UK in breach of a deportation order,

8.   the asylum claim is regarded as manifestly fraudulent,

9.   any of the evidence adduced or provided in support of an asylum application is regarded as manifestly false,

10. the claim is regarded as frivolous or vexatious.

It is being suggested that applications which fall under the above categories will more or less be classified from the outset as *lacking merit.*

22.3   Fast Track Procedure

Where an appeal is subject to this procedure, then:

● appellant must lodge his Notice of Appeal within 2 days of receiving the decision being appealed against (whereas if not under fast track, an appellant has up to 7 days to lodge his appeal).

● the Home Office on receiving the appellant's Notice of Appeal will speedily send it to a Special Adjudicator, the Notice of appeal, interview notes and copies of any documents referred to in the decision to refuse,

● once the special adjudicator receives the Notice of appeal from the Home Office, he will usually within 3 days after such receipt serve on the appellant a Notice of the date, time and place fixed for the Hearing of the Appeal (whereas if not under Fast Track, the special adjudicator has up to 5 days to do this),

● a special adjudicator should the appealss hear and provide his determination within 7 days of receiving the Notice of Appeal from the Home Office (whereas if not under fast track, a special adjudicator has up to 42 days to do this). This time limit can, however, be extended by the special adjudicator,

- usually special adjudicator's determination is sent by post (which may take about a month) but under the fast track procedure, such determination may be made on the hearing day.

- where such an appeal is dismissed, there is no right of appeal to the Tribunal.

22.4 b} REMOVAL TO A SAFE THIRD COUNTRY

Asylum seekers are expected to make their application at the first safe country of their arrival. Therefore, where an asylum applicant is found to have arrived from a third safe country, not having applied for asylum there, the merit of his asylum claim in the UK may not usually be considered and can be removed to that safe country, even in the absence of evidence that he would be admitted to that safe third country.

A safe third country is a country [1]:-

1) Where the asylum applicant is not a national or citizen, and

2) Where his life and liberty would not be threatened by reasons of his race, religion, nationality, membership of a particular social group or political opinion, and

3) Of which its government would not send asylum applicant to another territory otherwise than in accordance with the UN Convention.

Once the Home Office has certified a third country to be safe as described above, he is entitled to remove the asylum seeker or require him to leave the UK. Certain provisions of immigration law which protect asylum seekers from being removed or being required to leave the UK will no longer prevent the removal of such a person for whom a third country has been certified safe.

The protection which is therefore removed from such claimants can be summarised as follows:-

- protection of asylum claimants from deportation or removal from the UK from the time of their applications up to the time of the Home Office decision[2] ,

- protection which operates to put a stay (suspension) on removal directions where an appeal is pending[3] .

The effect of the new provision is that where a country is certified safe such a person, for all intents and purposes, has no asylum application for consideration in the UK and therefore can only appeal against the Home Secretary's certificate and not against a refusal (if any) of his asylum application. This right of appeal against the 3rd Country Certificate is only exercisable from outside the UK.

22.5   Appealing Against a Certificate

An appeal can be pursued against the Home Secretary's certificate for removal to a third safe country. This can only be done from outside the UK and on the limited grounds as follows:-

1)   that the Home Office acted unreasonably in issuing such certificate[4],

OR

2)   that the Home Office has acted unreasonably in not withdrawing the Certificate[5].

22.6   Important Points to Note

1)   The chances or prospects of succeeding with an appeal against the Certificate are, in most cases, not promising.

2)   Although the remedy of Judicial Review is available before removal from the UK, the courts do not usually look favourably on applications for reviews where appeal rights are yet to be exhausted[6].

22.7 c}   NEW IMMIGRATION OFFENCES AND INCREASED PENALTIES

22.8   Offences

New offence of obtaining or seeking to obtain leave by deception has been created. Therefore, a person may be charged with this offence if:-

1.   he seeks leave to enter the UK by deception[7],
2.   he obtains leave to enter the UK by deception.
3.   he seeks leave to remain in the UK by deception,
4.   he obtains leave to remain in the UK by deception.

This means that people coming in and those who are already in the UK can be caught by this provision. It also means that people who have genuinely obtained leave to enter or remain and subsequently engaged in deception in order to extend or vary such leave will equally be caught by this provision, for example, obvious marriage of convenience.

Further offence is created of assisting[8] :-

● asylum-seekers, and

● those seeking to obtain leave by deception.

This offence is created in place of limited offence of assisting illegal entrants. It therefore covers persons who, knowingly, are concerned in the making or carrying out arrangements for:-

1.   a)   securing the entry into the UK of anyone who he knows to be an asylum- seeker,

b)   securing the entry into the UK of anyone who he has reasonable cause for believing to be an asylum-seeker,

c)   facilitating the entry into the UK of anyone who he knows to be an asylum- seeker,

d)   facilitating the entry into the UK of anyone he has reasonable cause for believing to be an asylum claimant.

2. a) securing the entry into the UK of anyone who he knows to be an illegal entrant,

    b) securing the entry into the UK of anyone who he has reasonable cause for believing to be an illegal entrant,

    c) facilitating the entry into the UK of anyone who he knows to be an illegal entrant,

    d) facilitating the entry into the UK of anyone he has reasonable cause for believing to be an illegal entrant.

3. a) securing the obtaining of leave to remain in the UK by anyone whom he knows is not entitled to such leave.

    b) securing the obtaining of leave to remain in the UK by anyone whom he has reasonable cause for believing not to be entitled to such leave.

    c) facilitating the obtaining of leave to remain in the UK by anyone whom he knows is not entitled to such leave.

    d) facilitating the obtaining of leave to remain in the UK, by anyone whom he has reasonable cause for believing not to be entitled to such leave.

Facilitating means contributing towards or making something easier to achieve, while securing is the final accomplishment of the task. This suggests that a number of assistance other than in situations specifically excluded as mentioned below may fall foul of these provisions. For example, the spouse who is the British Citizen of an obvious marriage of convenience may be prosecuted for securing and facilitating the obtaining of leave to remain in the UK by deception (or for an attempt or conspiracy of same.

22.9   Those Excluded from Criminal Liability

A person is excluded from liability from the above provisions where he is assisting an asylum claimant:-

- otherwise than for gain, in other words, he did not assist with a motive to profit.

- in the course of his employment by a bona fide organisation whose purpose is to assist refugees.

22.10   Increased Penalties

The maximum prison term for certain immigration offences is six months, while the maximum fine which can be imposed in alternative or in addition to the prison sentence is now £5000.00   Thus illegal entry and similar offences, general offences in connection with the administration of immigration Act 1971, and offences connected with Ships or Aircrafts or with Ports, also attract penalties with the same maximum sentence[9].

22.11   d} NEW POWERS FOR POLICE AND IMMIGRATION OFFICERS

22.12   (i) Arrest without Warrant

The number of offences for which a police constable or an immigration officer may arrest without warrant have now increased.   A police or immigration officer is now empowered to arrest without warrant anyone he has reasonable grounds for suspecting to have committed:

a)   an offence of illegal entry,
b)   seeking leave to enter the UK by deception,
c)   obtaining leave to enter the UK by deception,
d)   seeking leave to remain in the UK by deception,
e)   obtaining leave to remain in the UK by deception,
f)   an offence of remaining beyond time limited by leave (Overstaying)
g)   an offence of failing to observe conditions of leave (e.g. Working without Permission)

22.13   (ii) Search of Premises with Warrant

A police officer can obtain warrant to enter premises, if need be by force, to arrest someone for the purpose of searching for and arresting a person whom he has reasonable grounds to suspect to have committed any of the offences stated in figure 22.12 above. The offences listed above are treated in the same category as serious offences as Murder and Rape and the requirement of reasonableness (not a high degree one) may lead to abuse by the Police, particularly in relation to ethnic minority communities.

22.14   e}   RESTRICTION ON EMPLOYMENT

All immigrants require one form of permit or another before they can work or establish business in the UK. This permit may be in form of a document issued by the Department of Employment or the Home Office.

The effect of the new law is to impose a duty on employers to ensure that employees have appropriate permission to work in the UK. This will definitely result to what is known as "Operation Show Your Passport/Work Permit".

22.15   Criminal Liability

An employer who employs an immigrant without the appropriate permission to work shall be guilty of an offence punishable by a fine of up to £5000.00 [10]. This provision has taken effect from the 27th January 1997, and it has been directed the 'Operation Show Your Passport/Work Permit' should not affect those already in the employer's organisation.

The language of the new provision covers all employers, including companies and their employees, directors or members whose consent, connivance or negligence contributed to the commission of this offence. Apart from placing too much burden on employers this provision would encourage unwelcome interference into the affairs of employees. It may also allow for indirect discrimination especially where a particular employee becomes target of grulling scrutiny.

22.16   Defence For Employers

Where an employer is charged under this provision, it shall be a defence for him to prove that there was produced to him a document which related to the employee which was of a description specified in an order made by the

Home Office (such document may presumably include a P45, Passport, and NI number), which allows such employee to work in the UK.

Employers must, however, be very careful so as not to discriminate against anyone because of his colour. If an employer has any doubt about whether a document from an employee will provide a defence, he can telephone a special helpline, on:

0181 649 7878.

The helpline will not be able to provide personal information about an individual, and will not provide advice on matters relating to employment law, work permits or the avoidance of racial discrimination. The helpline will be available to take calls from Monday to Friday, 9am to 5pm. Calls will be answered in turn and should be available from the 6th January, 1997.

Furthermore, anyone who is discriminated against because of his colour may seek advice from an employment lawyer.

Please note that this law only affects those who are employed and not those who self employed.

22.17   HOUSING AND WELFARE BENEFIT

22.18   Housing

The new law provides that housing accommodation should not be made available (by housing authorities) to immigrants unless they are of a class specified in an order (rules/documents) made by the Home Secretary.

Immigrants outside the said class shall, therefore, not be entitled to accommodation or housing assistance even where they are threatened with homelessness or where they have a priority need for accommodation.

Furthermore, immigrants outside the said class shall be disregarded in determining whether another person is homeless, threatened with homelessness, or has a priority need for accommodation. For example, where a British Citizen applies for housing, the presence of his relatives or friends in an overcrowded accommodation shall not be taken into consideration if the relative or friend is of the class to be specified in the said order.

22.19   Child Benefit

The new law states categorically that no immigrants within the meaning of the Asylum and Immigration Act 1996 shall be entitled to Child Benefit for any week unless he satisfies prescribed conditions. Immigrants under the 1996 Act means a person who requires leave to enter or remain in the UK.

22.20   Other Benefits

Please note that under the new social security rules which came to force on the 24th July 1996, benefits (such as income support/job seekers allowance, unemployment and Housing benefits) will no longer be paid to asylum-seekers whose applications for asylum have been refused by the Home Office, or to anyone who makes an asylum application having entered the UK for other purpose. A person affected by this law may, however, seek advice and assistance under the National Assistance Act 1948.[11]

FOOTNOTES

1.   *Asylum & Immigration Act 1996 S.2(2) a-c.*

2.   *Immigration Appeal & Asylum Act 1993, S.6*

3.   *Immigration Act 1971, paragraph 3, Sch.iii, paragraph 28, Sch.ii*

4.   *s.3(1)a 1996 Act*

5.   *s.3(1)b 1996 Act*

6.   *Secretary of State for Home Department, Exp. Swati 1986, 1 ALL ER 717*

7.   *Immigration & Asylum Act 1996, S.4*

8.   *Immigration & Asylum Act 1996, S.5*

9.   *Immigration & Asylum Act 1996, S.6*

10.   *Immigration & Asylum Act 1996, S.8*

11.   *National Assistance Act 1948, S.21(1)*

**Beware of Bogus Immigration Representatives
and those claiming to know someone at the Home Office**

USEFUL ADDRESSES AND TELEPHONE NUMBERS

Nationality

Nationality Division
Home Office
3rd Floor
India Buildings
Water Street
Liverpool
L2 0QN

Tel: 0151 236 5200
Fax: 0151 255 1160

Home Office Regional Public Enquiry Offices

Belfast
Olivetree House
Fountain Street
Belfast
BT1 5EA

Tel: 01232 322547

Birmingham
Immigration Office(Cargo Terminal)
Birmingham Airport
Birmingham
B26 3QN
Tel: 0121 606 7345

Glasgow
Admin Block D
Argyll Avenue
Glasgow Airport
Abbotsinch, Paisley PA3 2TD
Tel: 0141 887 2255

Harwich
Parkestone Quay
Harwich
Essex
CO12 4SX

Tel: 01255 504371

Liverpool
Graeme House
Derby Square
Liverpool
L2 7SF
Tel: 0151 236 8974

Norwich
Norwich Airport
Ifers Lane
Norwich
NR6 6EP
Tel: 01603 408859

Useful Addresses / Telephone Numbers

Ports of Entry Immigration Service and Detention Areas

City Airport (London) Immigration
Tel: 0171 474 1395
Fax: 0171 511 2363

London Heathrow

Terminal 1
Case Work   0181 745 6809
Arrivals control: 0181 745 6800
Fax: 0181 745 6814

Terminal 2
General: 0181 745 6850
Casework: 0181 745 6860
Fax: 0181 745 6877

Terminal 3

General: 0181 745 6900
Casework: 0181 745 6932
Fax: 0181 745 6943

Terminal 4
Switchboard: 0181 745 4700
Casework: 0181 745 4724
Fax: 0181 745 4705

Queens Building Detention Centre
0181 564 9726/7   (Detainees)
0181 745 6484   (Group 4)

Harmondsworth
Detention Centre
Building JA: 0181 564 7790
                       0181 564 7799
Building DA: 0181 897 8040 (detainees)
Group 4:   0181 759 9727

Dover East
Immigration: 01304 244900
Fax: 01304 213594

Dover South-EastPorts
Surveillance Team
Tel: 01304 216405

Dover Detention Holding Area
Tel :   01304 240246
Fax: 01304 216 303

Dover Hoverport
Tel: 01304 240246
Fax: 01304 215343

Dover Harbour Police Station
Tel: 01304 206260

Belfast City Office
Airport switchboard: 01849 422886
Immigration Ext: 4093
Tel: 01232 322547
Fax: 01232 244939

Bristol
Tel: 01275 472843
Fax: 01275 474434

Cardiff
Tel: 01222 481080
Fax: 01222 494979
Airport: 01446 710485
Fax: 01446 710606

Cheriton Detention
(Channel Tunnel)
Tel: 01303 282600
Fax: 01303 282610

East Midlands Airport
Tel: 01332 812000
Fax: 01332 811569

Edinburgh
Tel: 0131 344 3330
Fax: 0131 335 3197

Gatwick North
Switchboard: 01293 892500
Casework: 01293 892545
Asylum: 01293 892515
Fax: 01293 892560

Gatwick South
Switchboard: 01293 502019
Casework: 01293 502654
Fax: 01293 553643

Glasgow
Tel: 0141 887 4115
Fax: 0141 887 1566

Gravesend
Tel: 01474 352308
Fax: 01474 534731

Holding Room
Tel: 01293 524284
Beehive: 01293 569772

Hull
Tel: 01482 223017
Fax: 01482 219034

Leeds/Bradford
Tel: 0113 250 2931
Fax: 0113 250 0949

Liverpool
Tel: 0151 236 8974
Fax: 0151 236 4656

Luton
Tel: 01582 421891
Fax: 01582 40521

Index

Index

Index

Index